NOT ON OUR WATCH

THE MISSION TO END GENOCIDE
IN DARFUR AND BEYOND

NOT ON
OUR WATCH

Don Cheadle & John Prendergast

HYPERION
NEW YORK

ISBN-10: 1-4013-0335-8
ISBN-13: 978-1-4013-0335-8

Hyperion books are available for special promotions, premiums, or corporate training. For details contact Michael Rentas, Proprietary Markets, Hyperion, 77 West 66th Street, 12th floor, New York, New York 10023, or call 212-456-0133.

Design by Renato Stanisic

FIRST EDITION

10 9 8 7 6 5 4 3 2

CONTENTS

CONTENTS

ACKNOWLEDGMENTS

When we say we wouldn't have been able to write this book without the help of the following people, we really mean we wouldn't have written this book without their help. Another way to put it is that there would be no book without the following people. Is there any other way to make this clearer?

We are indebted to Heather Bourbeau and Colin Thomas-Jensen, who helped us write certain sections of the book and edited us mercilessly. We were very lucky to have Gretchen Young as our editor at Hyperion. Our book agent, Joe Veltre, hooked us up with just the right situation. And we had the best research team any two bumbling coauthors could ever hope for, including: Caroline Andresen, Patrick Arnold, Lindsey Carter, Chrissie Coxon, Annie Denes, Rashid Galadanci, Lindsay Joiner, Jamie Morgan, Kevin Murungi, Susana Rodriguez, Julia Spiegel, Taylor Steelman, David Sullivan, Leora Ward, and Sara Weisman. Others who have contributed in various ways include Kay Liberman, Lenore Zerman, Bonnie Abaunza, Semhar Araia, John Norris, Robert Malley, Jean Coleman, Alexis Hyder, Valerie Nussenblatt, Lisa Rogoff, and Caitlin Wall.

To all, we are in your debt.

Don Cheadle and John Prendergast
DECEMBER 2006

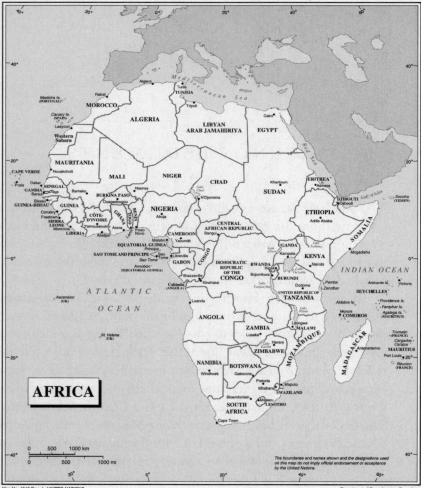

AFRICA

Map No. 4045 Rev. 4   UNITED NATIONS
January 2004

Department of Peacekeeping Operations
Cartographic Section

The boundaries and names shown and the designations used
on this map do not imply official endorsement or acceptance
by the United Nations.

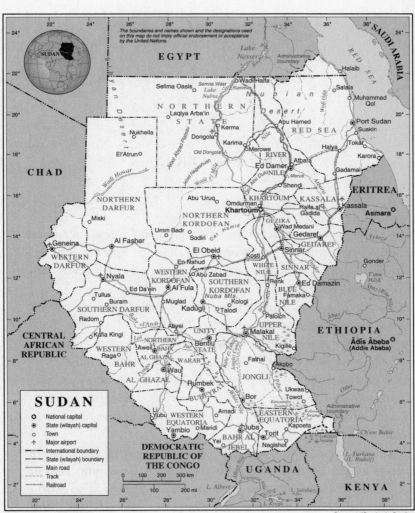

SUDAN

- ✪ National capital
- ◉ State (wilayah) capital
- ○ Town
- ✈ Major airport
- ⎯⎯ International boundary
- ⎯·⎯· State (wilayah) boundary
- ⎯⎯ Main road
- ⎯⎯ Track
- ╫╫╫ Railroad

The boundaries and names shown and the designations used
on this map do not imply official endorsement or acceptance
by the United Nations.

EGYPT

SAUDI ARABIA

CHAD

CENTRAL
AFRICAN
REPUBLIC

DEMOCRATIC
REPUBLIC OF
THE CONGO

UGANDA

KENYA

ETHIOPIA

ERITREA

Lake
Nasser

Libyan Desert

Nubian Desert

NORTHERN STATE

NORTHERN DARFUR

NORTHERN KORDOFAN

WESTERN DARFUR

WESTERN KORDOFAN

SOUTHERN KORDOFAN

SOUTHERN DARFUR

KHARTOUM

GEZIRA

KASSALA

GEDAREF

SINNAR

WHITE NILE

BLUE NILE

RED SEA

RIVER NILE

UNITY STATE

WARAB

JONGLI

UPPER NILE

BUHAYRAT

AL GHAZAL

NORTHERN BAHR AL GHAZAL

WESTERN BAHR AL GHAZAL

WESTERN EQUATORIA

BAHR AL JEBEL

EASTERN EQUATORIA

Selima Oasis

Semna West
Lake
Nubia

Wadi Halfa

Salala

Halaib

Muhammad
Qol

Laqiya Arba'in

Kerma

Abu Hamed

Port Sudan

Suakin

Nukheila

Dongola

Karima

Merowe

Atbara

Haiya

Tokar

Karora

El'Atrun

Old Dongola

Ed Damer

Gadamai

Abu Dulu

Shendi

Abu 'Uruq

Omdurman

Khartoum

Halfa al Gadida

Kassala

Asmara

Miski

Umm Badr

Sodiri

Wad Medani

Gedaref

Al Fasher

El Obeid

Kosti

Sinnar

Gonder

Geneina

En Nahud

Nyala

Abu Zabad

Al Fula

Renk

Ed Damazin

Ed Da'ein

Famaka

Ed Damazin

Tullus

Buram

Muglad

Kadugli

Kologi

Talodi

Radom

Abyei

Paloich

Malakal

Kafia Kingi

Awell

Bentiu

Kigille

Raga

Wau

Fathai

Akobo

Rumbek

Bor

Ukwaa

Towot

Li Yubu

Amadi

Maridi

Yambio

Juba

Kapoeta

Yei

Torit

Nagishot

Map No. 3707 Rev. 7   UNITED NATIONS
May 2004

Department of Peacekeeping Operations
Cartographic Section

0   100   200   300 km

0   100   200 mi

FOREWORD

I am a Jew who remembers when my people in German-occupied Europe were condemned to isolation, hunger, humiliation, unspeakable terror, and death. Until almost the end of the war, nobody came to our rescue.

I am member of the human family who remembers that 800,000 human beings were massacred in Rwanda in 1994. They could have been saved, but nobody came to their rescue. The leaders of the world knew of the perpetrators' intention and their victims' vulnerability, but they failed to respond. Everything was known, and to the shame of civilized society, hundreds of thousands of men, women, and children were abandoned and then slaughtered.

I am writing this now because in Darfur, Sudan, families are being uprooted and starved, children tormented and murdered in the thousands, and women raped with impunity. The world knows that the non-Arab peoples of Darfur are dying by the thousands, yet, in the eyes of the victims, the world remains indifferent to their plight.

I refuse to remain silent while leaders of the world make excuses for failing to protect the people of Darfur. I am writing to voice my compassion for the victims and my anger at leaders who are timorous, complacent, and unwilling to take risks. Remember: silence helps the killer, never his victims.

Darfur is today's capital of human suffering. Darfur deserves to live, and American citizens are providing it with reason to hope. Not to help, not to urge our elected officials to intervene and save innocent lives in any manner possible and needed is to condemn us on grounds of immorality. Our failure to speak out to end the ongoing genocide in Darfur would place us on the wrong side of history. And that thought must seem intolerable to all of us.

For the sake of our humanity, SAVE DARFUR!

Professor Elie Wiesel

INTRODUCTION:
When Ordinary Becomes Extraordinary

SENATOR BARACK OBAMA AND
SENATOR SAM BROWNBACK

Issues that transcend politics in Washington, D.C., are rare. However, there is one such cause that is worth putting political differences aside for. It is a cause that is more important than winning elections or raising campaign money. It is a cause that gets too little press attention despite the massive human consequences. The cause is Darfur.

Darfur is home to the first genocide of the twenty-first century. After the genocide in Rwanda, in which 800,000 people were killed, the world said we would not tolerate this ever again. Amazingly, the words "Never Again" have continued to be uttered in the months—and now years—that have passed since 2003, when the killing started in the remote western region of Sudan. We continue to hear people say this genocide cannot continue, but it continues every day. Up to 400,000 have been killed and millions displaced.

Why should Americans care about human suffering in Africa or anywhere else?

First of all, preventing, suppressing, and punishing genocide is a moral imperative. Both personally, and as a nation, we cannot sit idly by as innocent people are indiscriminately killed and forced out of their homes by violence.

The second reason genocide should matter to Americans is that we have all made a promise. "Save Darfur" is not simply a slogan; it is an American commitment. The fact that other countries choose to look away from horrors such as those in Darfur does not allow us to shirk our responsibility.

Third, eradicating genocide will make Americans safer. When we look out at the sea of humanity forced to live off handouts in UN refugee camps in Chad or Sudan, it is easy to forget that stopping genocide is not simply about charity; it is about creating a safer world for American children as well as for the refugee children stuck in the squalor of exile. History has taught us that regimes that target their own people rarely confine their murderous ambitions within their borders. Moreover, the victims—those who have been attacked not for anything they have done as individuals, but simply because of their religion or their ethnicity— tend not to go quietly into the night. Some radicalize, taking up arms against their assailants, and, eventually, joining criminal or even terrorist networks. The violence spreads; the innocents suffer.

So what does it take to stop genocide? What does it take to make the world listen and respond? It takes a number of important tools, including diplomacy, financial resources, and effective security forces. And in a world where these resources are finite, it often takes pressure—pressure from ordinary individuals standing together for an extraordinary cause—to mobilize these resources. In short, it takes you.

We are inspired by the occasions in U.S. history when citizens, community leaders, and politicians have united in the struggle for truth, justice, and basic human dignity—in expanding civil rights, in helping bring an end to apartheid, and in speeding the fall of the Berlin Wall. We are sobered by the chapters in America's past in which we have let injustices and atrocities unfold on our watch. As members of Congress representing different states and different constituents, we have been heartened, during what can feel like dark times, to hear loud, persistent, and inspirational voices from all corners of our nation calling for action to end the massacres in Darfur. These voices have come from men and women of all ages, religions, and national backgrounds. We in Congress have heard this remarkable range of voices, and although we don't always align on the details of foreign policy, we are committed to moving forward to help halt this genocide.

While Darfur is a current and pressing crisis, and while the anti-genocide movement in the United States has grown in response to today's horrors, it must expand its reach and its range. Just as surely as we know that hate-mongering individuals will strike out against the innocent in the future, we must also know that you will be there to sound the alarm, to hold your leaders accountable for their sins of omission, to move us away from slogans to concrete measures that save lives.

Genocide is an exceptional crime. It will only be overcome if "extraordinary ordinary" voices unite to summon the world's leaders to action.

PREFACE: ON OUR WATCH

"Not on our watch." What does this phrase mean and why have we chosen it as our title? The origin of the phrase is nautical; it refers to sailors who take turns sharing the responsibility of being "officer of the watch" aboard a ship. Whether this responsibility is requested or thrust upon the officer, it is to be taken very seriously, as any wrongdoing that occurs on his or her "watch" will result in a demerit or bad mark, even if the officer was not directly involved in the incident. For better or worse, the buck stops here. "On your watch," on your record.

The phrase has since been coopted in myriad ways, from managers talking to staff, to captains briefing cops, to teachers cautioning students, and even to parents warning their children that no misconduct will be tolerated while they are in command. And during President Bush's first year in office, when reviewing a report on the Rwandan genocide, he wrote in the margins, "Not on my watch." Perhaps he was putting his team on notice that he would not be the commander "of the watch" while a similar genocide rolled on. Maybe it was just a shot across his predecessor's bow, an observation to be passed around in the circle that a "bonehead" move like this, allowing genocide to occur while you held the reins, would never go down on this president's watch. It might have even been jotted down as a reminder or note to himself: "Note to self: thwart genocide."

We don't know the answer, but we do know this: as you read these words thousands of innocent people in Darfur are being systematically targeted for extermination. Their crime is that they are from specific non-Arab ethnic groups that are deemed to be sympathetic to rebel groups in Darfur; the "officer of the watch" aboard this ship: apparently no one. Aside from the humanitarian aid workers caring for the war's victims, the only people who can claim any such accountability are the African Union members stationed in Darfur and its surrounding areas. In their case this accountability is only as strong as their mandate, which does not allow them to engage the enemy, but rather simply to share reports with the United Nations on the results of the almost daily marauding runs. The UN's "watch," in turn, is hampered by its member states' reticence to intervene in the affairs of a sovereign nation, despite the fact that it was precisely the need to confront this kind of crisis that led to the creation of this international body.

So whose "watch" is it? Who stands on deck aboard this world-ship, assuming responsibility for the actions that occur during the shift? To us, the answer is clear: the responsibility of the "watch" lies with those who take it up. Neither of us is a president, world leader, general, or captain of a gunboat, but we wish to take up the "watch," and we know that there are thousands, maybe millions, like us who desire to tell their children and grandchildren that at a time when there was a terrible thing called genocide, to which those in power turned a deaf ear and blind eye, people like us spoke so loudly, in numbers so great, that we could not be ignored.

We take our "watch" as seriously as any officer on board and believe in our deepest hearts that the power of the collective can override the reservations of the few, regardless of position or prominence. We pray that we can steer clear of demerits on our record, keep bad marks at bay, and with the words that follow help us all to be worthy of our roles as officers "of the watch." We did not start this fire, but let us work together to put it out.

For those of us who don't want to just talk about it and want to BE about it, the buck stops here.

Glossary of Abbreviations

ACOA: American Committee on Africa

AFL-CIO: American Federation of Labor and Congress of Industrial Organizations

AIC: American Islamic Congress

AJWS: American Jewish World Service

ARV: Antiretroviral

ASAP: Afrobeat Sudan Aid Project

AU: African Union

CalPERS: California Public Employees Retirement System

CODEL: Congressional Delegation

DAC: Darfur Action Committee

DATA: Debt AIDS Trade Africa

ECOWAS: Economic Community of West African States

EU: European Union

FDA: Food and Drug Administration

FOTC: Friends of the Congo

G-8: Group of Eight

GIF: Genocide Intervention Fund

GI-Net: Genocide Intervention Network

ICC: International Criminal Court

ICRC: International Committee of the Red Cross
IDP: Internally Displaced Person
IGAD: Inter-Governmental Authority on Development
IMF: International Monetary Fund
IRC: International Rescue Committee
JWW: Jewish World Watch
LRA: Lord's Resistance Army
NAE: National Association of Evangelicals
NCP: National Congress Party
NATO: North Atlantic Treaty Organization
NGO: Non-Governmental Organization
NIF: National Islamic Front
NYSE: New York Stock Exchange
PEPFAR: President's Emergency Plan for AIDS Relief
SLA: Sudan Liberation Army
SLM: Sudan Liberation Movement
SPLA: Sudan People's Liberation Army
SPLM: Sudan People's Liberation Movement
STAND: Students Taking Action Now: Darfur
STOP: Slavery That Oppresses People
UNAIDS: Joint United Nations Program on HIV/AIDS
UNHCR: United Nations High Commissioner for Refugees
UNITE: Union of Needletrades, Industrial, and Textile
    Employees
USAS: United Students Against Sweatshops
WFP: World Food Program

1

Challenges and Choices

It was sometime round midnight in a little village in southern Sudan, and the only link to the rest of the world within a five-hundred-mile radius was one satellite phone, so when it rang it was a bit of a shock to everyone.

Don dispensed with the formalities. "My man, you are not easy to find."

"Obviously, hiding from you is not as easy as I thought," John countered.

Despite his attempt at a cool demeanor, John was excited. After Marlon Brando and Mickey Rourke (John is well aware that he has issues), Don was his favorite actor, and the fact that the two of them were about to go on a trip together to Chad and across the border into the western Sudanese region of Darfur was firing him up.

However, Don wasn't making a social call. He was concerned that the mission that we were going on with a bunch of members of Congress was only going to spend several hours in the refugee camps in Chad, and he wanted to stay longer. "You gotta rescue it," Don instructed John.

John looked around to see what tools he had at his disposal in that little southern Sudanese village, but all he could hear was the *ribbit, ribbit* of the Sudanese frogs. "I am in the middle of nowhere. Give me twelve hours."

A few hundred dollars of satellite phone calls later, a much more substantial and lengthy trip was planned. We also managed to get Paul Rusesabagina,* whom Don had portrayed in *Hotel Rwanda,* and Rick Wilkinson, a veteran producer for ABC's *Nightline,* to come with us and help interpret and chronicle our first journey together.

Our trip to witness the ravages of genocide in Darfur was not the first brush with that heinous crime for either of us. Don had visited Rwanda post-filming, and John had been in Rwanda and the refugee camps in Congo immediately after the genocide.

As we listened to the stories of the refugees who fled the genocide, we sensed what it might feel like to be hunted as a human being. These Darfurians had been targeted for extermination by the regime in Sudan on the basis of their ethnicity. Although well-meaning and thoughtful people may disagree on what to call it, for us the crisis in Darfur is one that constitutes genocide.[†]

---

*Paul was the manager of a hotel in Rwanda's capital, Kigali. In 1994, an extremist government set in motion a plan to exterminate Rwandans who were ethnically Tutsi and non-Tutsis who sympathized with them. Paul was a member of Rwanda's other main ethnic group, the Hutu. When genocide consumed Rwanda in 1994, Paul protected more than one thousand Rwandans from near certain extermination at the hands of extremist Hutu militias. *Hotel Rwanda* tells his courageous story.

[†]Throughout this book, we will use the phrases *crimes against humanity* and *mass atrocity crimes* interchangeably, treating *genocide* as one particular extreme manifestation of such crimes. Whether the crimes against humanity committed in Darfur should be regarded as genocide has been the subject of some debate. A United Nations Commission of Inquiry and several reputable research and advocacy organizations—including the International Crisis Group, Human Rights Watch, and Amnesty International—do not use this description. They have a number of good arguments, perhaps best summed up by Gareth Evans, the President and CEO of the International Crisis Group and member of the UN Advisory Panel on Genocide Prevention, who argues that, here, as in a number of other cases, use of the term genocide can be unproductive, non-productive, and even counter-productive. Unproductive, because there are always lawyers' arguments about whether the legal definition in the UN Convention on the Prevention and Punishment of the Crime of Genocide has been satisfied, and this can be a real distraction from the immediate imperative of protecting the victims of what everyone agrees are crimes against humanity. (The Convention definition requires that certain acts be "committed with intent to destroy,

Enough is ENOUGH. We need to come together and press for action to end the violence in Darfur and prevent future crimes against humanity. Through simple acts and innovative collaborations, we can save hundreds of thousands of lives now.

That is our fervent hope, and our goal.

Darfur: A Slow-Motion Genocide

Genocide is unique among "crimes against humanity" or "mass atrocity crimes" because it targets, in whole or in part, a specific racial, religious, national, or ethnic group for extinction. According to the international convention, genocide can include any of the following five criteria targeted at the groups listed above:

- killing
- causing serious bodily or mental harm
- deliberately inflicting "conditions of life calculated to bring about its physical destruction in whole or in part"
- imposing measures to prevent births
- forcibly transferring children from a targeted group.*

The perpetrators of genocide in Rwanda took one hundred days to exterminate 800,000 lives. This was the fastest rate of *tar-*

---

in whole or in part, a national, ethnical, racial, or religious group," and it is extremely hard to establish that element of specific *intent* to destroy non-Arab groups in Darfur.) Non-productive, because, as the U.S. response to Darfur illustrates, even when the term is invoked there is no legal obigation under the genocide convention for countries that use the term to actually do anything. And counterproductive when expectations are raised that a particular situation is genocide, but then lawyers' arguments prevail that some necessary element is missing, as was the case with the UN commission in Darfur: in these circumstances the perpetrators of what are unquestionably mass atrocities or crimes against humanity achieve an utterly unearned propaganda victory. All of this demonstrates that right-thinking people can disagree about the use of the term genocide. What we and these organizations all totally agree on, however, is that mass atrocities are being committed in Darfur, as well as in the Congo and northern Uganda, and were being committed in the 1990s in southern Sudan, Liberia, Sierra Leone, Angola, and Burundi. In those last five countries, international and local efforts have combined to being about an end to the atrocities and the wars that generated them, giving all of us hope that horrors in Darfur, northern Uganda, Congo, and Somalia can also soon be ended, and future catastrophes prevented.

*Convention on the Prevention and Punishment of the Crime of Genocide.

geted mass killing in human history, three times faster than that of the Holocaust.

JOHN:

In mid-2004, one year into the fighting and six months before the trip Don and I took to Chad/Darfur, I went with Pulitzer Prize–winning author Samantha Power* to the rebel areas in Darfur. At the same time, U.S. Secretary of State Colin Powell was visiting government-held areas in the region. But unlike Secretary Powell, Samantha and I went to the part of Sudan that the regime didn't want anyone to see, and for very good reason.

Before the genocide, Darfur was one of the poorest regions of Sudan, and the Saharan climate made eking out a living an extreme challenge. But these difficulties only made Darfurians hardier and more self-reliant, mixing farming and livestock rearing in a complex strategy of survival that involved migration, intercommunal trade, and resource sharing.

It had been over a year since the genocide began, so Samantha and I expected certain evidence of mass destruction. And we were indeed witness to burned villages where livestock, homes, and grain stocks had been utterly destroyed, confirming stories we had heard from Darfurians at refugee camps in Chad.

Yet no amount of time in Sudan or work on genocide

---

*Samantha was a journalist in Bosnia during the horrors of that war, and her frustration with the failure of the United States to lead a strong international response to the atrocities being committed compelled her to research and write a book about America's response to genocides throughout the twentieth century. Her book, *A Problem from Hell: America and the Age of Genocide* (Basic Books, 2002), won the Pulitzer Prize. Samantha showed that time and again U.S. leaders were aware that crimes against humanity were occurring but failed to take action. After she and John traveled to Darfur in 2004, Samantha wrote an article for the *New Yorker* magazine that won the National Magazine Award for reporting in 2005.

ever prepares anyone sufficiently for what Samantha and I saw in a ravine deep in the Darfur desert—bodies of nearly two dozen young men lined up in ditches, eerily preserved by the 130-degree desert heat. One month before, they had been civilians, forced to walk up a hill to be executed by Sudanese government forces. Harrowingly, this scene was repeated throughout the targeted areas of Darfur.

We heard more refugees in Chad describe family and friends being stuffed into wells by the Janjaweed in a twisted and successful attempt to poison the water supply. When we searched for these wells in Darfur, we found them in the exact locations described. The only difference was now these wells were covered in sand in an effort to cover the perpetrators' bloody tracks. With each subsequent trip to Darfur, I have found the sands of the Saharan Desert slowly swallowing more of the evidence of the twenty-first century's first genocide.

To us, Darfur has been Rwanda in slow motion. Perhaps 400,000 have died during three and a half years of slaughter, over two and a quarter million have been rendered homeless, and, in a particularly gruesome subplot, thousands of women have been systematically raped. During 2006, the genocide began to metastasize, spreading across the border into Chad, where Chadian villagers (and Darfurian refugees) have been butchered and even more women raped by marauding militias supported by the Sudanese government.

Sadly, the international response has also unfolded in slow motion. With crimes against humanity like the genocide in Darfur, the caring world is inevitably in a deadly race with time to save and protect as many lives as possible. In the fall of 2004, after his visit to Sudan, Secretary Powell officially invoked the term "genocide."[*]

---

[*]Testimony before U.S. Senate Committee on Foreign Relations, September 9, 2004.

He was followed shortly thereafter by President Bush.* This represented the first time an ongoing genocide was called its rightful name by a sitting U.S. president. And yet in Darfur, as in most of these crises, the international community, including the United States, responded principally by calling for cease-fires and sending humanitarian aid. These are important gestures to be sure, but they do not stop the killing.

We believe it is our collective responsibility to re-sanctify the sacred post-Holocaust phrase "Never Again"—to make it something meaningful and vital. Not just for the genocide that is unfolding today in Darfur, but also for the next attempted genocide or cases of mass atrocities.

And there are other cases, to be sure.

Right now, we need to do all we can for the people of northern Uganda, of Somalia, and of Congo. Though genocide is not being perpetrated in these countries, horrible abuses of human rights are occurring, in some ways comparable to those in Darfur. Militias are targeting civilians, rape is used as a tool of war, and life-saving aid is obstructed or stolen by warring parties. Furthermore, by the time you pick up this book, another part of the world could have caught on fire, and crimes against humanity may be being perpetrated. We need to do all we can to organize ourselves to uphold international human rights law and to prevent these most heinous crimes from ever occurring.

That is our challenge.

Raising the Political Will to Confront Crimes Against Humanity

Preventing genocide and other mass atrocities is a challenge made all the more difficult by a lack of public concern, media coverage, and effective response, especially to events in Africa. Crimes against humanity on that continent are largely ignored or treated

---

*White House press releases, September 9, 2004.

as part of the continent's political inheritance, more so than in Asia or Europe. The genocide in Darfur is competing for international action with human rights emergencies in Congo, Somalia, and northern Uganda—conflicts that along with southern Sudan have left over 6 million dead—but the international response to these atrocities rarely goes beyond military observation missions and humanitarian relief efforts, which are insufficient Band-Aids.

Crises like these need the immediate attention of a new constituency focused on preventing and confronting genocide and other crimes against humanity. Of these four conflicts, only Darfur has generated sustained media and public attention. Images of innocent Darfurian civilians—men, women, and children—hounded from their homes by ravaging militia have triggered significant activism on the part of Americans and citizens around the world. But these public expressions have not, by the time of this writing, at the end of 2006, yielded a sufficient international response. The United States government has yet to take bold action to protect the victims, build a viable peace process, and hold those responsible for this genocide accountable.

There is some positive momentum building. At the United Nations World Summit in 2005, member nations agreed to a doctrine called the Responsibility to Protect, or R2P. R2P states that when a government is unable or unwilling, as is the case with Sudan, to protect its citizens from mass atrocities, the international community must take that responsibility. We believe that this doctrine, developed by a high-level panel cochaired by Gareth Evans (the president of the International Crisis Group, where John works) and Mohamed Sahnoun (former Algerian diplomat and UN special advisor) commits us all, as individuals and nations, to do our part to fulfill that responsibility.

During our visit to Darfur and the Darfurian refugee camps in Chad, we heard story after story of mind-numbing violence perpetrated by the Sudanese government army and the Janjaweed militias they support. We heard of women being gang-raped, children being thrown into fires, villages and communities that had existed for centuries being burned to the ground in an effort to wipe out the livelihoods and even the history of those communities. We heard things that simply should not be happening in the twenty-first century.

In one of the refugee camps in Chad in 2005, we met Fatima, forty-two, who described how she had to escape her village of Girgira in western Darfur after her mother, husband, and five children were all killed by the Janjaweed militias. She said she feared the government would kill her as well. In desperation, she walked for seven days to a refugee camp. She couldn't walk during daytime hours because of the Janjaweed gangs. She hid under trees and plants. Despite all this, she wanted to return home, but she wanted to be sure it was safe. Having lost everything, she no longer trusted anyone, even the African Union troops deployed in Darfur.

Omda Yahya, a tribal leader we talked with from Tine, also saw all his children die in a violent raid on his town and in the subsequent escape to "safety." His town, he says, was attacked by men on horseback, planes dropping bombs, and armies on foot. He fled with many of his tribe, and after more than fifteen days of walking without food or drink, they arrived at a refugee camp. "We lost our village. They burned it. If we get all our possessions back, then after that we can go back. But now we don't think it is safe to go back."

How do we respond to these horrors?

What we've learned is that there are three pillars to fostering a real change in human rights and conflict resolution policy: field research to learn what is really happening in the conflict zones and what needs to be done, high-level advocacy to deliver the message to the people who determine policy, and domestic political pressure from a constituency that cares about these issues and takes them up with their elected officials.

This last one often goes missing. Sustained and robust campaigns by organized citizens are needed for maximum impact. Fostering these constituencies must be our focus.

Will the United States lead efforts to protect people when they are being systematically annihilated by predatory governments or militias? Will we punish the perpetrators of crimes against humanity? Will we promote peace processes with high-level envoys and other support? None of these options is beyond the realm of the possible; they are simply matters of political will. If U.S. citizens and therefore the government answer yes to these questions, millions of lives will be spared in the coming years.

The good news is that much of the suffering could come to an end. It is within our power. If the U.S. government takes a lead role during each crisis marked by crimes against humanity, our chances to prevent or end these crimes increases dramatically. If the U.S. government had taken a leading role in three areas of policy—peacemaking, protection, and punishment—these crimes could have been prevented or stopped. If U.S. citizens and their government increase their activism and work to build an international coalition to stop mass atrocities, major changes are possible.

Despite what you may see on the evening news, there are encouraging signs of progress. Indeed, sparse and sporadic news coverage of Africa focusing solely on crises there has led to a "conflict fatigue" associated with the continent as a whole.* By ignoring the positive news, U.S. and European media risk fostering a dangerous tendency to dismiss the entire continent as hopeless. So when wars erupt and their attendant human rights abuses emerge, the response—if there even is one—is often tentative and muted, and conflict-ridden countries easily descend into a free-fall. We think these conflicts are not just an affront to humanity; they are the greatest threat to overall progress throughout the African continent.

Yet despite the many obstacles, there is good news coming out of Africa every day. There has been a move away from dictator-

---

*Despite how Africa is often portrayed in the mainstream media, there is much good news. The journalist Charlayne Hunter-Gault's new book, *New News Out of Africa: Uncovering Africa's Renaissance* (Oxford 2006) tells the other side of the story.

ships toward democracy in many countries, and a commitment on the part of many African governments to fiscally responsible economic policies focused on alleviating poverty. Peace agreements have been forged in countries which only a few years earlier had been ripped apart by war and crimes against humanity. Witness the tragic tales of Liberia, Sierra Leone, Angola, Mozambique, southern Sudan, Rwanda, and Burundi, all of which had horrific civil wars that came to an end, laying the groundwork for huge positive changes.

So that is the point. If we can prevent and resolve these wars that lead to such devastation, one of the biggest reasons for Africa's misery and dependence will be removed. By giving peace a chance, we give millions and millions of Africans a chance.

We have identified the Three Ps of ending genocide and other crimes against humanity: Protect the People, Punish the Perpetrators, and Promote the Peace. (We will describe these in detail in Chapter 9.) If the government of the world's sole superpower, the United States, motivated by the will of its citizens, takes the lead globally in doing these three things, crimes against humanity can come to an end.

The decisions we need to make to protect those who are suffering are clear, and the sooner we decide, the more lives will be saved.

That is our choice.

Overcoming Obstacles to Action

So if it is as easy as that, why don't we do it? Mostly it is what we call the Four Horsemen Enabling the Apocalypse: apathy, indifference, ignorance, and policy inertia. The U.S. government simply doesn't want to wade too deeply into the troubled waters of places like northern Uganda and Congo. We did once, in Somalia, and the resulting tragedy of Black Hawk Down—when eighteen American servicemen were killed in the streets of Mogadishu—made everyone nervous about recommitting any effort to African war zones we don't fully understand.

As we all know by now, during the 1994 genocide in Rwanda,

American citizens—to the extent that they even heard about what was happening—largely averted their eyes, and as a result the U.S. government did nothing. Similar averting occurred during the 1975–1979 genocide in Cambodia, from 1992 to 1995 in Bosnia, and even during the Holocaust. As our friend Samantha Power documented in her book on genocide, *A Problem from Hell: America and the Age of Genocide,* this is the usual response to horrific crimes against humanity—disbelief in the totality of the horror and a genuine hope that the problem will go away.

Somalia's Black Hawk Down actually provides the wrong lesson. Instead of running away from these crisis zones, we could protect many lives, and do so much good, if we gave a little more of our time, energy, and resources, in ways that understand the local context. In most cases, we don't have to send 30,000 U.S. Marines every time there is a problem, though working with other countries to apply military force is sometimes necessary. Diplomatic leadership in support of the Three Ps (Protection, Punishment, Peacemaking) is what it takes to make a substantial difference.

Beyond indifference and the ghosts of Somalia, responding to Darfur has an additional obstacle. Sudanese government officials, who were close to Osama bin Laden when he lived in that country from 1991 until 1996, are now cooperating with American counterterrorism authorities. The regime in Khartoum rightly concluded that if they provided nuggets of information about al-Qaeda suspects and detainees to the Americans, the value of this information would outweigh outrage over their state-supported genocide. In other words, when U.S. counterterrorism objectives meet up with anti-genocide objectives, Sudanese officials had a hunch that counterterrorism would win every time. These officials have been right in their calculations so far. As of this writing, near the end of 2006, the United States had done little to seriously confront the Sudanese regime over its policies.

In order to win the peace in Sudan, we must first win an ideological battle at home. We must show that combating crimes against humanity is as important as combating terrorism. Often, as in the case of Sudan, the pursuit of both objectives doesn't have to be mutually exclusive. History has demonstrated that Sudanese government officials change their behavior when they face genuine international diplomatic and economic pressure. If we worked to build strong international consensus for targeted punishments of these officials to meet both counterterrorism and human rights objectives, they would comply.

The policy battle lines are clear. On the one hand are the forces of the status quo: officials from the United States, other governments, and the UN who are inclined to look the other way when the alarm bell sounds and simply send food and medicine to the victims. They believe that the American public and other citizens around the world do not care enough to create a political cost for their inaction. These officials are allowed to remain bystanders because of complicit citizens who know about what is happening but do not speak out, giving the officials an excuse to do nothing.

On the other hand are a growing group of Americans, a ragtag band of citizen activists all over the United States who want the phrase "Never Again" to mean something. They want the first genocide of the twenty-first century, Darfur, to be the last. Led principally by Jewish, Christian, African-American, and student groups, they have slowly begun to organize. Yet far more needs to be done to overcome the institutional inertia in U.S. policy circles. These groups are joined by an even smaller but determined core of citizen activists in other countries who are trying to build a global civil society alliance to confront crimes against humanity.

Who wins this battle will determine the fate of millions of people in Darfur and other killing fields.

That is our mission.

A Citizens' Movement to Confront Mass Atrocity Crimes

Our friend Nicholas Kristof of the *New York Times* has written about a "citizens' army fighting to save" millions of lives in Darfur. After describing some of the extraordinary efforts of ordinary citizens around the country, including fund-raising by young American kids, Nick wrote, "I don't know whether to be sad or inspired that we can turn for moral guidance to 12-year-olds."*

Well, we are inspired.

Samantha Power has written about the "bystanders" who do nothing when genocide occurs and the "upstanders" who act or speak out in an effort to stop the atrocities from continuing. Her book highlights the "upstanders" and "bystanders" of the last century. We all have the capacity to be "upstanders." The more of us there are, the better the chances that these kinds of crimes will not be allowed to occur in the twenty-first century.

It is up to us.

For us, Don first got interested in these issues through the movie he made, then through connecting up with John, who had gone through his own process of growing awareness and discovering a whole universe of Americans who are getting involved and trying to make a difference. We want to show that it is possible to care enough to change things. We want to remove all excuses and impediments to individual action, because such actions— collectively—do make a difference.

Throughout American history, social movements have helped shape our government's policy on a variety of issues. Often in the beginning, their appearance was not widely recognized as much of a movement. We believe we are witnessing the birth of a small but significant grassroots movement to confront genocide and—we hope, over time—all crimes against humanity wherever they occur. A campaign like ENOUGH is but one manifestation of that effort, and we describe many others later in the book.†

---

*"Heroes of Darfur," *New York Times,* May 7, 2006.

†The ENOUGH campaign was founded by a small group of friends and colleagues who had grown weary of watching the world reinvent the wheel every time mass atrocities lurched onto the world's television screens. There is no reason that we collectively cannot do far better and save countless thousands of lives in the process. ENOUGH seeks to strengthen the efforts of grassroots activists, policymakers, advocates, concerned journalists, and others by giving them up-to-date information from on the ground in

Student groups are forming on hundreds of college campuses (and hundreds more high schools) specifically to raise awareness and undertake activities in response to the genocide. Synagogues and churches are holding forums and starting letter-writing campaigns all over the country. National organizations—some faith-based, some African-American, some human rights–related—are running campaigns in every city. Celebrities are getting involved, taking trips and speaking out against the genocide. After all of the hollow pledges of "Never Again" dutifully made by politicians and pundits, networks of concerned Americans are taking matters into their own hands and demanding policy makers do more to end the crisis in Sudan.

One of the best things about this growing movement is that it is nonpartisan. So much of the venom that marks Washington these days—the red state/blue state divide—has been set aside. We always hear how politics makes strange bedfellows. How strange it must have been for some of the conservative evangelical members of Congress to find themselves agreeing with some of the most liberal members the Congress has ever seen!

How the world responds to genocide and other mass atrocity crimes represents one of the greatest moral tests of our lifetime. In the face of genocide halfway around the globe, can American citizens—acting individually and in groups—possibly aid in stopping these atrocities?

Absolutely!

We continue to be convinced that the growing chorus of outrage, from Florida to California, can stop war crimes and reduce the cries of agony in places such as Darfur. The U.S. government can take a leading role in stopping atrocities, in most cases without putting U.S. forces on the ground in large numbers. However, the only means by which U.S. policy can change, and thus the only

---

countries of concern and offering practical pressure points to end the violence. The initial efforts focus on a trio of countries: Sudan, the Democratic Republic of Congo, and the situation in northern Uganda. To learn more go to www.enoughproject.org.

way mass atrocity crimes can end, is if U.S. citizens raise their voices loud enough to get the attention of the White House and force our government to change its policy.

To encourage and embolden you, our readers, to join in this movement to bring an end to genocide around the world, we offer *Six Strategies for Effective Change* that you as an individual can employ to influence public policy and help save hundreds of thousands of lives:

- Raise awareness
- Raise funds
- Write letters
- Call for divestment
- Join an organization
- Lobby the government

Ultimately, this book is about giving meaning to *Never again.* In short, this is a handbook for everyone who thinks that one person cannot make a difference, for those who feel that what happens half a world away is not their responsibility, and for everyone who cares but doesn't know where to start making a positive difference.

We want to tell that story.

First, though, in the interest of full disclosure and since it is, after all, *our* book, we will tell you *our* stories. . . .

2

Two Paths Out of Apathy

Don's Path

MARCH 2004

JOHANNESBURG, SOUTH AFRICA

I'm standing at the South African Airlines ticket counter in the Jo-burg airport, wife and children in tow. "DC!"

I spin around and come face-to-face with Desmond Dube, his wife and son trailing along behind. "Ah *hah*," says I.

"Told you."

I've known Desmond now all of three and a half months—the amount of time it took to shoot the film *Hotel Rwanda* in South Africa and Rwanda—but we've made fast friends. When we first met, I had the earphones of my iPod jammed into my ears, eyes closed, listening to Babatunde Olatunji and stressing about my character, Paul Rusesabagina. Des tapped me on the shoulder.

"What's that?"

"An iPod."

"I-*what?*"

The iPod was a rarity in Johannesburg at that time, and Desmond had never seen one before. I gave him a brief tutorial and let him hold on to it for a minute while I rehearsed. By the time my scene was through, Desmond was asking me how and where he could get an iPod—immediately. I checked around and found that there were indeed a small number available in town but at almost twice the price as in the U.S. The next day, I reported the news and offered to arrange to have a much cheaper iPod sent over from the States as my gift to him, but Desmond wouldn't hear of it and insisted on paying whatever the cost. Desmond Dube was a big star in Jo-burg; his local television show had been top-rated for several years. He was a man proud and able to pay for what he wanted when he wanted it. Dig it. And anyway I could still get the thing full price and discount it to whatever sum I thought reasonable, "gifting" the difference to him without his knowledge. *Pride—check, altruism—check,* we struck a deal.

News of iPod trafficking spread across the set, and in two weeks' time I had at least eight requests from local cast and crew wanting to get in on the cut-rate U.S. hookup. Everybody insisted on being fair, paying the full U.S. price and not a dollar less, which after FedEx, customs fees, tax, and tax on customs—all overages I obviously absorbed . . . Well, I actually hadn't planned on that much altruism. I called the local shops to see if I could just get the iPods at the exorbitant rate they were offering, now cheaper than having them shipped from home, but wouldn't you know it, they'd all sold out, no shipments arriving for weeks. Great. So be it. Sure, I'd already dropped a load on a thousand gifts for the cast and crew, but Tom Cruise had given motorcycles to people he worked with on films, right? Didn't Keanu pay for some crew member's kidney operation or something? Wasn't I a Big Baller? Least I could do was eat the extra couple of grand for my newfound African homeys. My only caveat was that I get the cash from the folks in U.S. dollars. My wife and I had already bought every conceivable artifact, mask, and fair item with the rand (South African currency) I had amassed with my per diem (a stipend paid to performers on productions that are on location out of town), and I wasn't looking to collect more SA currency only to get killed on the exchange. Everybody understood and agreed, so I went ahead and put the follow-up orders in, even though a recurring theme had accompanied each request: "You must understand, it's very difficult converting this rand into U.S. dollars." Not the most encouraging news, but still I was sympathetic.

Working a six-day week with only Sundays off made banking near impossible. Even when they were open, converting cash in South African banks as a black South African can be *tricky* to say the least. Even the connections my friends knew of on the so-called "black market"—their term, not mine—took Sundays off. However, somehow, everybody managed to get their money right and into my hands before I headed home—except for Desmond.

Week after week, Des trickled dough to me—a fiver here, ten spot there—always with the assurance that the final oowap was on its way and not to worry. I suggested more than once that he just let the iPod be my gift to him and let the money slide, but he rebuffed me every time, once saying, "You think I need the charity?"

Now, standing at that ticket counter looking at seating with visions of the LA hustle and bustle crowding in, I had all but forgotten about it. But sure enough, Desmond strode in at the wire grinning like the cat that ate the cassava.

"Ah *hah*," says I.

"Told you," says he, throwing it back to me.

I could make out the familiar faded green of U.S. currency sticking out both sides of his fist. Yet even with my less than perfect vision, I could clearly see that it was light. With no accompanying look of apology or regret, Desmond pressed the $50 into my hand. "Get you the rest when you come back."

The wink he gave me was my cue to smile, so I did. I hoped he was right. I said good-bye to Des's wife and baby as he said good-bye to mine, and one hour later, Cheadle and company were headed to California.

Then somewhere over the ocean, it happened: déjà vu—not the one that hits you when somebody says something familiar to you, but a familiar *feeling* of the moment sidled up. Unease. This feeling I had come to recognize over the years. Like surviving the temporary pain in your stomach, paying you back for that burrito you ate at the taco stand, it was one I'd also become accustomed to breathing through and riding out. But this time was different. This feeling came out of the blue and the breathing wasn't working. This one was telling me that I had unfinished business in Africa, and it wasn't the $150 between friends.

FALL 2004
LOS ANGELES AND TORONTO, CANADA

This autumn in LA followed hotly on the heels of *Ocean's Twelve*. My family and I traveled to five countries in four months, and fun as it was, we were all still looking forward to returning to our brand-new-ish, dream–cum–money pit, nightmare–cum–pseudo dream house in the canyon. School was right around the corner, hard apples were in season, and all in all, autumn in LA was good. But fall was about to trip me up, placing me front and center on things I had only played at a few short months ago.

Earlier that summer, while we were still shooting in Italy, *Hotel Rwanda* director Terry George brought over a rough cut of the film and screened it for a few of us. He also brought along Paul Rusesabagina, who, unfortunately for me, sat beside me in the darkened theater. I've never been more nervous in my life. Every sound and gesture I made on that screen seemed either too big, too small, or just too *something* with me being in such close proximity to the man who actually did the things I was acting. It was very difficult watching the film with one eye while trying to gauge the reactions of the very stoic figure on my right at the same time. At some point I just gave up and forced myself to focus on the movie. (Actually, first I gave up looking at the movie and turned sideways in my seat to look directly at Paul, felt stupid, *then* turned forward and focused on the film.) No matter what I say at the press junkets, I am the harshest critic of any film I am in, especially one in which I'm the lead, so even without Paul sitting right there next to me the experience would have been painful.

Two hours later the lights came up and no one was talking. Now, there are many different types of "silence," but the two most common following the screening of a rough cut are the one of awkward embarrassment as people try to make it to the door or the kind when people don't yet want to speak for fear of trivializing the moment with some insipid comment that attempts to sum it all up. When Paul reached over and gently squeezed my arm, I allowed myself to believe the silence was the good one. But when I saw Scott Caan (tough-as-nails actor, and son of James Caan) sniffling into his sleeve, I knew the film had struck a chord.

Days removed, I found myself playing the movie over and over in my head, as much for its content as for the fact that we had done it at all. Terry had been trying to hustle interest and money for the film for three years before finally devising the spiderweb of financing with Alex Ho (producer) that got us into production— and even then only because Alex personally bankrolled our first day of shooting to keep us afloat. We fought an uphill battle against weather, the extras rioting (and rightly so), the payroll being stolen *twice,* and the normal things that plague all films with similar budgets shooting in foreign lands on tight schedules. But we knew we had a strong story to tell and at the very least could "get out of the road and just tell it," as Terry often put it.

There were and are thousands of stories in Africa from every imaginable walk of life and unimaginable as well. Our story was about one man and his desire to save his family and the greater family of man as best he could—that much was surely true and came clearly through. But would it pass muster out in the world? Would anyone even care to hear about it? If the response to the Rwanda genocide itself was any indication of how the film would be received, we had just made the most expensive home movie on the planet.

Paul, Terry, and I sit outside a little pub on the sidewalk drinking beers and spinning winter scenarios. Paul looks past Terry to me. "So, Don, what do you think about the Oscars?"

"The Oscars. What do you mean?"

"Will we be there?"

"Oh, man, I don't know."

Terry coming in now: "Yeah, hold on there, Paul. First we gotta get people to see it. Africa movies ain't exactly . . . you know . . ."

I knew. "Yep."

Paul, shaking his head. "No. People will see this."

I changed the subject to foreign beers, putting the Oscar talk to bed for the time being. It was enough for me that we had achieved at least our first goal—to tell the story. Award recognition was far from my thoughts; I agreed with Terry that we faced an uphill battle just getting butts in the seats. I have always been a cynic when it comes to those kinds of accolades anyway, seeing them as a kind of dessert that's nice to have but not at all necessary after a satisfying meal. Little did I know how important that kind of recognition can be for the life of the film. For us, in fact, the Oscar nominations would become life support.

I got the call from Terry sometime in August confirming that our film had indeed been accepted into the Toronto International Film Festival, so I needed to pack a bag. This was great news for us. This is a major festival for "serious" films like ours as well as being a serious marketplace to hawk your film and, for us, find foreign distribution as well. The life of the film can often be decided here, and we were all feeling the joy and the pressure.

School was just starting back up for our daughters, with thousands of miles of travel not yet out of their little bodies. We were very lucky this year; putting them in school during the filming in Africa had worked out just as good as the sisters traveling around with us during *Ocean's Twelve*. But they would sit out Toronto with Mom, even if it wasn't for another two weeks yet.

Bridgid and I fell asleep with the lights on talking all that night about Africa and the movie we'd made. Life was good.

September in Toronto was a quickening for me, as I had two films at the festival, with *Crash* premiering there as well. *Hotel Rwanda* was one of several Africa-themed films there that year—one of two about Rwanda. Paul Rusesabagina and his wife, Tatiana, were scheduled to attend, and you could cut the hype with a knife. Press from around the world had assembled for this event, and I felt the pessimist in me staking claim to my ego, sweating my credibility quotient once again being in such close proximity to the real McCoy. I had earlier considered "doing away" with Paul—not harming him, mind you, but offering him money to go MIA until after the screening, so as not to court comparison. But I punked out, hesitated, and now the film was about to unspool in front of a packed house. Damn my civility. Whatever fate awaited me served me right.

I headed off in the limo to the screening with Sophie Okonedo, who played Tatiana in the film, her face on high animation, talking a mile a minute. I was thankful for the banter, which was calming me down. The experience of filming the movie had thrown us together, both of us feeling the weight of what we'd taken on, praying we'd come out the other side worthy of the task. Tonight, however, Sophie wasn't worried. She was reminding me of the night she, Chiwetel Ejiofor (from *Dirty Pretty Things* and with whom I would later work), and one of his friends were roaming around Soweto, South Africa.

They had just left a party and begun wandering aimlessly around the streets, which can be a crazy thing to do in SA, or even LA for that matter. Sophie began to hear faraway singing, and the three followed her ears through the labyrinthine neighborhood to a little house where nearly a hundred souls were gathered in the small front yard, singing praises to the Lord. Sophie and company had walked up to the fence to get a closer listen, when they were spotted and immediately ushered in as if they had been expected. Folks began pulling them along through the crowd, telling them

"She's back in the back." One man took over, guiding them through the people and telling them, like someone out of a fable, that the "old woman" had told the singers gathered there to expect the company of three strangers and to welcome them in once they'd arrived. This was the moment when those who are thoughtful would look to reason, but these were three artists, so curiosity trumped caution and they waded deeper into the house, finding an elderly woman who gestured to them to come close. She sat them down and told them that earlier that night she'd had a vision of strangers coming to visit and that they were a good omen for her "people"—practitioners of a sect of Judaism. The woman questioned them for a short period of time, and after she was convinced of their purity of purpose, she told them to follow her outside. The large group surrounded the three and resumed singing, but a different tune and tempo now. Though Sophie and her friends didn't know the language of the song, they felt the singers' intent (the pail of water that was thrown in their faces serving as punctuation): they were being blessed. They laughed and smiled their wet, blessed selves all the way home, as well they should have—God is good. This hadn't been a polite sprinkle-of-holy-water blessing; it was a bucketful of safety that would eventually get us through all the adversity that was to come during the filming of this movie, in Sophie's opinion. Now, she said, it was the spirits of Rwanda that were giving us permission to testify, or maybe even demanding we do. We were protected and supported, she assured me, by their grace. Talk like this from Sophie is what brought me to the theater feeling that we might be all right after all.

Still, I was as nervous as a sinner in a Sunday service.

"Let's go smoke a cigarette, Sophie. This is . . ."

"Too right."

We stepped into the lobby and did our best to smoke and not care, but we failed miserably, comparing notes on the audience's reaction and rushing back in, our being outside of the screening proving harder than being in. We braved the remainder of the film with me about chewing a hole in my bottom lip the entire time.

In the box next to Terry, Sophie, and me sat Paul and Tatiana, hard to read, quiet and reserved, their behavior, even now as their lives played out on screen, consistent with what I had come to know over the last year. During our time together I would often watch Paul and Tatiana when they weren't looking, checking for signs of post-traumatic stress to break through their pleasant veneers. But I only ever caught the aftershocks of their horrific experience rising to the surface twice: once while they were watching the actors who portrayed the Interahamwe (a Hutu militia) rehearsing their parade at our base camp and then again at our first cast/crew party.

During rehearsals, Paul and Tatiana had been asked by Terry to observe the Interahamwe parade to assure authenticity of the scene. Drawn by the drums and singing, Sophie and I made our way to the narrow road outside to watch as well. I stood next to Paul, who again was a cipher, quietly watching, though it quickly became clear that Tatiana wasn't comfortable with the demonstration. After only a few moments of the processional's passing, she shook her head, saying, "I can't, I can't . . . ," and retreated inside. Paul stayed behind, his lips almost imperceptibly moving, quietly muttering to himself. The actor in me was burning to ask him what specifically he was feeling, but it felt too rude at that time. Paul spoke up without prodding.

"It looks very good, *hey*? Very real."

"Um . . . yeah . . ." was all I could muster. Paul had opened the door, but I was still too cautious to step through.

Then Paul was shaking his head and saying, "I don't like it. It is hard to watch."

But watch it we did as it passed by, South African, Burundian, and even Rwandan extras singing songs of intimidation and Hutu dominance. (We later learned that some of the members of the parade were actual members of the Interahamwe who had participated in the genocide of 1994. No wonder it looked so real.)

The second time I witnessed how close it all was to the surface for Paul and Tatiana was a few days later at our cast/crew party.

Antonio Lyons, the actor playing Tatiana's brother (and nearest in resemblance to his character out of all of us), came up to her full of enthusiasm, introducing himself: "I'm Thomas!" Tatiana burst into tears, as if the ten years since the deaths of her sibling and his wife had not passed. It took a half hour to calm Tatiana down and persuade her to rejoin the party. To her credit, and a testament to her and Paul's resilience, they were soon dancing with the rest of us—all outward signs of sorrow gone, which is the way I remember them 99 percent of the time—pleasant, open, and happy. Paul and Tatiana, along with Odette Nyiramilimo and Jean Baptiste Gasasira, two of their closest friends in Rwanda at the time, survivors of one of the worst massacres in human history, shared their stories with us freely and more often than not displayed a gentle kindness and a genuine love for life that I initially didn't expect from survivors of such horrors. I expected much more rancor, bitterness, a desire for revenge even. In retrospect, however, I have come to understand another equally natural reaction to their tragedy—relishing every moment and celebrating life

As the final credit rolled over the screen to Wyclef Jean's song, the crowd began clapping very enthusiastically. Sophie and I were grinning ear to ear. I looked over to Paul and Tatiana. Their expression was the same as it had been at the top of the screening: a cipher. Terry jumped up quickly and moved to the edge of the box, waving his arms at the crowd for them to quiet down. It took a minute, but finally they calmed to hear what he had to say.

"Thank you, thank you . . . I just wanted to say that we have special guests here, the two people whose lives were featured in the film tonight, Paul and Tatiana Rusesabagina."

I've never witnessed a four-minute standing ovation before. I've been in a two-minute and changer before that was really more like two minutes, ten seconds strong, with the last ten being a mix of polite the-performers-can-still-see-you applause and people making for the aisle. This was not that. When Paul and Tatiana raised their joined hands, the crowded house literally threw its applause and shouts toward the two. They both stood there politely soaking it in, framed by the spotlight from the front, outlining them in a very fitting halo when viewed from behind. After about two minutes (*real* sixty-second minutes—time it for yourself; it's long), in a completely unplanned gesture, Paul reached over and took my hand, Tatiana found Sophie's, and they pulled us both into their spotlight. I didn't know quite what to do. I was embarrassed to have been brought into a moment that was so clearly a display of affection and gratitude meant for Paul and Tatiana, but I knew of no way to remove my hand from Paul's without looking like an ungracious jerk. The feeling of having that much concentrated energy pouring out at you is hard to describe. My emotions ran the entire gamut over the next minute I stood next to Paul feeling small. The overriding sensation I had, however, was one of joy for Paul and Tatiana finally seeing their story on the big screen and knowing that even if only these few hundred gathered here witnessed it, the tale was told. Eventually, I couldn't take it anymore and sheepishly backed out of there waving to the people whose applause didn't subside for another full, *real* minute.

Our film was quickly picked up by an overseas distributor and everyone was talking about February: Oscar season. I started getting calls from the U.S., from people who had heard the buzz and couldn't wait to see the film, including a congressman from Orange County, Ed Royce, who believed *Hotel Rwanda* could be a rallying point around which to draw attention to the recent troubles in Darfur. *Darfur? Where's that? There's genocide occurring there as well?* Then closely on the heels of the question, I got that feeling again, coming more sharply into focus. I am far from done with Africa. Or was it Africa that wasn't yet done with me?

DECEMBER 2004
LOS ANGELES, CALIFORNIA

I met with Congressman Ed Royce at an MGM screening, and he invited me to join a congressional delegation traveling to Darfur to see firsthand the fallout from the weekly attacks by the Sudanese military and the Janjaweed on the civilians of western Sudan. Ed proposed that we visit refugee camps and speak with local government leaders as well as members of a far too minimal and largely ineffectual African Union security force. Despite coming together to protect the refugees in and around the camps, the AU's toothless mandate prevented them from using force against the marauders, relegating them to little more than observers, reporting to the UN about incidents they could do nothing to stop. And all of these incidents occurred in an area roughly the size of Texas that the AU's two thousand or so members were far too few to adequately patrol.

On the face of it, the situation looked hopeless and I was not exactly sure why I was being asked along. I mean, I understood that being a "celebrity" (still feels ridiculous to refer to myself as one) carries with it the ability to draw the public's attention to various issues, but this wasn't promoting the hottest new hip-hop artist or fashion line we're talking about, this was bearing witness to murder on a mass scale. What could *I* do to stem this current tide of oppression that ranking members of Congress on both sides of the aisle had been unable to stem? All I did was act in a movie. However, I agreed to go, apprehensive about what I might see but relieved to finally identify what had been eating at me all this time. I was about to get "involved."

JANUARY 2005
WASHINGTON, DC

The CODEL (congressional delegation) flies first thing tomorrow morning, but tonight is spent with my sister Cindy out and about in DC. I don't get to see her very often to my great regret, as her busy teaching schedule and my sporadically busy filming schedule are in heavy competition. Cindy is older by thirteen months and funnier, smarter, and wiser than me by about thirteen years. We have lived on opposite sides of the country now for about ten years, though she spent approximately one year in LA with my family in a failed "nanny" experiment—a job too small for her many talents. Cindy also spent that year alternately teaching at a local school and tutoring elementary school students, several of them with special learning challenges. I love it when I'm tooling around town and get stopped by someone who I believe to be a fan and it turns out to be a parent of one of these children who could care less about me but heaps praise on my sister for the work she's done with their child. That's a *real* review.

After about an hour of meandering due to indecision—a Cheadle family trait—we settle on Ruth's Chris Steak House. Over drinks we discuss our very busy separate lives, Africa in general, and Darfur specifically.

"What are you going to do when you're out there?"

"Visit several refugee camps, meet with some of the displaced leaders there as well as the AU. The congressmen and -women are then going on to Khartoum to sit down with some government officials, but John and I are going to stay back on the Sudan-Chad border. Paul Rusesabagina is going too."

"That's cool. What's your goal?"

"Well, to get a firsthand account of what is happening there from the people suffering from it every day. Hopefully, we can then put our collective minds and the congressmen and -women's collective powers together to come up with some kind of strategy to present to the current administration that will stem the tide of this genocide." My sister, God love her, never really one to play her cards close to her vest, gives me a look filled with both skepticism and sympathy. She and I are both aware that this particular battle will probably be fought uphill in a rainstorm with boots made of papier-mâché.

"Well, at least we can give the people there a forum to air their troubles. And with *Nightline* tagging along, we can document their stories and put those all-too-ignored words and pictures in front of an American audience."

She's still unconvinced, so I go on.

"You never know what will move people to respond. However hard it is, we still have to try to add our light to the sum of light."

"Wow." Impressed now. "The first part was kind of extra but I like that 'sum of light' thing."

I admit to her that I stole the phrase from the film *The Year of Living Dangerously,* and I can't remember if they stole it or who they stole it from. She asks me if there's anything she can do to help. Before I can answer, the waiter returns with our embarrassingly huge steaks, and the juxtaposition of these two medium-rare monsters with our conversation about genocide, famine, and poverty makes each bite a little difficult.

We soon shift into catch-up mode, and our talk begins to flow between family and friends, food and memories. But I'm just a little behind the whole time, words and thoughts not coming to me very easily. I'm stuck back on Africa and my papier-mâché boots.

When Congressman Ed Royce first suggested the Africa trip, I thought it would be an amazing opportunity to smell, touch, and feel what I had only read about or seen on TV and in movies. And though that specific opportunity hadn't changed, my sister's skepticism was eating at me. The possibility that we could travel many thousands of miles in an attempt to make a difference, yet return no closer to realizing our goals than when we left, hadn't ever seriously occurred to me. Don't get me wrong; I'm not Pollyanna-ish about how things work in the world. I wasn't expecting instantaneous results in Sudan simply because the CODEL was making this expedition with Don Cheadle along for the ride. But the idea that we could make a very concerted effort for change and fail anyway, the specter of it, threatened to push me from being a pessimist to being a fatalist, letting me permanently off the hook. Looking at that nearly made me sick. It was scarier to me than doing nothing at all.

I'd always hurt for Africa and her tortured past/present. Even if one had only cursory knowledge of the continent, you'd know that it is rife with stories of civil war, famine, and disease. Being a Black man, I had always carried a fair amount of guilt, justifiably or not, for not having done a great deal more than I had for the mother-land. But up until now, my perceived powerlessness had protected me. It buffered me from ever feeling too bad about my inaction when a call from the televangelists arose or when an invitation to a $5,000-a-plate dinner for Africa-related issue X came across my desk yet found its way into my circular file. Africa's woes were overwhelming—far too big for me to grapple with. I imagine there are many like-minded individuals experiencing the longing to "do something" for Africa but feeling too small to effect any real change given the scope of the continent's problems. Others I'm sure have shared my skepticism regarding the conduits through which dona-tions flow, having heard accountings of disreputable organizations skimming off the top or worse, donated money, food, and supplies falling into the hands of the very criminals and warlords who cre-ated the grave need for assistance in the first place. And the question of where to start is overwhelming to ponder: Whose need is the greatest? Which country, which war, what issue?

Before, I would have put away the porterhouse in front of me in a heartbeat, guilt-free, no problem. Can't do anything about it. Why worry? Let's eat. Not so easy now. I grinned, chewed, and joked my way through dinner and kept it all to myself. This wasn't guilt that was eating me up now; it was the resounding drum of ambivalence starting to pound in me.

Later that night I was trying to buy some hand-crank radios to deliver to the refugee camps so that the people could listen to their tunes and news stories without needing batteries or electricity. We tried a couple of sporting goods stores before we found some at REI, but they only had about twenty-five of them. There was no conceivable way that would be enough radios, but some was bet-ter than none. The store owner recognized me and talked loudly enough to draw the attention of his employees, who began ques-tioning me about what I was buying and what I was doing in their neighborhood. It gave me the perfect opportunity to talk about Darfur and our trip and what we were hoping to do. A few of the guys had seen *Hotel Rwanda* and were interested in what I had to say about how a place called Darfur was in an eerily similar situation, how it was definitely reminiscent of the reluctance to act on the part of the international community toward what had been officially declared a genocide. This discussion ran all the way through the boxing of the radios and the swiping of the card.

Nine o'clock now and the last stragglers are driving off as Cindy and I stuff the oversized boxes into her compact car. We're playing a king-sized game of Tetris like a mutha, but we manage.

"Don't you feel like your mission has already started?"

"What mission?"

"To get the story out to as many people as you can. What you just did in the store, wasn't that a part of it?"

"I guess so."

"It's similar to what you were saying about the stories that *Nightline* will bring back except you're not waiting for the show to air. You are the storyteller. You are being active now."

That one word stopped me from telling her that I had only an hour ago seriously contemplated fatalism. One word snapped me to attention: Active. Steven J. Brown, political lobbyist turned hedge fund manager, had mentioned the word before to me, almost as an aside. "Being an activist for Africa is no small thing. Are you sure you're ready?" No, I wasn't ready, and I wasn't one, given that the word "activist" in my mind was reserved for people who would possibly put themselves in harm's way to defend justice. I wasn't *there*. Activists always took up the gauntlet for the rights of the meek over the tyranny of the strong. The reward for activists could be a paradigm shift toward justice, true, but often as not the result could be professional suicide, if they were lucky, with grave bodily harm or death never completely off the table. I wouldn't cast myself in that movie. My idea was to gain insight, leverage celebrity, and keep it movin'. I feel for the people, but my own family serves as my chief and primary concern. I was hardly anybody's activist. But I was active. Active begets activism and creates an activist? No. It's got to be harder than that.

At my sister's home, the conversation and conversion contin-ued. "You're not going into any real dangerous areas, are you?"

"There's no way we'd get clearance if we were. These are all congressional members traveling and we have a military escort *and* we're going to have news cameras with us. I don't think any-thing's going to happen."

"You should bring cameras to the camps. Individual video cameras."

"Why?"

"So that the Darfurians can film what is happening themselves. What would be the impact if the Internet was suddenly flooded with all these home movies of bombers doing runs on their villages or Janjaweed attacking children and women, everybody running for their lives? All of that?"

I needed to think on that for a minute but answered immediately anyway, Joaquin Phoenix's character in *Hotel Rwanda* leaping to mind.

"Everyone would be probably be shocked. Some would be out-raged. Few would act."

But her question sent me down a tour of tangents. Would footage from the Nazi Holocaust, if it were to have been strewn across some information highway equivalent to the Internet in the forties, have ended that genocide? It would have been as ghastly a sight as any horror movie that's come out in the last twenty years, more so for being real. Could we have stood by so long then? When I was in junior high school I saw the Holocaust-themed documentary *Night and Fog*. It messed me up. The prisoners in those camps were on a one-way trip to death by work, starvation, medical experimentation, or execution, and everyone in that audi-torium knew it but them. I wished I could go back in time and scream at them, "Those are not the showers! Rush those guards! They're lying to you!" I have never been as affected by images in my life save for a *Frontline* documentary on Rwanda I saw many years later. Moving pictures.

But more recently, did news footage of the ethnic cleansing in Bosnia play any role in the United States' decision to intervene? Fifty years after the rise of the Nazis, we were as a people familiar with the existence of ethnic cleansing, even if we didn't know the particulars of the Bosnian conflict. Did the 1992–1995 audiences of news watchers in any way shame policy makers in the U.S. to action, the echoes of Russia and Germany reverberating in their hearts and minds?

Perhaps it is a quantitative question, however, and the numbers of dead and dying in this current ethnic cleansing are perceived as being simply too small to get involved. Or could it be the Darfurians' international position that is the real impediment to action? The government of Sudan has simultaneously been labeled by the U.S. an ally in the war on terror as well as a purveyor of modern genocide; the extreme opposition these viewpoints occupy has created a skewed impression. The U.S. has also claimed that it is loath to interfere in the affairs of a sovereign state, a fair-weather policy at best when, no matter the possible implications and political intricacies, the West *does* choose to intervene when a boon can be derived. What boon then beyond justice can be derived from Darfur? In the face of all this, what good could images really do?

Cindy's question also got me thinking about the 1935 movie *Triumph of the Will,* which Leni Riefenstahl shot, documenting the Nazi Party's rise to power. Intentionally or not, that work promoted the perceived and then fully realized power of the Nazis. But could it in some way work in reverse? Could genocide footage from Darfur and Chad showing that the strength *these* purveyors of death enjoy lies in their ability to act with impunity—not from their power as a truly formidable force—could this inspire other nations to act? Would we challenge cowardice as readily as we were emboldened to face down tyranny?

Though it seemed like only seconds I had been ruminating on all this, it must have been longer.

"You falling asleep?" Cindy asked.

"No."

"Where'd you go?"

"Everywhere."

Nine o'clock now, post shower and cold cereal, and it's time to make my way downstairs to load my pillowed-under eyes and oversized boxes into the waiting van. I board the already full bus that would be shuttling us to the airport and on to our private military escort plane. Several members of Congress are in attendance. Jim McDermott, a Democrat from Washington State, has spent much of his time in Congress dealing with African affairs. Barbara Lee, a California Democrat, is sitting near the back. Over her shoulder sits Diane Watson, another Democrat from California. Both of them are on the House Committee on International Relations Subcommittee on Africa. Betty McCollum, Democrat from Minnesota, is here as well. She also has a seat on the Committee on International Relations, where she promotes U.S. leadership to confront the HIV/AIDS pandemic. Last but not least is California Republican Ed Royce, the then vice-chairman of the Subcommittee on Africa. He is a strong supporter of the African Growth and Opportunity Act, which reduced import quotas on African goods as large parts of the continent began moving toward free markets and political democracy. And then there's me, starring in the grown-up version of *Sesame Street*'s "one of these things is not like the others." I hope to God nobody asks me a question about Chad or Darfur and my answer reveals my absolute ignorance on the subject. Just in case, I've front-loaded the complimentary response "I'm here to learn." It's hardly a lie.

The trip had been described as a fact-finding exercise, which was exactly the type of trip a neophyte like me needed. I had only just begun to investigate the situation and was familiar with only a few of the players involved in the conflict. I knew I had much to learn. But then something happened as I began to take stock in my traveling companions. My seeds of fatalism began searching for purchase: "What knowledge could this fact-finding trip *really* yield, and to what end?"

The U.S. die had already been cast for Darfur policy-wise, hadn't it? Weren't we actually going to bring back incontrovertible evidence of "genocide," so named by our government because of the mountain of evidence, of an incontrovertible nature, that already existed to support the finding? It was a riddle wrapped in a mystery inside an enigma of diplomatic doublespeak. Yet here we were, on our way. It didn't all add up. The congressional members couldn't have been counting on free publicity to highlight their empathetic and compassionate souls, given that the trip had been planned for months and *Nightline* had only recently agreed to accompany us (cutting it very close to the wire, in fact). So why were they going? Maybe what made the trip inviting was the fact that it was politically safe for the representatives on both sides of the aisle; these people hailed from a government that had used the word "genocide" while referring to Darfur yet ignored all international conventions that called for direct action against it. This mission could be the perfect opportunity for a politico to pick up compassion points without being saddled with the need for results. For a fledgling fatalist, skepticism was as comfortable as an old shoe, and I had gone from enthusiastic participant on our journey to pessimistic passenger in only the time it took to walk down the bus aisle. *Dammit! now I gotta take this long-ass trip with these people who aren't really looking to change the game, they just want to assuage their guilt and have the opportunity to claim the moral high ground come election time. "At least we've gone to Africa to see the horror up close." I can hear them now.* Whoa. I can hear *me* now. I had just "them-ed" them. I let their new moniker roll around in my mind for a hot second. I was good with it, but I always allow for the fact that I could be wrong.

After the short bus ride, "them" and I board a military charter, rounded out by an automatic weapon–toting security force. Nice. We're headed first to Entebbe, Uganda, and eventually to Chad.

Before long the film *The Battle of Algiers* begins to play over the cabin's television screens. It is an amazing movie about the Algerians' fight for freedom against the French in the 1950s, and I couldn't for the life of me figure out why we were watching it on this trip. True, the CODEL was going on to Algiers after Chad and Sudan, but the subject matter of this film jangled greatly out of tune with the mental profile I had compiled of my travel companions. We were flying to be witness to the ravages of genocide in Darfur, accompanied by sound and pictures of young, brown men and women, not cardboard caricatures but human beings depicted evenly, preparing bombs to explode in markets, restaurants, and bars. I thought my *head* would explode. Maybe the people on this CODEL were different. Maybe they were about opening their eyes to seek understanding, to move toward positive change. Maybe these people were actually trying to do something here. Could they be "Us"s?

When we landed in Entebbe to refuel, our group went into the airport's waiting area, where we met a marine unit stationed in the region, shocked as hell to see "that guy that came out in *Boogie Nights*" ambling around tryng to get cell phone reception. We took some pictures together; I finally found a T-Mobile–friendly corner, and a short time later we hopped back on the plane to finish the last leg of our trip.

JANUARY 2005
CHAD

As our transport slowly taxied down the runway, I peeked out the window and found two things that stood in stark relief against the dusty tarmac: the *Nightline* camera crew filming all the proceedings and a long, stringy-haired, six-foot-and-change white man strolling casually up to the plane like he was walking down the street to the local convenience store to get the paper. John Prendergast looked right at home.

I first met John in November of 2004 at the Holocaust Memorial Museum in Washington, D.C., which was hosting a screening of *Hotel Rwanda*. Sophie, Paul, Tatiana, and Terry had all assembled for the event, with hundreds in attendance. Bonnie Abaunza, a seriously dedicated human rights advocate working with Amnesty International, was navigating us through the maze of people and making sure we were meeting the folks we needed to, when she brought me over to John, hanging out with his running buddy, and U.S. ambassador-at-large for war crimes issues, Pierre-Richard Prosper. I only mention height because within five minutes of our meeting these two "important" people, the conversation devolved into a healthy round of trash-talking about basketball. They'd heard tell of my basketball prowess—a tale told by an idiot, full of sound and fury, signifying nothing—and proceeded to look down on me (literally), recounting tales of hardwood heroism, challenging me and any other human being I knew to a game of two-on-two. I told them that I knew Magic Johnson, Michael Jordan, and many of the Lakers and Clippers but would only need to pull somebody from my weekend crew to face down a couple of Beltway braggers who clearly only had height going for them. Needless to say, we were fast friends. Segueing out of ball and back to matters at hand, John downloaded me on his extensive experiences in Africa and said he wanted me to consider him an ally-in-service for whatever Africa-related task I might take up. I pocketed the info, and when the Darfur trip arose, he was an early call.

Now, seeing him confidently rolling up, throwing his arms open wide with a "Buddy!" and no apparent worry clouding his mug, I was sure I was in the company of another "Us." Seconds later our "Us" would be complete as Paul Rusesabagina, smartly dressed as always, stood nearby with a "My friend!" of his own to welcome me. I'd known he would be accompanying us, but I was still completely blown away. This man had come through a fire that most would greatly resist even mentally replaying, never mind reliving through the experiences of these people we were about to meet. If he could bring himself to this task, who was I to entertain fatalism? I was humbled in the company of all that had made this journey—people committing much more than empty sentiments to try to change for the better the world in which they lived. It would most probably be a thankless job and one with a most uncertain outcome. But standing on the ground in Chad, I found myself smiling, happy to be among doers, lucky to be pulled into the current of Us.

John's Path

I hate waking up early. I'm an unapologetic, unreformed vampire, hard-pressed to lay my head on the pillow before 3 A.M. Let's just say it isn't easy to get me out of bed anywhere in the vicinity of the crack of dawn. So when I first heard the sound of banging on my hotel door on a scorching July morning in Khartoum in 2003, I wasn't pleased. I knew the zealous housekeeping staff liked to finish their work before it got too hot, but they knew from experience that my room was usually the last one they would have access to on any given day. But when the knocking persisted and even got louder, I knew I had to surrender and find out the reason for the urgency of the knuckles on my door.

I opened the door and my friend the bellhop practically tumbled into the room, breathlessly proclaiming that this time I had gone too far. "You've been declared an enemy of the state," he blurted, with a mixture of satisfaction and concern. "The foreign minister is saying your security cannot be guaranteed. That is decidedly not good."

My first reaction was logistical. Having been in more than a few jams over two decades traveling in war zones, I usually liked to make sure I had a good escape plan, just in case the temperature rose a little too fast. Over the years, I'd been shot at, bombed, mortared, imprisoned, beaten, threatened (credibly, I would hasten to add), deported, surveilled, chased, and defamed a hundred ways till Sunday. (My mother's prayer group saying the rosary for me is probably the main reason I am still alive today.) But this "enemy of the state" thing was a new one, and I didn't know for sure what the next move would be.

The bellhop wasn't finished. Apparently, my appearance on the Arabic television equivalent of CNN, Al-Jazeera, went over like a lead balloon with the authorities. I had emptied my rhetorical chambers into the camera the day before, saying that the leaders of the regime should be tried for war crimes in front of an international tribunal for what they were doing in Darfur and what they had done in the south of the country. This was an unwelcome message at the time, as the regime was doing its best to clean up its image around the world and trying to keep what it was doing in Darfur under the radar screen. My eyewitness account to Al-Jazeera, broadcast live from Khartoum, appeared like a rabid skunk at a white linen picnic. The daggers were drawn quickly. The bellhop was sure my life was in danger, even though he was clearly pleased with the message I'd delivered, given that his own family had been victimized in a village raid a year earlier by government-backed militia in Darfur.

My second reaction was one that I had unfortunately had a few too many times in my life: "Another fine mess you've gotten yourself into, J.P.!" It was hard to imagine the chain of events that led me to that moment. I will try, however, starting with the ideas and influences that eventually came to shape my character. They originated early on, in the dark basements of the houses I lived in as a kid, where I would voraciously consume comic books about my heroes who took on evil to protect the helpless. The Mighty Thor, Captain America, Batman, Daredevil, and the Silver Surfer were all guys who hated injustice and put their lives on the line for it. They all had certain powers that they used in the service of others, often to the detriment of their own lives. When I was a kid, I used to read about these superheroes like there was no tomorrow. I wanted to be like them somehow, wanted to stand for something good. I was especially drawn to the darker characters, the ones with significant personal flaws, those who were running from something yet throwing themselves into their mission. Their humanity, their vulnerability, made their commitment all the more appealing. I always felt that many of their powers were just exaggerations of things certain human beings were capable of under extreme pressure (with the possible exceptions of flying, shooting spiderwebs out of hands, turning green, and picking up entire buildings). When I would hear about things like floods in Bangladesh or famines in Africa, I wondered why someone like my superheroes couldn't save the victims.

But of course there are no superheroes in that sense and we don't really "save victims." It is about working with others in defense of justice and human rights. And that means some element of sacrifice, even if it is just a few minutes on a computer to write a letter. After the Al-Jazeera interview, the correspondent asked me, "Aren't you worried for your safety? I keep hearing about you running into trouble. Why do you do it?" My response: "Anger. I can't accept that we just stand idly by while entire peoples are being extinguished because of the actions and advantage of a few people. Every time I think I will walk away from this and become a sportswriter, focusing on my beloved Kansas City Chiefs, I see something like this and it just flames me up again. I'm doomed to do this for as long as I live."

But last I checked, the contract for this book doesn't say "autobiography," so I will spare you the details of my childhood. Save that one for some future movie of the week. The far distant future. Or maybe my baby brother Luke can write it; he remembers everything. I mean everything. For the purposes of this story, however, the journey really begins later, in my early twenties, when I was a somewhat clichéd rebel without a cause and a crusader in search of a mission.

After bouncing around the United States and going to four different universities, I ended up back in my adopted hometown of Philadelphia, working for a congressman and going to Temple University at night for my fifth and final undergraduate stop. (Papa was a rolling stone, a frozen food salesman to be exact, and this apple didn't land too far from Jack's tree.) I was doing all kinds of stuff focused on urban problems in the United States: my job with the congressman allowed me to get involved in many things. I also was a Big Brother to kids in the Big Brother/Little Brother program, as well as to kids I met in the homeless shelters where I was volunteering. (That's the next book.)

I loved my work and loved what I was studying at school on urban policy, but in 1983 a story broke that changed my life forever. The famine in what is now Ethiopia and Eritrea* emerged into the public consciousness very slowly, as these kinds of issues do, if they ever do at all. I kept seeing these pictures of mass starvation (mostly on those post-midnight fund-raising paid programs that organizations buy to highlight the horrors they are trying to ameliorate with their food and medicine) and reading into them messages of a world that just didn't care enough to do whatever was necessary to end the suffering of those people. There were images of hundreds of thousands of homeless Ethiopians and Eritreans in makeshift camps—people living and dying in the worst circumstances humanly possible. I was overwhelmed by the pictures; all of my empathetic and protective tendencies went into overdrive. I hadn't studied any of these issues, but I knew at the bottom of it all there must lie a massive core of injustice, overlaid by a blanket of apathy.

In 1984, I decided to go to Africa to investigate for myself. After reading all those comic books and believing in the ultimate triumph of good over evil, it was time for Captain America's number one fan—naive but determined—to spring into action. I believed very innocently then that if the United States would just get involved, we could fix everything.

---

*The "Ethiopian Famine" of '83–'85 resulted from the tactics of war pursued by the Ethiopian regime at the time against Eritreans fighting for independence and Ethiopians fighting for a more inclusive government; these tactics were exacerbated by drought. Many of the war tactics used by that regime have been replicated by the Sudanese government in Darfur. For more information and a cheap plug, see John Prendergast and Mark Duffield, *Without Troops and Tanks,* Red Sea Press (Lawrenceville, 1994).

My education was about to begin.

The only place to which I could get a visa on short notice was Mali, a country well to the west of Ethiopia but suffering a major food crisis as part of the Sahelian drought. I knew no one in Mali, with the exception of Mark Heim, a Peace Corps volunteer with whom I had played soccer during one year of high school (before I dropped out of that school . . . starting to see the pattern?). I am not sure what the hell I was thinking I would or could accomplish, or even how I thought I would learn what I would need to do to make a difference.

But fate, or God, intervened. On the plane ride over, a Malian guy appropriately named Mohammed came up to me and told me he remembered me from playing basketball at the Georgetown gym during my freshman year of college. I guess since I had long hair then too, and I played very flamboyantly. He understood immediately that I was just a twenty-one-year-old kid who wanted to learn and to help, and he took it upon himself to make sure my introduction to Africa 101 was the right one.

He worked for the Agricultural Department of Mali, so he showed me how Malians themselves were trying to deal with their own problems. Nonetheless, tariffs and subsidies in Europe and the U.S. made it impossible for them to compete as farmers. Right away, I started to see the unfairness of the relationship between Africa and the rest of the world. I moved into one of his houses, as he had three little huts in which his three wives lived. He moved one of them into another house, and the chickens and I took over the third hut. Eventually I met an American guy, Jeff Gray, a fellow hoopster who worked for an American organization called Africare, and he let me accompany him as his assistant as long as I would talk with him about basketball and Philadelphia, and we headed into the Sahara Desert to initiate water projects for the people all the way up toward Timbuktu, a place I thought existed only in fairy tales.

Coming back to the U.S. after that trip was difficult. I couldn't think about anything else but Africa. I would tell my stories of adventures in Africa to my Little Brothers from the program, and they would tell me their stories of growing up in Philly and D.C. The core inequity, discrimination, and maldevelopment were shared, but Africa's place at the very bottom of the global priority totem pole drove me to want to return, to be somehow part of changing that deadly cocktail of neglect and exploitation.

I went back the next year to Zanzibar to take a volunteer job on a youth employment project. Zanzibar was paradise, but I wanted to go somewhere in which my initial interests in confronting war and famine were at play. So I next went to Somalia, and that is where the worm really turned for me. That is where I saw the Cold War being played out, where the U.S. was cynically using Africa in its geostrategic chessboard, with the Somali people acting as the pawns. My government was pouring money into a military dictator who was brutally repressing and killing his own people. I spent time volunteering in an orphanage and watched babies die needlessly of malnourishment and disease.

My reaction was one of pure anger. Anger at the injustice that was actually killing people. Anger at my own government for not only not intervening to stop it, but instead actually pouring gasoline on the fire by providing arms and money to the perpetrators. I had never seen anything as nakedly unfair as that, and with such devastating consequences. I decided then that I would dedicate the rest of my life to attacking that injustice in whatever way I could. The lightbulb finally went on. I could sit there and try to help save the starving babies, or I could go back to the U.S. and work on policies toward Africa that would ensure that babies didn't have to starve.

Of course, seeing the pictures in 1983 of millions of starving Ethiopians was an extraordinary pull factor in influencing me to make my first trip to Africa. My basic humanitarian tendencies were certainly triggered massively by the level of helplessness of those who had been targeted and hunted in the context of the war-induced Ethiopian famine (one of the deadliest in the world during the last century). Simplistically, at that time I just wanted to help, wanted to figure out the best way to get life-saving aid to those most in need.

But it took me a few more years to figure out that while food and medicine were crucial, they were not the sole solutions. I began to see the political roots of the lack of response from my country and the larger Western world. I was greatly helped in seeing that, as a very naive twenty-two-year-old, by the organization of the Live Aid concert in 1985, but particularly by the organizer, a musician-turned-radical-politician, Bob Geldof of the Boomtown Rats, who would later help organize the Live 8 concerts in 2005.

Geldof appeared to me like a force of nature. He was on the cover of my beloved *Rolling Stone* magazine and many others, swearing at the political leaders who were obstructing a meaningful response to the famine and its roots. He took on the system; in fact he spit on the system, damning it for not caring in the face of such human deprivation. And he attacked our apathy and ignorance, swearing that he wouldn't sleep until everyone woke up to the horrors that the people of Ethiopia were living on a daily basis.

Geldof helped shake up the status quo and force a larger response to the crisis. He slammed the issue of starvation into the face of the larger public in Europe and America. And he changed forever the face of celebrity involvement in crises.

With his long hair, huge ego, gutter mouth, irreverence, and unyielding passion for the people who were suffering so badly, Geldof was a heroic figure, perhaps unexpected, but a role model anyway for the ability of one person to make a major difference in the world. He challenged politicians to live up to their pledges, and challenged us as regular people to help him make a difference. I felt his call, and the call of the Ethiopian and Eritrean people, to respond to this emergency. They were dialing 911; Geldof was just a dispatcher, and I took it as a challenge and a responsibility to respond. I wouldn't have missed that call for the world.

What I saw on the ground in Somalia, combined with what I

perceived Geldof and his allies to be accomplishing, was a powerful combination for me, a catalyst for what became my lifelong commitment to promoting peace and human rights in Africa. Which leads me back to Sudan.

In mid-2003, before conferring upon me the title of "enemy of the state," Foreign Minister Mustafa Osman Ismail (aka "Mr. Smile") and I were in his opulent house in Khartoum, sitting by the Nile River. He insisted there was nothing wrong in Darfur, noting that the Americans concerned with Darfur were the same people that erroneously accused Iraq of having weapons of mass destruction. We argued over the basic facts of the Sudanese situation. I told him of emerging evidence of systematic crimes against humanity perpetrated by the militias in Darfur and of evidence that these militias were armed and supported by the government. He denied everything, with that patronizing tone and ever-present smile that earned him his well-deserved nickname.

But having seen the early results of genocidal policies in Darfur, I felt compelled to speak truth to power, to Al-Jazeera, to the world. Damn the personal consequences.

I made it out of Khartoum in one piece, thanks to one of the Marines from the U.S. embassy who rushed over soon after the bellhop rousted me out of my troubled reveries. He drove me to the airport and made sure I got out safely. In the three years since then, the regime hasn't given me a visa to go to Sudan legally. Nonetheless I've gone back repeatedly into rebel-held areas of the country, gathering stories, trying to shine a spotlight on some of the world's worst atrocities.

Sudan is indeed where all the world's worst atrocities come together, like a perfect storm of horrors. War, slavery, genocide— you name it. But particularly genocide. Beyond the Sudanese government and other perpetrators of mass atrocities, however, the "bad guys" in this story are apathy, ignorance, indifference, and inertia. It is up to us to overcome them.

Darfur represents the first genocide of the twenty-first century. The 911 call has gone out again. And Americans, particularly younger ones, are starting to respond in ways I could never have imagined twenty-something years ago. Across this country, people are objecting to a political system which has made responding to Darfur a low priority, and they are succeeding in overcoming the apathy based on sheer ignorance of the situation. At the public education events I participate in at campuses nationwide, students come up to me now with the same look I had back in the 1980s when I first saw the pictures of the Ethiopian famine. They say how they are inspired by the crisis to do more, from just doing something immediately like writing a letter, all the way to changing their majors and their career ambitions to pursue human rights advocacy, conflict resolution, or humanitarian action. In person and in e-mails, they express a desire to get involved somehow, to lend their hearts, minds, and commitment to the ultimate just cause, and to live a meaningful life. The hunger out there for meaning is extraordinary. It is perhaps the most fulfilling part of my work. We've gone through Generation X and Generation Y, but if Generation Z is in formation, and the massive outpouring of student action over the Darfur genocide is any indication, we have very good reason to hope in the future.

When I first went to Africa and saw the extraordinary suffering, the massive numbers of people that had been forsaken and forgotten, what little connection I felt with God disappeared. Like so many others that have witnessed such scenes of absolute deprivation and unfairness, I became angry at any construct that would have a god somehow in charge of all this. That angry and studied agnosticism held for nearly two decades. It has only been in the last three years, corresponding ironically to the time of the Darfur genocide, that I have begun to reconnect to my faith.

I remember going into a cathedral in Khartoum during that fateful trip in the summer of 2003. There I witnessed a vigil of hundreds of southern Sudanese praying for peace. I stayed after everyone had left and knelt in the pew, reading stories from the Gospels about Jesus, about redemption, about second chances, about forgiveness, about sacrifice, the themes that resonate so powerfully with southern Sudanese. I remember watching the pigeons (They looked like doves. Wait a minute, are doves actually pigeons? Are pigeons actually flying rats? Never mind, you get the point.) flying around in the church, as I reflected on the mistakes I had made in my life and the sadness I had caused, hoping that this redemption was real. And mostly I just felt an emptiness born of twenty years of traveling and battling, often on my own, in my personal and professional life, and I felt a peace creeping in as I read about Jesus's life and his teaching. Though the particular window through which I view God is Christianity, surely only just one window into the divine, one of the most gratifying things about working on Darfur issues in the U.S. is the way people of all major faiths—particularly Muslims, Jews, and Christians—come together in respect and partnership around a common cause and are motivated by their faith to pursue what is right.

Early on, I had been a bit incredulous as to the real possibilities of citizen action in moving governments to act. Then, as I saw student and religious groups and others really responding and mobilizing to these different crises, and as I started to see policy change, I began to believe in the power of ordinary people to make a difference. Perhaps it is too much to hope, but if these students and the thousands of other new activists on behalf of the defenseless have their way, the first genocide of the twenty-first century might also be the last, or at least the last one that doesn't provoke an appropriately strong response.

DON:

*O*ur first day in Africa is pretty much a bust as far as me doing anything of real substance. We all have a very brief briefing in the Le Meridien hotel banquet room, where we are brought up to speed on the latest developments in the region by U.S. Ambassador Marc Wall. Though the Nightline camera is rolling, no one appears to be playing to the folks at home. Everyone is focused on the task at hand; it's all business. The briefing yields little more

*than my research has already revealed, and I am looking
forward to going out to the desert to see what I came to see.
The meeting wraps up in relatively short order, and we pile
into our escorted cars and head out to meet Prime Minister
Moussa Faki of Chad.*

*There is much pomp and circumstance when we arrive,
but the moment is followed by confusion as it becomes
evident that all in our company are not welcomed into the
tiny room where this meeting is to be held. I never did find
out if the prime minister's representatives' decision-making
process was based on our perceived hierarchy or if it was
simply that the room was too small to accommodate us all.
Regardless, I offer to stay outside, not nearly as excited
about listening to a political figure as I am about listening
to the stories from the people on the front lines of the
conflict. I slightly bow my head respectfully and try to back
out but I'm grabbed at the last second by Congresswoman
Watson, who must've thought I was being polite because
she pulls me in behind her. Before I can protest, the door is
shut on all of us in the stuffy little room and the prime
minister's man begins to speak. Apparently, I'm not going
anywhere.*

*The setup was very interesting, with the prime minister
sitting at the front of the room dressed in what I believe to
be traditional finery, swatting at small flying pests with a
horse-tailed wafter, his assistant standing next to him in an
ill-fitting suit. The meeting went on for what felt like an
hour and maybe was. Prime Minister Faki was speaking in
slow, even, thoughtful tones, almost as if he believed the
pace of his speech might help us to better understand his
language, but all the monotone cadence did for us in this hot
little room was hasten our way toward the heavy-lidded
respite that after over twenty hours of travel we all so very
much crave. Between my super long blinks—blinks I tried to
disguise by nodding my head thoughtfully up and down as if*

deeply affected by the words his equally inflection-less translator was spooning out—I caught sight of my fellow travel companions also bobbing for sleep, Ms. Watson chief among them. When she and I finally made eye contact, I mouthed, "Thank you," getting a shrug in return. If she had known what we were in for, I'm sure we both would have opted to stay and play with the kids who had shown up outside the gates almost the second our cars pulled into the compound. It wasn't that the information we were receiving was irrelevant to our trip, but the manner in which it was disseminated was for me strangely similar to the way many politicians on this side of the world do their thing: too many words representing too little action for too few (my present company excluded, of course). I wished we could have forgone all of this diplomacy and gone right into the camps, but that's a lot like being without transportation and needing to catch a ride to the bank with your friend. If he wants to stop at the cleaners first, it's better just to grin and bear it. Tomorrow will come soon enough.

It doesn't. Though we're leaving at the crack of dawn, the time change, nerves, excitement, or a combination of all three has me up way before the sun, far earlier than any self-respecting farmer would dare begin his chores. Tired of tossing and turning, I sit up and turn on the TV. Just three channels work on the set; two of them have the same program, CNN news, and the other one is in Arabic, but somehow just having the fuzzy thing on helps to calm me down a little bit. I try to get into the real images on the screen so that the imagined ones of traumatized refugees can recede into the background. Being this close to it has me spooked now, or maybe it's the local gendarme standing guard outside my door with a machine gun for my "protection" that's working my nerves. Heavy. I sit staring at the screen until the phone rings for my wake-up call a half hour later. It's 4:30 A.M.

We convene in the hotel's modest banquet room once again, and everyone's pretty chatty this morning despite the early hour. The feeling in the breakfast line is one of purpose, the primary goal of our travel just hours away.

After a short drive up the road, we're back at the airstrip, this time headed first to Abeche, where we will deplane and then board a smaller aircraft before continuing on to Tine, a town on the Chad/Sudan border where the African Union has one of their outposts. We board the Beechcraft 1900 and everybody picks a seat. John sits behind me to the left. He's furiously writing away on anything that will hold ink—napkins, scraps of paper, gum wrappers . . . I ask to trade seats with Rep. Betty McCollum so I can get a closer look at John's Russell Crowe–like Beautiful Mind *behavior.*

"What is all that?" It takes him a second to shift gears.

"Hey, Buddy. Just trying to collect my thoughts here." I gather from all the references to Darfur I can make out on the scraps of paper that John wants to make sure he's ready for the cameras. But it's not a ruse; the man knows his stuff.

"Thrall me with your acumen," I say, hitting him with a poor Tony Hopkins impersonation as Hannibal Lecter from The Silence of the Lambs.

"Do what to my what?"

"It's from Silence of . . . *Forget it. What are you writing about?"*

3

Sudan's Backdrop to Genocide

As we stood together in Darfur's golden sand, the stark reality hit us squarely over the head: the Sahara is rolling slowly southward. The desert is advancing, rendering access to basic resources such as land and water a matter of life or death. If you have access to those resources or the support of those in political power, you survive. When there is no democracy, no peaceful way of accessing power, then in Sudan, as in so many other places around the world, people pick up guns to win back their rights. In Darfur, the government of Sudan armed that country's far deadlier version of the Ku Klux Klan, the Janjaweed, a mixed bag of bandits and racist ideologues whose ethnic cleansing of all non-Arab people is mostly motivated by the desire to take over land and steal livestock. John has talked with young Janjaweed recruits. They felt they had no economic alternative. These were the same feelings of the young members of the militias that committed the genocide in Rwanda. Cynical leaders can exploit economic destitution and desperation, and like macabre, racist pied pipers lead people right over the moral cliff.

Since achieving independence from Great Britain in 1956, Sudan has been a country at war with itself. The genocide in Darfur is only the latest in a series of horrific conflicts. Sudan's civil wars unfold in a depressingly familiar pattern. The Khartoum government's counterinsurgency strategy has nearly always begun with killing and displacement on a massive scale. When the international community starts to take notice and the spotlight shines on government atrocities, the regime then scales back the military assault and the chess game begins. They manipulate ethnic dynamics, sowing internal divisions within the opposition. They manipulate American, European, and African diplomats, buying time through disingenuous negotiation to gain the upper hand on the battlefield. And they manipulate humanitarian assistance, hiding behind the iron curtain of state sovereignty to deny humanitarians access to territory where vulnerable civilians need help.

The ruling National Islamic Front (known today as the National Congress Party) has taken state-sponsored brutality to extraordinary levels, but the systematic hoarding of wealth and power by elites in Khartoum and the endless violent campaign to silence a deprived and angry population have deep historical roots.

Colonial Times—Sowing Seeds of Discord

Sudan is the largest country in Africa, straddling the cultural divide between the Arab and Arab-influenced societies of northern Africa and the societies south of the Sahara. Sudan's geography and its 41 million citizens are correspondingly diverse. Follow the Nile River from Sudan's northern border with Egypt to its southern border with Uganda and you travel from scorching desert landscapes to swamps and rain forests. The people you meet along the way are equally varied. More than 50 percent of Sudanese describe themselves as black or "African," and nearly 40 percent are Arabs. Sunni Muslims are 70 percent of the population and Christians are at least 5 percent, with the remainder adhering to traditional belief systems.

From the early fifteenth until the twentieth century, the northwestern region of Darfur was a prosperous independent kingdom of the Fur people. (In Arabic, *Dar* means "home," and Darfur therefore is "home of the Fur.") Successive Fur leaders, called sultans, extended the kingdom's control southward from the Sahara. Colonialism put borders around Sudan's diverse geography and people for the first time, creating a number of difficulties. In 1899, Britain and Egypt assumed joint authority over Sudan: Britain managed affairs in the south and let the Egyptians control the north. As a result, the two regions developed unique cultural and religious characteristics. While the Egyptians encouraged the spread of Islamic values in the north, the British developed a "Southern Policy" to reduce Islam's influence, encouraging Christian missionaries to work and promoting the English language in southern Sudan. In 1916, the British government decided to extend its own control to include Darfur, and the colonial administration annexed the sultanate. Working through local political leaders, the British established a so-called "Native Administration" that loosely controlled Darfur.

When the British government began to withdraw from Sudan after World War II, British officials reconnected the north and south and handed power to the northern elites. Northern Sudanese officials quickly replaced the British administrators in positions of influence in the south. At this time, Darfur was arguably less developed than the south, and the people of Darfur were suspicious of any central authority in Khartoum. Southerners were equally wary of northern intentions. The consolidation of power in the northern city of Khartoum at the expense of the south and the west only confirmed this distrust. The battle lines were drawn, and southerners rioted and rebelled in 1955, just before independence.

Sudan's First Civil War—A Nation Born into Conflict

Internal conflict overshadowed any celebration when Sudan became independent on January 1, 1956. Two years later, the national army took power by force. General Ibrahim Abboud's regime crushed political opposition and began efforts to Islamize the south through violent proselytization. Southern ex-soldiers and policemen formed a guerrilla army—the Anya-Nya (meaning "snake poison" in the local Dinka language)—to resist northern aggression. The Anya-Nya found sympathy among the southern population. Soon, the government's violent counterinsurgency intensified into full-blown civil war between the government's forces and the rebels.

In October 1964, a popular uprising in the north toppled the military regime, but new civilian leadership failed to reach a political settlement with the south and the war intensified. Throughout the mid to late 1960s, numerous foreign powers began to funnel money and weapons to the government, to the Anya-Nya, or to both. As in many African countries, the Cold War was not "cold" at all. The government maintained its close ties to the Middle East, but the Soviet Union would become Khartoum's main patron. Even in 1969, when the military again took power by force, General Jaafar al-Nimeiri's new government increased Sudan's trade with the Soviet Union and other communist states. Khartoum relied on Moscow for weapons, and Moscow asserted its strategic influence in the region. Meanwhile, the Anya-Nya rebels drew support mainly from Israel and from neighboring countries such as the Congo, Uganda, and Ethiopia.

When communists failed in a July 1971 coup attempt, Khartoum's ties with the Soviets deteriorated and its relationship with the United States and Western Europe improved. Without Soviet military support, Nimeiri recalculated the attractiveness of war with the south and conditions for peace improved. Just months after the failed coup, Nimeiri's government entered direct negotiations with the Anya-Nya in Addis Ababa, Ethiopia. In March 1972, the two sides ratified the Addis Ababa peace agreement which provided substantial power and wealth sharing between the two sides. Darfur at this time was neglected by Khartoum and desperately impoverished, and the Addis Ababa agreement was not the first peace deal in Sudan that failed to resolve the root causes of conflict in all of Sudan, namely the hoarding of wealth and power in Khartoum.

A War Interrupted

Unfortunately, peace in Sudan did not hold for long. Though a military strongman, Nimeiri had very little popular support in the north. A group of powerful Islamists, supported by Libya among other governments, formed a strong and organized northern opposition. Sadiq al-Mahdi, a former prime minister, led another failed coup attempt in 1976. Nimieri's subsequent attempts to appease the Islamists and generate political support among northerners led him to appoint al-Mahdi and several leading Islamist opposition leaders to important government posts (usually at the expense of southerners who had achieved their positions under the Addis Ababa agreement). Nimeiri allowed opposition leaders living in exile to return to Sudan, including members of the Muslim Brotherhood, a radical religious fundamentalist organization. The extremist Islamist scholar Hassan al-Turabi became attorney general, and an Islamist influence spread within the government.

The pressure from the Islamists to renege on the peace agreement was compounded by the discovery of oil in southern Sudan. Driven by greed, northern elites sought to monopolize and maximize oil profits: they resented the provisions in the Addis Ababa agreement that gave the south a degree of financial autonomy as well as the right to collect the central government's taxes on commercial activity there. Nimeiri's increasingly uncompromising cabinet demanded that he replace southern troops with northerners in areas with significant oil deposits. Then he stole southern proceeds from an oil licensing deal and set in motion plans for a pipeline to take oil from the south to Port Sudan, for export or for processing in northern refineries.* These attempts to cut southerners out of the oil profits exacerbated underlying tensions.

Southerners began to express their frustration with the Nimeiri government, and northerners became increasingly anx-

---

*Ann Mosely Lesch, *The Sudan: Contested National Identities* (Bloomington, 1998) as cited in *God, Oil & Country: Changing the Logic of War in Sudan* (International Crisis Group, 2002), page 12.

ious about the power of southerners in the military. In January 1983, Nimeiri ordered a southern-based battalion to abandon their weapons and redeploy to the north. The troops refused their orders, negotiations to resolve the dispute failed, and in May 1983 Nimeiri ordered his army to attack the insubordinate southern troops. Outmanned and outgunned, the mutineers fled with their weapons, and similar uprisings and desertions continued across southern Sudan. The southerners sought refuge in neighboring Ethiopia and united to form the opposition Sudan People's Liberation Army (SPLA).

Return to War: The Sudan People's Liberation Army and National Islamic Front

On June 5, 1983, Nimeiri issued an order that annulled the Addis Ababa agreement. In what is now a familiar pattern of betrayal, the government of Sudan simply turned its back on a signed treaty, and regional autonomy was instantly wiped out. Khartoum reestablished and consolidated control over the administration, finances, and armed forces of the south. Further, Nimeiri's order declared Arabic, not English, the south's official language. Later that year the Nimeiri government passed the infamous "September laws" that transformed Sudan into an Islamic state, imposing Islamic law (Sharia) on the entire country and subjecting even non-Muslims to harsh penalties. The result—another civil war.

Southerners rallied behind the SPLA and its charismatic leader John Garang, who was a member of the Dinka ethnic group, the largest group in southern Sudan. Orphaned at the age of ten, he joined southern rebels in the first civil war when he was only seventeen. Always an excellent student, he left Sudan to complete his secondary education in Tanzania and won a scholarship to study in the United States.

He returned to Sudan to rejoin the rebels. After the Addis Ababa agreement, he joined the Sudanese military and rose quickly through the ranks. When southern troops mutinied in

May 1983 and formed the SPLA, Garang emerged as the movement's natural leader. His vision for Sudan was broader than simple demands for southern autonomy. Instead, he sought to transform Sudan into a democratic state that respected the diversity of its citizens.

Civil war escalated between the government and the SPLA, and a new civilian government was installed in Khartoum. Under Garang's leadership the southern rebels took control of much of southern Sudan. Yet by June 1989, as both sides recognized that total victory would be nearly impossible, a constitutional conference to address the south's grievances and end the war seemed imminent. Meanwhile, as we will see below, simmering resentments and escalating violence in Darfur were largely ignored.

Later that month, however, Sudanese dreams of a lasting peace were dealt a near fatal blow on June 30. Brigadier General Omar Hassan Ahmed al-Bashir seized power in a military coup engineered by the National Islamic Front (NIF) and its front man, the former attorney general Hassan al-Turabi. The Bashir government moved swiftly to violently crack down on political dissent, abolishing parliament, banning opposition political parties, arresting opposition political leaders, and clamping down on the press. Anyone who was judged a threat to the Islamists faced arbitrary detention. Most gruesomely, the government tortured and killed its opponents in secret "ghost houses" and prisons.*

The National Islamic Front pursued with renewed vigor the radical agenda to make Sudan—north and south—an Islamic state. Non-Muslims in the south would be converted through the barrel of a gun if need be, as the government intensified the war with the SPLA and, ultimately, with the people of southern Sudan. The crimes committed by the National Islamic Front during the next fifteen years of civil war put Bashir's Islamo-fascist government alongside Nazi Germany, the Khmer Rouge in Cambodia,

---

*Millard Burr and Robert O. Collins, *Requiem for the Sudan* (Boulder, Westview Press, 1995) as cited in *God, Oil & Country* (International Crisis Group, 2002), page 14.

Milosevic's Yugoslavia, and the genocidal government in Rwanda as one of the twentieth century's most murderous regimes.

It was during this war with Garang and the SPLA rebels that the Sudanese government practiced and perfected the genocidal violence that it later unleashed on Darfur.

The Second Civil War—Sharpening the Tools of Genocide

Divide and Destroy

Government officials, especially members of the pervasive military intelligence services, sowed and continue to sow divisions and increase tension between the ethnic groups that oppose the Sudanese government. The logic is simple: rebels are less effective in fighting a civil war with Khartoum if they are fighting among themselves. And if the motivations of the government are genocidal, as is often the case in Sudan, exploiting ethnic tensions and pitting one group against another is an effective way to exterminate people from certain ethnic backgrounds.

In its war with the SPLA, the government skillfully engineered ethnic splits within the rebels and encouraged a "war within the war." Military planners in Khartoum devised a counterinsurgency strategy that used ethnically based militias against the SPLA rebels and civilians who supported them in the south. The government armed, trained, and provided logistical support for horse-mounted militias, giving these proxy forces total impunity and encouraging them to attack civilians from Garang's Dinka ethnic group. (Although other ethnic groups belonged to the SPLA, the Dinka were considered the rebels' backbone.)

The Dinka's historical ethnic rivals in southern Sudan are the Nuer, and the government armed Nuer militias to attack Dinka civilians and divide the insurgency. The attacks decimated the SPLA's ethnic base by destroying Dinka livelihoods and the social fabric of their community. In the mid and late 1980s, before the National Islamic Front came to power, government-backed Arab militias had relentlessly attacked Dinka villages, leading to widespread famine in southwestern Sudan. The National Islamic Front government continued to use ethnic militias against its southern enemies, and learned some valuable lessons it would later apply to Darfur: do not support militias too transparently, in order to create a degree of separation between the regime and its militia proxies.

To attack its enemies and civilians inside Sudan, the Sudanese government also supported human predators from neighboring countries, including the sadistic Lord's Resistance Army (LRA), a notorious Ugandan rebel group responsible for grotesque human rights violations that include cutting off victims' lips and ears and raping small girls. The LRA rebel leader Joseph Kony sees himself as a Moses-like figure, sent by God on a mission to impose the Ten Commandments on northern Uganda. His distorted view of the Old Testament—literally an eye for an eye—is a recipe for human rights violations on a macabre scale. Kony's army is composed principally of abducted, tortured, and brainwashed children whom he forces to commit horrific atrocities.*

When we visited northern Uganda together in 2005, we met former child soldiers in Kony's army with terrifying stories. The Lord's Resistance Army has created a generation of children afraid to sleep in their own beds. Each night before the sun set, we saw thousands of Ugandan children march in grim procession along dusty roads that took them from their rural villages to larger towns. The children and their parents were terrified that the Lord's Resistance Army would abduct them and force them to hunt down their friends, families, and loved ones. The children we met—called "night commuters"—spent their nights in churches, empty schools, makeshift shelters, and alleyways.

The government of Sudan provides the Lord's Resistance Army with weapons and sanctuary. In exchange, Kony and his henchmen attack the SPLA and civilians in southern Sudan. The president of Uganda, Yoweri Museveni, supported the SPLA dur-

---

*For a background on the LRA see Crisis Group Africa Report 77, *Northern Uganda: Understanding and Solving the Conflict*, April 14, 2004.

ing the war with Khartoum, and Sudanese support for the Ugandan rebels is also meant as revenge.

Twentieth-Century Slavery

Government-supported militias in southern Sudan had a sinister ulterior motive in attacking Dinka villages: taking slaves to use for domestic labor and field work in northern Sudan. During the colonial era, one of the largest exports from Sudan was human beings. It's difficult to imagine slavery existing at the end of the twentieth century, but for the killers in Khartoum, slavery made sense, as it terrified southerners and created economic incentives for northern militias.

The Sudanese government had a name for the slave trade: intertribal abductions. The government denied both its involvement in and the existence of an organized campaign to perpetuate slavery. Instead, Khartoum feebly claimed that "tribal hatreds" were behind the systematic kidnapping of Dinka civilians. The exact number is not known, but an extensive survey by Sudan experts John Ryle and Jok Madut Jok documented at least 12,000 abductions from 1986 to 2002.* The total number remains unknown.

The militias would fan out on horseback to raid villages within a fifty-mile radius of the railroad that ran through the south, killing and raping and then galloping away with human cargo. The trains that ran along the line became known as "slave trains." The captives were often taken to camps, where Sudanese from the north or buyers from overseas would come to purchase or trade goods for slaves. Younger boys and girls were usually used as farmhands or as domestic laborers. Older girls and women were usually taken as "wives" or concubines, often subject to rape and sexual abuse. Living in subhuman conditions, the slaves were cut off from their families, stripped of their religion and culture,

---

*This research is available at http://www.riftvalley.net/inside/projects.htm. The U.S. Department of State's 2002 report on slavery in Sudan, "Slavery, Abduction, and Forced Servitude in Sudan," is available at http://www.state.gov/p/af/rls/rpt/10445.htm.

denied access to an education, and forced to become Muslims. Some tried to escape, but capture meant torture and possibly death.*

In 1998, vicious militia attacks aimed at abducting civilians were partly responsible for a devastating famine in southeastern Sudan. Thousands died from starvation, while relief workers struggled mightily to reach vulnerable people, but these efforts regularly encountered a more menacing resistance than Sudan's harsh landscapes.

Starvation as a Weapon of War

The NIF government employs vicious tactics to achieve its strategic objectives, including inflaming intertribal conflict, slavery, and the denial of humanitarian food assistance. Despite the presence in southern Sudan of one of the world's largest and most expensive humanitarian operations, Khartoum was able to deny food to millions of southern Sudanese by manipulating humanitarian access. The regime tried to starve the civilian supporters of the rebels into submission. This genocidal policy led to the deaths of 300,000 people in 1992–1993, in an area of southeastern Sudan that became known as the "starvation triangle," and another 250,000 in southwestern Sudan, in the area of the slave raids. This tactic was honed and perfected over the years and used in the genocide in Darfur with deadly efficiency.

To employ starvation as a weapon violates international law under the Geneva Conventions, but the government of Sudan has never been bothered by the rules that govern warfare. Starvation in war-torn regions of Sudan is less a by-product of indiscriminate fighting than a government objective—the wholesale liquidation of civilian populations—largely achieved through the diversion and denial of humanitarian food assistance. State-sponsored mass murder has

---

*The tactics employed by the militias during the 1990s are well documented in reports by the UN Special Rapporteur on the Situation of Human Rights in Sudan.

moved to the bureaucratic level, with the government vetoing relief flights destined to provide food to starving civilians, forcing many people to flee. And as the south was emptied of its citizens, like the Lost Boys (see page 115), the Khartoum government gained greater access to oil, which helped finance its continuing war.

The Curse of Oil

The discovery of oil in Africa can be a blessing or a curse, as is the case in southern Sudan. Against all odds and predictions, the Sudanese regime—backed by Chinese, Malaysian, and Canadian oil companies—was able to forcibly clear out the populations of huge swathes of south-central Sudan in order to secure the way for the oil companies to begin exploiting the oil.* Hundreds of thousands of people were killed or displaced by these vicious scorched earth campaigns—in which everything is burned, including crops, villages, and houses—in the oilfields, and the manipulation of relief flights was an effective complement to government air strikes and ground assaults.

Oil exploitation has lined the pockets of mass murderers in Khartoum and financed the arms the government uses to terrorize its own citizens. More money from oil means access to more sophisticated weapons, and while the United States is forbidden by law from selling arms to Sudan, numerous other countries happily profit from Khartoum's barbarism. The Chinese even helped build weapons factories inside Sudan, creating a military-industrial complex.†

Nonetheless, despite staggering growth in government revenue since oil first began to flow, most Sudanese remain desperately

---

*Human rights and conflict prevention organizations—including the International Crisis Group, Human Rights Watch, and Amnesty International—have reported extensively on the link between foreign oil companies, the Sudanese government, and atrocities in the oil-producing regions. The role of Asian oil companies in Sudan is discussed in the Council on Foreign Relations Task Force Report No. 56, "More than Humanitarianism: A Strategic U.S. Approach toward Africa," 2006.

†"China: Winning Resources and Loyalties of Africa," *Financial Times,* 28 February 2006.

poor. The government's social development spending is dwarfed by international aid flowing in, and millions more people would starve without the support of international relief agencies that persistently fight bureaucratic obstruction to deliver assistance.

Many companies that have cut deals with Khartoum are from Russia and China—countries that occupy powerful and permanent seats on the United Nations Security Council and have very poor human rights records. These countries' cuddly relationship with hard-liners in Khartoum is based on greed, and protecting their interests comes at the expense of innocent lives. China in particular has used its position on the Security Council to protect the government of Sudan from sanctions and to prevent stronger action to end the atrocities in Darfur. This protection came despite the Sudanese government's long history of harboring terrorist organizations and radical Islamic groups.

Osama bin Laden's Refuge

The National Islamic Front sought to establish the country as a key capital of the militant Islamic world, developing close ties with many violent organizations inside and outside of Sudan and attempting to organize them into a cohesive Jihadist network. The NIF hosted annual meetings attended by terrorist delegates from Egypt, Algeria, Palestine, Afghanistan, and more than fifty other countries, including Osama bin Laden and other al-Qaeda leaders.*

Terrorists moved freely in and out of the country, and the Sudanese government hosted bin Laden from 1991 to 1996. His main protector while in Sudan was a man named Salah Abdallah Gosh, the current head of the powerful military intelligence organization and one of the architects of genocide in Darfur.

The Sudanese government allowed bin Laden monopoly stakes

---

*See John and Phil Roessler's report for the U.S. Institute of Peace, "Can a Leopard Change Its Spots? Sudan's Evolving Relationship with Terrorism," May 28, 2003, available at www.usip.org.

in some of Sudan's most profitable businesses, gave fake passports to al-Qaeda operatives, allowed terrorists to set up training camps, and transported terrorists and their weapons aboard Sudan Airways aircraft. Bin Laden plotted some of his later terrorist attacks while living in Sudan, and the profits he made there undoubtedly funded attacks against Americans and other Western targets.

Putting Pressure on Khartoum

In response to bin Laden's use of Sudan as a base of operations, a small group of people working for President Clinton began to focus on the regime. They argued that Sudan's support for international terrorist groups made it a rogue nation that needed to be pressured heavily. Susan Rice was a staff member of the National Security Council. Working for former White House counterterrorism czar Richard Clarke, she saw the threat that bin Laden's residence in Sudan posed to U.S. national security. Working closely with Madeleine Albright (who was U.S. ambassador to the UN and then secretary of state), she and others (including John, who worked for her at both the National Security Council and the State Department) managed to ramp up U.S. pressure on Sudan and were finally able to impose strong United Nations multilateral as well as unilateral sanctions on the leadership there. As a result of this years-long campaigning, the Sudanese government booted bin Laden out of the country and ceased much of their overt support for terrorist organizations. It is but one example of the Khartoum government responding to outside influence.

Near the end of the Clinton administration in 2000, the process unfolded to choose the new nonpermanent members of the UN Security Council. Sudan was Africa's consensus choice to represent the continent. Against the strong advice of all of the other Security Council members, President Clinton decided to oppose Sudan's ascension to the seat and tasked Ambassador Richard Holbrooke, U.S. permanent representative to the UN, with leading the diplomatic effort to find a replacement and defeat Sudan's candidacy, even though this had rarely been done in the history of the UN.

Two weeks of hard diplomacy from Ambassador Holbrooke, Secretary of State Albright, National Security Advisor Sandy Berger, Assistant Secretary Susan Rice, as well as Gayle Smith and John, finally produced a stunning verdict: the tiny island country of Mauritius defeated Sudan in the General Assembly on the third ballot. It was an incredible upset that demonstrated in no uncertain terms what the United States can do when it puts its political muscle behind its intentions. But there was more to come.

The "North-South Peace Process"

In late 2002 and early 2003, after nearly twenty years of horrific conflict, the United States and others pressed the Sudanese government and the SPLA to enter peace talks. Responding to growing public pressure from conservative U.S. Christian groups concerned about Christians in southern Sudan, George W. Bush appointed former Missouri senator John Danforth as his special envoy to Sudan. Danforth led U.S. efforts to push both sides toward an agreement, but, like the Addis Ababa agreement, the "North-South peace process" (as many people refer to it) did not address the grievances of northern Sudanese marginalized by the Khartoum government.

The Sudanese government's policy of economic marginalization and violent repression is not limited to the south, yet the peace talks between the SPLA and the government excluded numerous other constituencies in Sudan that opposed the National Islamic Front and its divisive policies, notably groups in Darfur. Opposition groups in northern Sudan, including those in Darfur, drew one simple conclusion from the North-South peace process: the only way to get what you want in Sudan is to fight for it. The Darfurians that took up arms to fight for their rights never imagined that the regime they were opposing would meet their mutiny with genocide.

DON:

The incredibly early drive the next morning is over a bumpy road of dust, the sheer volume of which clogs the filter and stops the car, stranding us in questionable territory. Our United Nations High Commissioner for Refugees guide that day chirps, "Don't worry, the Janjaweed take Tuesday off." His wry sense of humor lets you know he's been at it awhile now. It isn't necessarily gallows humor, but obviously you have to grow a thick skin to stay out here for the length of time most aid workers do and not completely come apart. The workers are in fact in a strange position. They are both highly sought after and needed for as long as they can take it, yet cautioned against staying too long. That would create the kind of burnout that can turn a young ambitious contributor into a nihilistic fatalist. But how long is too long when the people you have come to know, come to befriend, are suffering? Spend a year getting to know someone, cry with them, share a meal, a story, a laugh with them, then when "too long" comes, leave them to their fate—that's what these people reckon with. No good deed goes unpunished. Our guide to Am Nabak is in fact rotating back home at the end of this year's tour.

He tells us this while he fixes the car and gets us back under way. We ride through miles and miles of dust, terrain that only sustains scant vegetation and trees far too small and bare for shade. The Am Nabak refugee camp seems to slowly rise out of the dust. It is truly an oasis to the weary, distraught travelers, though you'd probably never use that word to describe what we're about to see. It is un-cinematic, stark and real.

"We ain't in Kansas anymore." John as Dorothy from The Wizard of Oz *now.*

"But I'm from Missouri."

"And we ain't there either."

Driving into the camp, we are immediately mobbed by

kids. I don't know what I expected our welcome to be, but I am soon told that whenever these UNHCR vehicles arrive there is a great flurry of activity because of what or whom they might carry—good news or bad. Or perhaps on a long shot, it could be an emissary from an agency, country, or municipality that has taken an interest in the Darfurians' plight beyond simple survival and instead promises to secure a real measure of relief through political intervention. There are also many beefs these inhabitants need to air, stories from the many daily arrivals, recounting their particular journey to the camp. Each tale is eerily similar to the others in its specificity and scope: first the planes, then the soldiers, then the marauders. Basic details of cruelty vary, but death for most men and rape for perhaps thousands of women are the consistent themes.

We pull to a stop in a cloud of loose earth and hop out into the throng. The cars are at the very least providing a break in the monotony, toting some odd-looking people to gawk at. The camp leader quickly approaches the car. I don't speak his tongue, but it isn't necessary to; he's clearly upset. Somebody once told me that spoken language actually comprises only a small part of communication, and watching this conversation I'm inclined to agree. It is clear that a case is being made for something serious to this man, and he wants results! Our guide nods his head in appeasement, his body language telling me that he understands. The entire time the Nightline *cameras roll, and I have to keep reminding myself that I'm not in a movie with special effects, lighting, and makeup but experiencing reality on a level I have never seen. When the* Nightline *cameraman hops out of the car with his equipment on his shoulder, red light steady to document the moment, many of the people, especially the young ones, shrink back. The little ones are smiling. I ask about it and am told that most of the kids have probably never seen a video camera.*

"You're not serious."

"Yes. You are one of the few outsiders who have ever been here except for relief workers. And never a camera crew that I can remember."

Right. What am I thinking? This isn't Bosnia or Somalia or Iraq; this is an itinerant refugee camp on the Chad/ Darfur border, nestled in the middle of nowhere, with very little international interest to protect its inhabitants. Who's filming them? Maybe those in the crowd who were exposed to a camera before believe by now that pictures must be taken solely for the benefit of the photographer, not the subject, as their lives go unchanged while the picture takers go. Why not turn away? Those remaining, however, the curious, are partitioned out almost in concentric circles, with the youngest forming the closest ring and the elders on the outermost, with each gradation in between fanning out in a spontaneous, human design. I walk slowly, taking it in. A father myself, I know better than to try to force some kind of exchange with these kids, although, probably because I am a father, I am hawklike, looking for an angle to do so.

We are introduced to Emile Belem, head of operations at Am Nabak as well as two other camps in the area. He's been here a year and today is his last day.

"When they come first to the camp and you approach them, you will see that they are very sad." Emile breaks it down.

"Very sad," I parrot.

"Now you see them, they are smiling, and this is, this is a very good image."

Images of my two safe-at-home, well-fed, educated kids are swirling around in my head, and reverberations of reality find another pitch to hum inside me. My daughters' faces are now joined by others. I feel my own face starting to shift, my expression beginning to change, but I'm maintaining, masking well the sorrow that's creeping over me for those little boys and girls whose faces remind me of my childhood—looking in the mirror of my sister and brother's faces, my cousins and friends. Faces taking me back to old pictures in only slightly newer family albums of happy times, Little Donald surrounded by the people he knew and loved most in the world. I hear the voice in my head speak up, the one my reason uses: "Maintain, Little Donald."

Just then, I catch the eye of a little boy, no more than ten or eleven, staring at me tripping. I hope he didn't vibe my slippery state. The last thing I want to do is somehow present a sour mug, a face wracked with pity when pity in this situation is a useless and obvious indulgence, insulting even, if no action follows it. I shake it off. This child is the first one since we've pulled up that's looked unwaveringly in my eyes. So I do what any clown would do: I make a silly face at him. Thankfully, he laughs, the wordless joke translating. Uh-oh. The Ham is loose. I got inroads now. I kick a rock over near him nonchalantly, still getting downloaded on camp specifics. When he kicks it back, though, I excuse myself from the tutorial; it's on! Pretty soon other little kids are jostling around the impromptu soccer match, laughing and giggling. John jumps in as well and we're having a nice little game now. One of the kids does a fancy between the legs move, and I reach out to give him a pound, and he pulls away, avoiding my contact and my culturally specific way of saying "good one," an outstretched fist. Toward a child, no less. Am I an idiot or what?

Don't they know I'm only five short generations away from being an African myself? When my six-foot-one, melanin-challenged traveling companion reaches out, I understand these kids' reservations. But me? For these kids, however, regardless of my skin and similar facial features, I

*am a "Them" from a foreign land and don't quite have
pound privileges yet, harmless though I know myself to be.
I turn their reticence into a game too, walking away like I
couldn't care less, then darting back to grab at them. The
kids think this is a laugh riot, and it trumps the soccer
game, carrying us deeper down the roadway and into the
heart of the camp, comprised of small, makeshift mud,
stick, and found-plastic homes. Completely bereft of any
adornment, only the most basic of structures serve as a
buffer to the harsh elements for their inhabitants, who
sometimes number eight or more. We settle near a small
area where women sit beside tarps laid out on the ground
with beans, grain, and small knickknacks strewn across
them. Is this a market? Emile goes off to find Fatima, the
woman we are to meet with today and interview for*
Nightline, *while John and I survey the camp over the tops
of the tiny heads huddled closer around us. The kids are
braver now. The older ones, and even the adults now, close
the circle behind them, and for a few minutes, that is all
that happens: them staring at us staring at them. I don't
know what to do at first, then I remember I am a clown,
here to entertain. I pick up a little stone, bend my arm back
so I can balance it on my elbow, and then swipe my hand
down fast, snatching the stone out of the air. Big reaction.
They want me to do it again. John chimes in.*

"You're a hit, buddy."

"I'm a seal. They just want to see how far I'll go."

*I do the trick a couple more times then hand the rock to
one of the kids, inadvertently inciting a pushing and
shoving match as they all want to take possession of the
stone, now apparently imbued with some kind of unique
otherness that it lacked just five minutes ago. The conflict
doesn't last long, however, as an elderly woman, perhaps a
camp elder (a small yet significant distinction), appears
from behind one of the small huts carrying the innards of a*

box spring overhead, its metal coils rusted and black. She throws the thing at our feet and begins an impassioned rant. I look around for Emile, but he's off dealing with camp business, and no one near can translate. John is no help.

"Do you have any idea what she's saying?" I ask.

"No. She looks pissed though."

She does.

"Maybe she's talking about what happened to her in her village," John adds.

"Maybe this bed and all her other possessions were destroyed by the Janjaweed." Sounds about right. Like I said before, trucked-in strangers like us often signify witnesses, and very likely her story was one she knew we needed to hear. But I had to take it further. "Could be. Or maybe she's looking for some payback and wants to tie one of us to that bed and set it ablaze."

I push John an arm's length away and point to him, hoping she'll understand my gesture as the sincere offering it is: "Take the white man."

"No, buddy. Her attackers look more like you than me."

"Sure. Now."

Emile calls us over. Fatima is ready to talk. I don't know if I'm ready to hear. Reading testimonials in source materials is quite another thing from looking into haunted eyes and seeing scabbed-over scars. Hotel Rwanda's real-life star, Paul Rusesabagina, stands close by. It's a good thing. I consider his strength and step under the awning of the lean-to for my education from Fatima.

4

From the Front Lines of Darfur

Conflict in Darfur has been simmering beneath the surface for decades. The roots of it are competition for land, access to water, and the Sudanese government's decision to manipulate local tensions for political gain rather than develop Darfur's economy to address worsening poverty.

As the Sahara crept farther southward due to desertification—the degradation of formerly productive land due to drought and overuse of the land—nomadic herders from the upper northwest of Sudan began to encroach on the agriculturally rich areas farther south. Tensions increased, as nomads and their herds of cattle and camels strayed onto local farms and drank from precious water supplies.

The land is a complex mix of people, and tribal affiliations have always been important. There are at least thirty-six main tribes in Darfur, and people identify themselves as either belonging to an Arab or a non-Arab tribe. Three of the largest non-Arab tribes—and the ones most directly targeted by the regime in the genocide—are the Fur, the Zaghawa, and the Massaleit. Victims and perpetrators in Darfur are all devout followers of Sunni Islam (in its Sufi incarnation as practiced in many parts of Africa). Arab and non-Arab identities are more political and cultural than racial, as centuries of coexistence and intermarriage have blurred the line between Arab and non-Arab in Darfur. Still, these groups retain separate identities.

For centuries the people of Darfur resolved local disputes through negotiation and customary law. Economic desperation was widespread and conflict over scarce resources was not uncommon, but violence never escalated to full-scale ethnic warfare. What destroyed this precariously balanced harmony was the Khartoum government, which in its pursuit of power by any means necessary turned the ethnic diversity of the Sudanese into a political instrument of genocide.

In the 1980s, the government of Sudan offered a glimpse of what was to come in Darfur when it began providing arms to Arab groups to fight against southern SPLA rebels. In 1987, the NIF government intervened in a local conflict between Arab nomads and non-Arab farmers from the Fur tribe. The Fur are the largest group in Darfur and have traditionally ruled the region. Arab nomad militia called the Janjaweed committed atrocities against the Fur and drove them from their land. The Fur formed a militia and fought back. The resulting two years of fighting eerily foreshadowed the carnage that would envelop Darfur fifteen years later.

This conflict in Darfur from 1987 to 1989 killed as many as twenty-five hundred Fur and five hundred Arabs. The Janjaweed militias stole forty thousand cattle—a precious commodity and a source of wealth for many Darfurians—and burned four hundred Fur villages. Many Fur representatives called the conflict "genocidal" and claimed that the Arabs were trying to destroy their economy and drive them from their land. A second conflict between Arabs and non-Arabs erupted in 1996, and again the government armed Arab militias to attack a non-Arab group, the Massaleit. Hundreds of people were killed, and 100,000 Massaleit villagers fled across the border, becoming refugees in neighboring Chad.

Atrocities against non-Arabs were increasing, and in Darfur

the citizens realized that peace talks between the government and the SPLA rebels would not change the NIF's destructive policy toward them. Non-Arab groups organized themselves militarily and formed the Sudan Liberation Army (SLA). In 2003 the SLA launched its first attacks against government outposts in Darfur. In response, the government of Sudan subcontracted the Janjaweed militias in another scorched earth counterinsurgency campaign. They let loose the hounds of hell, and gave them total impunity. The strategy is the oldest in the "art" of war: if you kill or displace all the people supporting a rebel group, you kill the rebellion. The result was genocide.

Who Are the Janjaweed?

The Janjaweed are a loose collection of thousands of mercenary fighters and career criminals who share a racist ideology with their paymasters in Khartoum. The NIF's powerful and pervasive security apparatus had used the Janjaweed effectively in other wars against Darfuri non-Arab groups, but this time was different. The SLA was a more organized fighting force than previous Darfur rebels, and left unchecked, they could have eventually posed a genuine threat to Khartoum.

Many young men from Darfur entered the Sudanese army and rose through the ranks to become commanders. The government trusted poor northerners to fight its war against southern-based rebels, but could government troops originally from Darfur be trusted to fight a war against people from their home area? When the government launched its counterinsurgency, with as many as 80 percent of its own troops from Darfur, government officials had strong doubts that the army would remain loyal. So rather than risk a mutiny, Khartoum turned to its trusted allies, the Janjaweed. The government needed more Janjaweed fighters to achieve its objectives, and it looked to the poorest reaches of northern Sudan for recruits.

Put simply, the government of Sudan cut a sinister deal. The regime promised land, livestock, war booty, and impunity to its Janjaweed allies. In return, the Janjaweed would attack villages belonging to the non-Arab Fur, Zaghawa, and Massaleit. To swell the ranks of its proxy army, the government released criminals from jail, recruited fighters from neighboring countries, and gave cash handouts of around $100 to anyone who would take up arms against Darfur's non-Arab tribes. The government provided the Janjaweed with new rifles and heavy weapons, and some of them even got uniforms.

The Janjaweed served a strategic purpose: to create anarchy and to inflame ethnic divisions and conflict. The government could then lie, say that atrocities were occurring because of historic "tribal" feuds, and still be believed. This fallacy, as it had in Rwanda and Bosnia before, allowed those in the international community who didn't really want to confront the killers to conveniently forget who set this destructive process in motion. It's divide-and-destroy.

These are fundamental elements of the regime's strategy for maintaining power: first they kill and displace as many as they can, until international condemnation reaches a tipping point, then they turn the ethnic diversity of Sudan into an instrument of war and political control. We have seen this time and again over the last two decades in Sudan: in southern Sudan, in the Nuba Mountains in central Sudan, and now in Darfur.

Government officials responsible for genocide in Darfur outsourced direct control and orchestration of Janjaweed activity and the divide-and-destroy policy to local government officials. These officials conjured up ways to stoke conflict between neighbors as if they were playing the board game Risk. Until the Janjaweed and regime officials are dealt with decisively, the situation will remain bleak. Darfur's tormenters will not reverse their policy of support for the Janjaweed, because they would have too much to lose politically and militarily, and the pressure from the international community remains too muted and weak to alter their calculations.

Descent into Genocide

The genocide in Darfur came in two waves. The first wave featured wholesale destruction of the way of life and livelihoods of the civilian supporters of the rebellion. The second wave has been marked by the manipulation of humanitarian access to survivors, aimed at slowly destroying their will to survive through mass rape and preventing their return home.

The government's military has coordinated closely with the Janjaweed and laid waste to Darfur's Zaghawa, Fur, and Massaleit populations. By the end of 2003, the Sudanese military and Janjaweed militia had slaughtered 70,000 people and driven more than 700,000 from their homes. The worst was yet to come.

The widespread campaign of atrocities and ethnic cleansing was extraordinarily evident. Nonprofit organizations such as the International Crisis Group, Amnesty International, Human Rights Watch, and the Sudan Organization Against Torture sent research teams to document the horrors: children thrown into fires, mass executions and gang rapes, rape survivors branded with a scalding iron.

When we spoke with the survivors of the genocide, most had similar stories. The attacks usually began before dawn. Government aircraft commenced the assaults by dropping crude bombs on villages, killing men, women, and children as they slept in their beds. In the chaotic aftermath of the bombings, government troops with hundreds of Janjaweed fighters would sweep into a village to murder the men, rape the women, burn the homes, loot the livestock, and drive the survivors into the desert. The attackers yelled racial slurs as they rampaged through the villages, and after they raped women they would often tell them that they would give birth to Arab children.

The Sudanese army and the Janjaweed methodically set out to destroy the livelihoods of Darfur's non-Arab peoples. To prevent people from returning to their villages, the Janjaweed poisoned the water supply by dumping bodies down wells. They destroyed crops and precious food supplies. Food availability dwindled, prices soared, malnutrition rates skyrocketed, and the government began its favorite, tried-and-true tactic of denying humanitarian assistance to its suffering citizens by cutting off their access to aid agencies.

Witnesses to Destruction

One of *New York Times* columnist Nicholas Kristof's trips to Darfur in June 2004 was particularly difficult and uncomfortable.

"I was sleeping outside on the ground, and there were tens of thousands of refugees who had just arrived at the border. They were seeking shelter under trees, and I started talking to them. Under the first tree were two brothers who had been shot. The one less injured had carried his badly wounded brother on his back for forty-nine days and was nursing him, trying to keep him alive. Under the next tree was a woman whose parents had been shot and thrown into the wells, and then her husband was shot in front of her. Under the third tree were two little children, aged four and one, who were orphans, their parents killed. Under the fourth tree was a woman whose husband and two small children had been killed, and then she had been gang-raped and mutilated to humiliate her forever. And then, as far as I looked there were more trees, and more families sheltering under them, with stories just as wrenching."

Nick adds, "Later, what I found most poignant was the women in Kalma camp who were willing to tell me, with sound and video running, using their names, that they had been gang-raped by the police. They risked humiliation and retribution, yet they had the guts to come forward because they thought it would help stop the assaults. I found that courage incredibly inspiring (and then agonized about whether to identify them; in the end I did not use their full names or identities because I didn't want to have them on my conscience if they were imprisoned and beaten)."

Shockingly, these women were not even safe at the displaced camp. In late August 2006, the International Rescue Committee reported that more than two hundred women had been raped in the Kalma camp over the previous five weeks alone.*

Jerry Fowler, former staff director of the Committee on Conscience at the U.S. Holocaust Memorial Museum, was witness to the horrors told by refugees in eastern Chad in the summer of 2005. In Bahay, in stifling 115-degree heat, he spoke with a woman who had two bullet wounds in her leg. She had just crossed the border with sixty families, all fleeing attacks by Sudanese government forces and the Janjaweed. Along the journey from her village to the border, she and a seventeen-year-old girl went to a well to get water. A government soldier was guarding the well, preventing anyone from getting a drink. The soldier grabbed the girl and began taking her away, and the other woman tried to pull her away from his grasp. He opened fire and shot the woman twice in the leg. The teenager was later found in the desert. Both her legs were broken and she was covered with blood.

At one point, Jerry was sitting in a hot tent, a sandstorm raging outside, and a woman was telling him her story of the attack on her village. At that moment, Jerry had the overwhelming urge to get out of the tent. He was emotionally and physically exhausted. As he grabbed his things and began to leave, the woman asked him about her mother. Did he know her? Had he seen her? Did he know how to find her? These were not rhetorical questions. The woman's name was Hawa. Her mother's name was Hadiya Ahmed. Whenever Jerry speaks publicly about Darfur, he mentions Hawa and her missing mother. He doesn't know if she was ever found.

John Heffernan from Physicians for Human Rights traveled to eastern Chad in May 2004 and recalls another refuge near the northern stretch of the Chad/Sudan border. John H. and his colleague Jennifer Leaning, a professor at Harvard and an emergency room doctor, drove south along the Chad border with Sudan be-

*IRC Press release, "Increased Sexual Assaults Signal Darfur's Downward Slide," August 23, 2006.

fore heading to the more forbidding north. After an eight-hour drive they arrived in a desolate locale near the northern stretch of the border. The travel was grueling, and the car was stuck in a *hubbub* (sandstorm) along the way. Both John H. and Jennifer were badly dehydrated, and it became quickly clear that Jennifer's condition was extremely serious. She needed fluids rapidly, and despite being hooked up to two IVs (with the assistance of relief workers) she was getting worse. "I'm losing ground," she told John H. The nearest clinic was three hours away.

As John H. and others worked to improve Jennifer's condition, he looked out at the scene around him. Unlike other official refugee sites he had visited in Chad, there was no camp here: only people huddled under trees. The 18,000 refugees had no shelter or health care, meager food supplies, and shared one dirty well with the livestock they had managed to bring across the border. Many animals—the livelihood and lifeline for many societies in Darfur—had not made it, and piles of burning carcasses among the refugees made for an awful scene.

Jennifer's condition began to improve, and as the car departed for the nearest health clinic, John H. thought to himself, If my friend almost died here, what chance do these people have? They were caught in a desert death trap, and it became clear to him that the victims of the conflict in Darfur were victims of genocide. John H. is currently director of the genocide prevention initiative at the U.S. Holocaust Memorial Museum's Committee on Conscience, where he works to end the genocide in Darfur and atrocities in places like Congo and northern Uganda.

In a horrible turn of events, African Union peacekeeping troops were also subject to the violence in Darfur. In January 2006, thirty Senegalese peacekeepers were attacked in Fatima's village, Girgira, after delivering a truck to another location. (We talked about Fatima in the first chapter.) The Khartoum government blamed Chad or Chad-backed rebels, while Chad's government said Sudanese government forces were behind the attack.

We walked among the rows of refugees in the Amna Bak refugee camp in eastern Chad, under the harsh desert sun, amid shacks constructed from sticks, plastic, and earth. Don tried to imagine what all these people had seen and felt. But it is unimaginable. Much as when he stood next to Paul Rusesabagina in Toronto at the film festival, he felt very small and humbled. One man, finishing his afternoon prayers, was restrained with metal shackles because he had been so traumatized by the bomb attacks on his village that he kept running into the desert, into danger and certain death. As if it might help make us understand better, some of the refugees had drawn posters, illustrating the ground and air attacks that drove them off their land and into this place. At the camp, water only comes from taps near the edge of the settlement, and bread comes from grain that is ground daily. Mud is mixed to keep walls of huts strong against the wind and the desert winter's biting cold.

In another camp we visited near the Chad/Sudan border, Tulum, the 21,000 refugees lived in tents rather than mud or wooden shacks, but their stories were just as brutal, and as in other camps, there was rampant disease, fear, and depression.

JOHN:

*O*n one of the trips I took to Darfur with Samantha Power in late spring 2004, we met a woman, Amina, cooking on the ground. She had fled her village during an attack. Her husband had been shot as soon as he left their hut. She had two of her children on her back and the other two in her arms as about twenty Janjaweed chased her on camels. First they ripped her five-year-old, Adom, from her, and when she stopped running and begged for her child, they told her they would shoot her. So she continued running away from her village that was up in flames. The Janjaweed then tossed Adom into the fire. He was screaming and calling her name, but she just kept running. Despite her speed, her seven-year-old, Asam Mohamed, was then taken and shot, once in his side and once in his back. She was never able to bury her children.*

Over the last three years, on a number of trips to the region, I have spoken with countless other women who recounted with surprising candor how while collecting firewood for the refugee camps, they were beaten by Janjaweed, threatened with knives, cut, and raped. The women went to the police to report the rapes, but nothing happened. Most victims don't trust the police and consider them as just another branch of the government that will rape, torture, and murder them. The government has even hidden Janjaweed fighters within the police, creating a sickening scenario of the attackers "guarding" their victims. These women had no other option but to go out again to these unsafe areas on a daily basis in search of firewood.

This fills me with an anger that can only be reduced when this genocide is halted and justice is served for the perpetrators, or at least those who orchestrated this madness. Until that happens, I will not stop sounding the alarm. In fact, I cannot stop. I hope you will feel the same way.

One of the most effective alarm bells I have had the opportunity to sound has been the CBS show 60 Minutes. *Correspondent Scott Pelley and his producers Bill Owens and Shawn Efran made a commitment to Sudan which allowed us to produce three shows in 2004 and 2006, reaching tens of millions of Americans. On the first trip Samantha and I took for 60 Minutes, we found a book bag full of notebooks in a partially burned hut in one of the destroyed villages. We brought the notebooks and other household items back to the United States, and the Holocaust Museum in Washington, D.C., and the Museum of Tolerance in Los Angeles both agreed to exhibit some of the items.*

Two years later, it finally occurred to me (not the sharpest knife in the drawer) that we should try to find the kid to whom the notebooks belonged and see if he or she was still alive. We got the notebooks translated from Arabic to English and found that the name of the kid was Jacob.

Scott and I decided to go in search of Jacob, to see if he was still alive and what had happened to his village, where we had found the notebooks.

Sometimes needles are found in haystacks. Searching throughout the refugee camps in Chad, we found someone with a name that matched Jacob's who had registered for food rations at a camp in northeastern Chad. After what at times appeared like a wild goose chase, we finally found Jacob in a humble mud hut in the center of one of the refugee camps outside of a town called Bahai. After getting over his initial consternation about the Martians who had landed in the middle of his refugee camp, Jacob was astonished to see the notebooks we handed over to him at the outset of our discussion. He was moved by the memories of his village and talked poignantly about the difficult choice he was making in not joining the rebels, but instead pursuing education in order to help bring about a political solution to the conflict.

At the end of our discussion, when we asked him what he wanted to do with the notebooks, he urged that we return them to the museums in order to teach as many people as possible about what had happened to his homeland.

Throughout 2003 and part of 2004, the government denied that there was a crisis in Darfur and enacted labyrinthine procedures aimed at blocking and delaying the establishment of humanitarian operations. As humanitarian workers applied for visas to travel to Sudan and assist victims of the conflict, the government's embassies and consulates around the world processed their requests at a glacial pace. Government customs delayed the release of vehicles, equipment, and relief supplies, including essential medicines. Khartoum blocked food shipments to Darfur and grounded some of the aircraft used to move food and relief supplies. When relief workers did eventually arrive in Khartoum, they had to apply for travel permits to get to Darfur, and the delays continued. Relief agencies had difficulty getting jet fuel for the few planes that they had permission to fly, despite the fact that the Sudanese military had little difficulty fueling its own planes and attack helicopters to bomb and strafe civilians.

As the Sudanese military and the Janjaweed squeezed the life out of Darfur, peace negotiations in Kenya between the government and the southern-based SPLA moved slowly ahead. An agreement seemed tantalizingly close, and the international community was reluctant to take strong action to end the killing in Darfur for fear that the government of Sudan would reconsider negotiations with the south. The Bush administration had invested considerable time, energy, and money to push the north-south peace process forward. Genocide in Darfur threatened to expose the problems with negotiations that excluded northern opposition groups.

In early 2004, policy makers made a lethal decision to conclude the peace agreement between the government and the southern SPLA rebels before focusing full diplomatic attention on Darfur. The National Islamic Front reacted by slowing down the negotiation process and accelerating their campaign of human destruction in Darfur. While U.S. diplomats tried desperately to seal a deal that would end the war in southern Sudan, Darfur was in flames. The Sudan government knew that the longer it could delay an agreement with southern rebels, the more time it would have to conduct the genocide in Darfur.

In March 2004, on the eve of the anniversary of the genocide in Rwanda, the top United Nations official in Khartoum, Mukesh Kapila, courageously compared the butchery in Darfur to the organized slaughter of 800,000 Rwandans ten years earlier. "I was present in Rwanda at the time of the genocide, and I've seen many other situations around the world, and I am totally shocked at what is going on in Darfur," he told a BBC radio program. "This is ethnic cleansing; this is the world's greatest humanitarian crisis, and I don't know why the world isn't doing more about it." Most commentators and diplomats dismissed his admonitions as the rantings of a frustrated bureaucrat, but Kapila turned out to be dead right.

Echoes of Rwanda

Only a familiarity with Rwanda could prepare us for what we heard and witnessed in Darfur. But John's twenty years in African war zones and Don's work on *Hotel Rwanda* (particularly his travel to Rwanda itself) were only partial desensitizers to the tales of cruelty and horror.

The worst stories, perhaps, were those of the brutal gang rapes that are the hallmark of Janjaweed attacks. Every day, hundreds of thousands of women in the displaced camps throughout Darfur face a Sophie's Choice: they can either stay in the relative safety of the camps and watch their families starve to death with no firewood to cook the little food donated by the international community, or they can leave the camps and forage for firewood, which will allow their families to eat another day but expose them to the probability of rape, sometimes gang rape, by Janjaweed militia.

These horrors can seem inexplicable and incomprehensible. But the why and how of genocide and other mass atrocities are often eerily similar. The two cases of genocide we are most familiar with are Rwanda and Darfur. Did the top regime officials in the Rwandan capital Kigali and Sudan's Khartoum just wake up one morning and decide to unleash genocide? Of course not. These genocides are the product of cold, rational, chilling calculations.

The story of the last forty years of Sudan has been one of war, famine, and human displacement. The genocide in Darfur represents a culmination of the tactics used by the current government in other parts of the country. Crimes against humanity don't just happen to people. There are planners, orchestrators, and perpetrators. They must somehow be stopped, and they must pay for their crimes.

The first category of stark parallels between the genocides in Rwanda and Darfur is why they have been perpetrated:

• The regimes in Sudan and Rwanda wanted to maintain absolute power by any means necessary, even if that meant perpetrating genocide.
• Both chose the oldest, most extreme method of counterinsurgency in the art of war: drain the pond to catch the fish. If you destroy the people from which your opposition comes, then you won't have much of an opposition anymore.
• Both wanted to send a message to any other potential rebels from any quarter: if you challenge us, herein lies your fate.

That is megalomaniacal, murderous behavior, but it is not irrational.

The second category of stark parallels between Rwanda and Darfur is how these two genocides have been perpetrated:

• Militias do most of the killing, to give the orchestrators—the governments—a degree of separation and hoped-for deniability. In the case of Rwanda, the Interahamwe militias did the dirty work. In Darfur, it is the Janjaweed.
• Specific ethnic groups are targeted because of their support for opposition groups or as a mechanism for mobilizing government support. In Rwanda, the Tutsi were vilified and targeted for extinction. In Darfur, three specific non-Arab ethnic groups were targeted initially: the Zaghawa, the Fur, and the Massaleit. We should know and remember their names.
• Intercommunal rivalries are stoked. This is a classic case of divide and conquer or, more specifically, divide and destroy. The governments in both countries sow divisions to keep potential opponents weak. Tutsi were pitted against Hutu in Rwanda, and in Darfur, Arab populations were encouraged to attack non-Arabs.

5

Citizens v. Government:
Knowing What We Are Up Against

"If every member of the House and Senate had received 100 letters from people back home saying we have to do something about Rwanda, when the crisis was first developing, then I think the response would have been different."

SENATOR PAUL SIMON IN RESPONSE TO
U.S. NONINVOLVEMENT IN RWANDA IN 1994*

What happens in the United States when there is a horrific crisis that requires global intervention, and not enough citizens and policy makers care for that to happen? Nothing. Sadly, U.S. and international inaction in the face of mass atrocities has a long, inglorious history. The Rwandan genocide was simply the most dramatic example of impotence and indifference.

It is frustrating to us how sparse and sporadic the news coverage is of Africa, which only makes headlines when another crisis erupts. This has led to a "conflict fatigue" associated with the

---

All Things Considered, National Public Radio, July 22, 1994.

continent as a whole. The truth is, however, that much of Africa is a good news story. There are positive stories that deserve air time, such as:

- The move away from dictatorships to democracy throughout Africa
- A proliferation of nongovernmental organizations contributing to the development of most African countries
- Effective roles in the war on terrorism by many African governments
- Peace agreements forged in countries which only a few years earlier had been ripped apart by war and crimes against humanity, such as Sierra Leone, Liberia, southern Sudan, and Burundi
- Serious methods by African institutions to combat transnational threats of disease and ecological degradation
- Commitment on the part of many African governments to fiscally responsible economic policies focused on alleviating poverty.

By ignoring the positive news, U.S. and European media risk fostering a tendency to dismiss the entire continent as hopeless. So when wars erupt and their attendant human rights abuses emerge, the response—if there even is one—is often tentative and muted, and conflict-ridden countries easily descend into a free fall. We think these conflicts are not just an affront to humanity, they are the greatest threat to overall progress throughout the African continent.

JOHN:
In mid-March 1998, as a young official at the National Security Council, I had the honor of participating in President Clinton's first trip to Africa, the longest overseas

travel of his entire presidency. President Clinton visited Senegal, Ghana, Uganda, Rwanda, South Africa, and Botswana over eleven days. I helped organize the visits to Rwanda and Uganda, and the Heads of State Summit during the trip. Led by Susan Rice at the State Department and Ambassador Joe Wilson at the National Security Council,* the objective of the trip was to highlight the positive aspects of and opportunities in Africa. Since all we ever see on our television screens is famine and war, President Clinton wanted to show the other side of Africa: democratic governments, reforming economies, extraordinary cultures, great investment opportunities, and the legendary resilience of Africa's peoples. Media, business executives, and legislators came on the trip to see the other side of the story.

The trip was a grand success. President Clinton came back psyched to do more for Africa. And then . . . WHAM! Wars erupted like the mother of all fireworks displays all across the continent, wars which made headlines because of the terrible atrocities committed. All of the plans to do more were laid to waste. The whole positive media spin turned poisonous, and support evaporated for new initiatives and investments.

Two realities slapped me in the face, hard, and helped refocus my life's priorities:

- *First, if conflicts aren't resolved, efforts to support Africa's development will be undermined repeatedly.*
- *Second, political will for supporting positive agendas in Africa has a great deal of competition from many other pressing priorities, so unless people like you reading*

---

*The trip also had the excellent support of White House staffers Robin Sanders and Erica Barks-Ruggles and Deputy Assistant Secretary of State Johnnie Carson.

*this book become more vocal, little will change in how
we respond to Africa.*

*The conclusion hit me in the middle of the forehead,
and it has only grown since that time. Quite simply, we
need to build a popular constituency for Africa.
Throughout my time in the Clinton administration, I saw
first-hand how difficult it was for senior policy makers to
marshal the attention and resources to address the hard
issues confronting countries beset by crimes against
humanity, because usually there are few U.S. political
constituencies pressing for action. In other words, there is
no political cost for inaction. That's precisely what Don and
I—and many others around the world—are trying to
change.*

*Bono, DATA (Debt AIDS Trade Africa), and the ONE
Campaign are going a long way toward doing that in the
areas of foreign aid, trade, and debt relief. Only recently has
an adequate effort begun to prevent crimes against
humanity. To that end, my longtime friend and colleague
Gayle Smith and I decided to launch an initiative called the
ENOUGH campaign, which we talk about later in the
book, in Chapter 8.*

So it is absolutely imperative that resolving conflicts and confronting mass human rights abuses be central objectives of U.S.
policy in Africa. However, the U.S. government usually does not
respond to cases of mass atrocities—particularly in Africa—
because of the previously mentioned Four Horsemen Enabling the
Apolcalypse: ignorance, indifference, policy inertia, and apathy.
When the American people—or influential subsets of them—do
not make noise about mass atrocities, then it is highly unlikely
that the U.S. government will do much more than express concern
and call on the parties to lay down their arms.

However, the case of Darfur is different. Americans—particularly a few important constituencies—have expressed great horror over Darfur and demanded more action. If this were a "normal" case, we activists could have influenced the policy makers and something viable might have been done. But Darfur has an added point of complexity. After the 9/11 terrorist attacks, the Sudan regime—out of fear of reprisals for their earlier support of Osama bin Laden and continuing contacts with other terrorist groups—intensified their counterterrorism cooperation with the U.S. government. President Bush wasn't kidding when he uttered the famous words "You're either with us or against us." In this case, Sudan is with us, and that bought the regime breathing room while it unleashed the genocide in Darfur.

A Pattern of Global Inaction

One of the most consistent responses to genocide and other mass atrocities by governments around the world is to deliberately portray matters as more complex than they really are. In this way, officials can delay difficult and bold decisions and justify inaction. Certainly, the dynamics of most conflicts are indeed complicated, but somehow when U.S. or other governments' interests are at stake, these administrations have found a way to understand and effectively react to the situation.

Another response by governments and the UN to crimes against humanity is to practice moral equivalency, treating perpetrators and victims equally, calling for cease-fires rather than calling for accountability. This is the unfortunate case in Darfur. As you can imagine, we need much more than rhetorical and balanced appeals to stop those willing to commit such crimes. Moreover, such equivalency ignores the international convention relating to genocide, which clearly states, "Persons committing genocide . . . shall be punished, whether they are constitutionally responsible rulers, public officials or private individuals." While military skirmishes by rebels or competing governments may have started a conflict, mass atrocities are always far beyond a reasonable and proportionate response.

Most often, governments and the UN Security Council posture, warn, and threaten, but they rarely act. The lesson is clear: you can kill as many as you want, and there will be no consequences. In 1992, we began to hear the term "ethnic cleansing" in relation to events in the former Yugoslavia. It was a term used repeatedly in criticisms of Slobodan Milosevic and in resolutions by governments and the UN Security Council. After many unfulfilled warnings, it was only after the mass killings at Srebrenica in 1995 that the international community took substantive actions to end the violence and bring a tentative peace, with the Dayton Accords.

Even if they feel domestic pressure to act, permanent members of the UN Security Council routinely use entrenched divisions as an excuse for inaction. The United States and the United Kingdom often allow opposition from China and Russia—a given on any human rights issue—to paralyze them, rather than confronting these states more forcefully as they do on issues of more direct national security interest. This was seen during the genocide in Cambodia in the mid 1970s, when Amnesty International and five governments (not including the United States or Western European nations) brought charges to the UN Commission on Human Rights. In spite of evidence that the Khmer Rouge intended to destroy Cham Muslims, Christians, Buddhist monks, and the Vietnamese and Chinese minorities, the Security Council, with anticipated vetoes by the Soviet Union and China, did nothing and the remaining major powers did not pursue other routes.

Lastly, during genocides and mass atrocities, outside governments apply humanitarian Band-Aids over gaping human rights wounds, citing the millions of dollars (sometimes billions) they provide in food aid to exonerate themselves from the responsibility to protect civilian life. Sadly, this is also the case with Darfur, as we shall see shortly. Food and medicine today are helpful, but are insufficient if a person's life is still in jeopardy due to violence.

"In the public portrayal of humanitarian situations our profession has often reduced massive suffering to a charitable appeal. The depiction of reprehensible brutality is simplified to merely needing benevolent relief. Humanitarian emergencies are not merely health crises, they are epidemics of human rights abuses," wrote Gerald Martone, director of humanitarian affairs for the International Rescue Committee. "We must communicate complex situations as moments for international action not merely remedied by Western do-gooders and the provision of supplies. Our communication should invite action, outcry, and engagement."*

Top Ten Current U.S. Excuses for Inaction

Throughout this latest genocide, the U.S. government has used each of the above tactics and added new justifications to avoid getting involved. After the U.S. government's declaration of "genocide" in Darfur in 2004, officials had to become even more creative in deploying excuses for inaction. We wondered why—after taking the bold and necessary step of actually naming a genocide a "genocide"—there was so little follow-through on the part of the Bush administration. Why was the government of the United States, intentionally and not, diminishing its own best intentions and setting up obstacles to constructive change?

As the genocide unfolded, American officials in the Pentagon, CIA, and State Department made excuses as to why the United States could not do more. They confidently asserted that their policies, given time, would stabilize the situation, bring peace to Darfur, and end the genocide. That confidence was badly misplaced. After returning from our first trip together to Africa, we pored over the rationales the U.S. government has

---

*Gerald Martone, "Neglected Crises: Playing the Blame Game," *InterAction Monday Developments,* Volume 24, Number 12 (July 31, 2006).

used to justify its weak response to the Darfur genocide, and we narrowed them down to ten lame excuses that were deployed throughout the first two years of the genocide. We wrote about these in the *Wall Street Journal*,* and we summarize the ten excuses here:

1. We're doing all we can.

In the same breath that Secretary Powell first invoked the term "genocide," he said the United States was already doing all it could to counter it: "We concluded—I concluded—that genocide has been committed in Darfur, and that the government of Sudan and the Janjaweed bear responsibility, and that genocide may still be occurring . . . however, no new action is dictated by this determination. We have been doing everything we can to get the Sudanese government to act responsibly. So let us not be too preoccupied with this designation. These people are in desperate need and we must help them."

This was an important and deliberate choice of words given that the Genocide Convention demands that signatory states do all they can to prevent and punish the crime. Article VIII of the Convention states that contracting parties (which include the United States and Sudan) "may call upon the competent organs of the United Nations to take such action under the Charter of the United Nations as they consider appropriate for the prevention and suppression of acts of genocide." In the two years after Secretary Powell's use of the term, as we write, not one meaningful punitive measure has been imposed on the orchestrator of the atrocities—the Sudanese regime.

---

*"The Darfur Genocide," *Wall Street Journal* op-ed, March 24, 2005.

2. More action would worsen the situation.

U.S. officials often said in meetings with us and others that if they pressured the Sudanese regime any harder, it would implode and the consequences would be grave. Graver than genocide? Regardless, this is specious, since the Sudanese regime is one of the strongest governments in Africa and in no danger of collapse. Its intelligence apparatus and military are among the largest on the continent, and any form of dissent is ruthlessly suppressed. It will not collapse if pressured. Like many governments committing atrocities, it would change its behavior.

3. Peace in the south will solve Darfur.

U.S. officials have said since the advent of the Darfur conflict that they needed to focus on getting a deal with southern-based rebels first and then they could turn their attention to Darfur. Following the signing of the peace agreement between the north and south in January 2005 (nearly two years into the genocide in Darfur), John Danforth, who served as President Bush's special envoy to Sudan, said, "John Garang, the head of the SPLM . . . plus the government of Sudan have both said that the key to solving Darfur is this north-south peace agreement. . . . So the focus now has to be on Darfur."* Knowing this was the order of priorities for the Americans, the Sudanese regime delayed getting a deal with southern rebels during 2003 and 2004 so that they could carry out the most violent phase of the genocide: the scorched earth village burning campaign.

---

*Mark Bixler, "Historic Peace Agreement: Q&A / John Danforth," *Atlanta Journal-Constitution,* January 12, 2005.

4. We don't support the ICC.

The U.S. has consistently said that there must be justice for the crimes committed during genocide. The International Criminal Court has opened an investigation, prepared a list of suspects, and appointed a judge for the situation in Darfur. But by not supporting the ICC (which alone has the mandate to investigate and prosecute the crime of genocide) with information and declassified intelligence, the United States has undercut its own stated position of seeking some measure of accountability.

5. The rebels are also to blame.

The United States has often said that the rebels in Darfur were as big a problem as the government, so as to reduce the pressure for responding more urgently to the genocidal actions of the regime. During the same 2004 Senate testimony in which he first used the word "genocide," Secretary Powell said, "At the same time, however, the rebels have not fully respected the cease-fire. And we are disturbed at reports of rebel kidnapping of relief workers."* Kidnapping is, of course, deplorable, but the continued government-sponsored Janjaweed attacks that razed entire villages, killed tens of thousands, and left thousands of women violated made the equivalency argument incomprehensible.

6. The African Union is taking care of the problem.

U.S. officials relied for too long on the African Union troops to try to stabilize the situation, rather than moving more urgently for a UN force that could protect

---

*Testimony to U. S. Senate Committee on Foreign Relations, September 9, 2004.

civilians from rape and killing. The AU forces, number-
ing about 7,200, are spread over an area nearly the size
of Texas, are low on funds, and lack appropriate fire-
power. Where the AU forces are concentrated, they
have been able to provide some security, assist humanitarian agencies with deliveries, and negotiate the release of abducted aid workers, but the region is just too
large and the forces too underfunded to be an effective
response to the Janjaweed and government forces.

7. We're giving lots of food aid.

The United States has consistently cited how much humanitarian aid it is providing to the victims of the genocide, remaining quiet about how to stop the abuses that
made the assistance necessary. During the foreign policy debate in the fall of 2004 between presidential con-
tenders George Bush and John Kerry, both were asked
what should be done about the genocide in Darfur.
After obligatory expressions of outrage at the horrors,
both basically said that they would increase humanitarian aid, leaving the causes unaddressed.

8. China and Russia will prevent real action.

The Bush administration has argued that it is often
blocked from doing more because China and Russia
will veto more potent international action on Darfur in
the UN Security Council. But the United States rarely
tests this threat. When the Americans plays chicken
with Russia and China, the two usually drive off the
road and abstain. For example, in March 2005, the Chinese and the Russians were confronted twice with juicy
veto opportunities but backed down when other members of the UN Security Council pushed them. In a rare
display of courageous action at that time, an almost inexplicable temporary stiffening of the spine, the Secu-

rity Council authorized targeted sanctions and referred the case of Darfur to the ICC.

9. Incentives are better than pressures.
The United States has argued that it must pursue a soft policy of constructive engagement with the Khartoum regime, rather than a punitive or isolationist approach. However, a policy of pressure has a proven track record with the Sudanese government, as we explained in Chapter 3 and will again show in Chapter 6. For instance, in the 1990s, the UN Security Council punished the Sudanese government with a series of multilateral UN sanctions for its support of terrorism, and the regime quickly changed its behavior, evicting Osama bin Laden from the country, dismantling the al-Qaeda commercial infrastructure, and cutting its ties with other terrorist organizations.

10. The situation will get better. Trust us.
Most insidiously, at many points during the three years after the genocide had begun, the United States argued that circumstances in Darfur were getting better, and that its policy—if given time—would result in peace and stability in the region. Each time officials made this contention, new horrors would come to light or new statistics would be released that would demonstrate the fallacy of this assertion.

Given the excuses used over the past three and a half years, the truth appears to be that combating genocide and other mass atrocities is simply not considered a national security issue by most elected officials. The United States government doesn't want to burn its leverage on confronting genocide. It would rather save it for issues like Iraq or Iran, as well as keep a friendly relationship with its counterterrorism pals in Khartoum. The only antidote to this searing truth—the only way the United States will take the kind of leadership necessary to end the horrors—is for there to be a political cost for inaction, at the voting booth. We need to make the temperature a little hotter, a little more uncomfortable for those politicians who would look away.

Just a few more degrees. Just a few thousand more letters. It is, frankly, that simple.

Further Obstacles to Meaningful Action

As stated previously, the predictable responses and pathetic excuses outlined above usually unfold in a policy environment of indifference, apathy, ignorance, and inertia (the Four Horsemen Enabling the Apocalypse). This is certainly the case in Congo, northern Uganda, and post–Black Hawk Down Somalia. But the Sudanese case is special. There have been additional strategic factors, not in the top ten excuses, that have constrained the U.S. response there.

First is the "Law of the Tool."* Because of the wars in Iraq and Afghanistan, most of our resources devoted to international military operations are being diverted to these conflicts. Consequently, there is little spare change left over for anything else. The Law of the Tool dictates that your response is driven by what tools you have, rather than what is really needed for the unique circumstances of a given crisis. Before the U.S.-led invasion into Iraq, Secretary of Defense Donald Rumsfeld argued that the United States had the capacity "to provide for homeland defense, to undertake a major regional conflict and win decisively . . . and simultaneously swiftly defeat another aggressor in another theater."†

---

*This is discussed in John's book *Frontline Diplomacy: Humanitarian Aid and Conflict in Africa* (Lynne Rienner, 1996).

†See Remarks as Prepared for Delivery by Secretary of Defense Donald H. Rumsfeld, for the House Armed Services Committee, Wednesday, February 5, 2003.

That was hubristic, to say the least. Now the military is stretched thin of personnel as the wars continue much longer than anticipated, further lessening the opportunity for the United States to engage in a meaningful support role for Darfur—a crisis that one could argue is far more real and pertinent than the reasons for going to Iraq. So the Bush administration has tried to sell Congress and the interested public on a policy that it could afford in Darfur, rather than on a policy that would end the genocide. President Bush's team hoped they'd get lucky and that the genocide would end, just as it appears they hoped good fortune would bless their Iraqi adventure. But in both places the president and his people were unlucky, and wrong.

The second strategic factor is what we view as the "New Cold War." Understandably, counterterrorism has replaced the Cold War as America's overriding foreign policy framework. Sudan flipped from being a sponsor and supporter of international terrorism in the 1990s to becoming a partner in counterterrorism activities after 9/11. Many of the senior Sudanese officials who now offer information to the CIA are also the principal orchestrators of genocidal crimes.* The CIA even flew one of those officials, Intelligence Chief Salah Abdallah Gosh, on a private jet to the United States for a week of meetings. Gosh is widely believed to be directly responsible for the government's policy to create and support the Janjaweed in Darfur, and he is at the top of a list of persons identified by the United Nations as responsible for atrocities. As important as information on al-Qaeda and other terrorist groups is, U.S. officials should not be able to justify this moral sacrifice on national security grounds. It should be in the U.S. national interest to oppose a regime accused of committing

---

*We published an opinion piece in the *Los Angeles Times* that discussed the collaboration between the United States and Sudan's intelligence services despite the genocide in Darfur ("Our Friend, an Architect of the Genocide in Darfur," *Los Angeles Times,* February 14, 2006). John wrote about the issue again for the *Washington Post* ("So How Come We Haven't Stopped It?," *Washington Post,* November 19, 2006).

genocide, particularly when it has a history of supporting groups that have targeted the United States.

The third strategic factor is what we call the "Samantha Power Principle." As Samantha wrote in *A Problem from Hell,* if there is no political cost for inaction in the face of mass atrocities, we will get inaction. There will be no structural change in how we respond to these horrors until enough citizens are willing to say, "We're mad as hell and we're not going to vote for you anymore!" Media coverage, or lack thereof, is certainly a factor in the lack of attention crises like Darfur receive from the public and policy makers. The media can help drive policy debates when the pictures and stories create an urgency to respond such as with the famine in Ethiopia and Eritrea in the 1980s.

Citizen Action in Action
So what can you do?

What can we do to change the "Samantha Power Principle"? By now, we have seen how indifference and ignorance can kill. A little knowledge and concern that produces some action can actually save hundreds of thousands—even millions—of lives. That was obvious in the context of Rwanda, when just a small deployment of force could have saved hundreds of thousands of lives. It could have started, as Senator Paul Simon devastatingly said, with one letter. In 1994, Congresswoman Patricia Schroeder received letters during the Rwandan genocide, but she echoed Senator Simon's lament over a lack of concern for the human victims. "There are some groups terribly concerned about the gorillas. But—it sounds terrible—people just don't know what can be done about the people."*

For years, both of us were a bit incredulous that citizen action could realistically move governments into action. Then, as the student groups and others really started responding and mobilizing

---

*Paul Richter, "Rwanda Violence Stumps World Leaders," *Los Angeles Times,* April 30, 1994.

and we started to see the stirrings of a response from policy makers, we began to believe again in the power of ordinary people to make a difference. The efforts of one individual—no matter how flawed, how scarred, or how seemingly small—can save huge numbers of lives. And when many individuals express the same desire for change, for action, for compassion, our elected leaders actually listen.

JOHN:

In late 2003, I went to Capitol Hill to meet with members of Congress. My message was focused on the "Never Again" theme and how it is being desecrated. A number of congresspeople told me that they cared about what was happening in Sudan and wanted to help, but Iraq was dominating the foreign policy debates and the president needed to save his leverage for Iraqi policy imperatives. It was quite clear: an African issue—even when genocide was involved—just didn't rise to the level of national security importance in most people's books. I asked them what it would take to change this reality. One of them replied honestly, "We have to hear it from our constituents. Make as much noise as you can, scream bloody murder, force us to care!"

This has been my experience for some time now, ever since I worked for a couple congressmen in the 1980s. The squeaky wheel gets the grease. If we can make enough noise and demonstrate that there will be a cost for those politicians who just ignore us, then we can change things. I've seen it happen again and again. This is the foundation of our democratic system. Either use it, or we lose it on the issues we care about the most.

If the voices of those working on behalf of Darfurians were initially too soft to be heard, they are now coming together and becoming too loud to be ignored. In the summer of 2004, the

United States Holocaust Memorial Museum and American Jewish World Service organized a Darfur Emergency Summit. John, Gerry Martone of IRC, and Elie Wiesel, the Nobel Prize–winning author and Holocaust survivor, spoke to the assembled. Elie Wiesel's passionate speech about the importance of being heard was a potent wake-up call. "How can I hope to move people from indifference if I remain indifferent to the plight of others? I cannot stand idly by or all my endeavors will be unworthy."* He told the group to stop using the phrase "Never Again" if they were not going to respond to Darfur. Because it *was* happening again. His words had a profound effect: for many, Darfur moved from being just another crisis to being a genocide. The cause suddenly had a different feel; people's sense of responsibility was triggered, and the Save Darfur Coalition was born. *The time had come to start forcing people to care, and to act.*

By 2006, in response to increased citizen advocacy, President Bush began feeling the heat. After sitting on the sidelines for three years as his senior officials searched for quick fixes within the narrow confines of the policy constraints outlined above, Bush began weighing in publicly. Obviously fed up with the status quo, he took many people by surprise, including his own top advisors, when he called for NATO to help protect civilians and stabilize the security situation in Darfur. "We need more troops," Bush said in February 2006. "And so I'm in the process now of working with a variety of folks to encourage there to be more troops, probably under the United Nations. But it's going to require, I think, a NATO stewardship, planning, facilitating, organizing—probably double the number of peacekeepers that are there now."† These unscripted public pleas Bush made were a direct result of citizen

---

*Save Darfur Coalition press release, "Diverse Coalition Issues Statement and Call to Action on Sudan," August 2, 2004. Available at www.savedarfur.org.

†White House Press Release, "President Discusses Global War on Terror," February 17, 2006.

advocates making their voices heard right up to the president. After that declaration, the debate intensified.

During the late spring and early summer of 2006, the situation in Darfur deteriorated significantly, even after a peace deal was signed between the government of Sudan and one of the three Darfurian rebel groups. Bush administration officials continued to give the president no workable options to ameliorate conditions in Sudan beyond the status quo, so the president's bold assertions were never followed up and operationalized fully.

We hope that such a bureaucratic fumble is never allowed to happen again. The only way to do that is by turning up the heat and making as much noise as we can about Darfur and other crises involving mass atrocities against our fellow human beings.

Through the stories in this book that show individuals making a difference in a variety of ways, we hope to inspire people to get involved. The smallest of actions—writing letters to Congress, meeting members in the district offices, penning op-eds, raising money—*can* make the biggest of changes—even galvanizing action to end genocide!

DON:

It seemed innocent enough. My manager asking me, "Do you want to be a presenter at the Live 8 concert in Philadelphia?"

This "super," worldwide concert was going to be an unprecedented, historical event.

It took all of a second for me to answer.

"Hell, yeah."

It wasn't until I stepped out of the wings and took my first step onto the stage in Philadelphia that I truly considered where I was and what I had agreed to. And that is absolutely the wrong time to consider anything other than reading the words off of the teleprompter. My little voice inside my head was thinking the same thing, and he must've been nervous too, 'cause he started yelling at me: "Just keep walking; you out here now, fool! Can't do anything about it at this point! Go! Get on your spot! Read the teleprompter! Oh yeah, and relax, man!"

I'd never been to Philadelphia before but had always wanted to see the city that one of the baddest groups in hip-hop, The Roots, placed at the center of most of their songs. So Bridgid and I—kiss, hug, love to the kids—hopped a plane and headed to the land of sound. We were a little giddy. We don't really do a lot of the celebrity life thing, so this major concert outing was very big for us. Incredible entertainment by some of the most exciting acts in the world, happening all around the world, yet free to the Philly folk, and in service of an inarguably noble cause. Wow. All that altruism sounded too good to be true. This was an enormous outpouring of energy and effort, promoters forgoing the opportunity to maximize their financial upside, all for Africa, no less? It didn't make sense on the face of it. I better understood the goals of the G-8 meeting next week: "Get money, baby!" But Bob Geldof was the creator of both Band Aid, the supergroup of popular musicians that raised millions through hit singles, and Live Aid, the huge concerts that had generated over $100 million for famine relief. If I was going to throw in with anybody in such a grand way as this, might as well be with him.

I'm introducing two acts tonight, Bon Jovi first (classic) with Kanye West to follow (Mr. Kanye "George Bush doesn't care about Black people" West? Love that). And punctuated throughout my introductions is the message of the evening: Wake up. Stand up. Get involved. Do the right thing. Speaking of which, after complaints that there weren't enough Black acts on the bill, Russell Simmons made some calls and changed the profile. Bono also called Jay-Z to ask him to pull more hip-hop artists into the mix, and was equally accommodated. I wondered if in four days

the G-8 Summit, the meeting of the most powerful people
in the world, would enjoy similar cooperation: "Yo, Chirac,
need more bases in the southern part of France. Cool?"

"You got it, GW. Anytime. Holla at your boy."

Probably not. How the world leaders would react to the
plea from the Live 8 family—to "Make Poverty History" by
wiping out debt for eighteen of the poorest countries in the
world, a $50 billion request—that remained to be seen. But
today in Philly, Alicia Keys, Linkin Park and Jay-Z, Maroon
5, Stevie Wonder (just to name a few), and dozens more in
ten such concerts all over the world, are lifting their voice as
one. Music as movement. Beautiful.

"And now, Jersey's own, Bon Jovi!!"

The Philly crowd screams in unison as if these orange
state boys were born and bred just down the block.

"See there? Listen to 'em. You did fine. OK. You're done.
You can go. . . . C'mon, move your—"

"Wait!" I scream back at my little voice, tired of being
pushed around. I take my eyes from the teleprompter and
let myself look up for the first time at the full expanse of
human beings grooving in front of me. Some say there were
600,000 people stretched down the parkway in front of the
Museum of Art. Others say 1.5 million. I say, "Damn, that's
a lot of people I don't care how you slice it."

And there's even more watching in stadiums, on streets,
television, and a live Internet stream—many, many millions
more, all listening to our prayers for peace, our calls to
action.

My voice crowds in. "All silently judging you. Get the
hell off the stage!"

Discretion being the better part of valor, I obey and
slink back to the wings just in time to see Beyoncé building
with Alicia Keys backstage. It's then that I know I've died
and gone to hip-hop heaven, a small sacrifice to be sure.

6

Activist Beginnings and Success Stories

"To stay quiet is as political an act as speaking out."
ARUNDHATI ROY, AUTHOR AND ACTIVIST*

Over the past two decades, many citizens' movements have sprung up in the United States and elsewhere that have addressed international issues with intelligence, creativity, dedication, and, most importantly, success. By examining activist efforts from around the world and even in Sudan before the Darfur genocide, we can learn what tools were successful during the recent past and apply them in the fight to end mass atrocities today.

Anti-Apartheid

Citizen activism played a crucial role in ending the apartheid system of racial discrimination in South Africa. We were overjoyed to see the climax of this incredible surge of activism—the fall of apartheid and the release of Nelson Mandela—and Americans played a role in making it happen. During the late 1970s, the media increased its coverage of the racial discrimination and increasing violence of the regime in South Africa. Americans wanted to

---

*Addressing an audience at UCLA, May 27, 2003.

do something to help end apartheid, and activist groups began a divestment movement to channel support for the cause into meaningful change. Activists recognized that convincing city and state governments to dump their stock in companies that did business with the white supremacist apartheid government would put financial pressure on those companies to stop doing business in South Africa. As a result, the South African government would become more isolated internationally.

In its early days, this divestment movement was largely student driven. Though condemned by university officials, student protests during the early and mid 1980s had the support of human rights, labor, and civil rights leaders, such as Rev. Jesse Jackson. When constituents began voicing their support for the students, the lawmakers responded. In 1986, Congress passed the Anti-Apartheid Act, which blocked the import of South African products and prevented new corporate investment in the country as well as U.S. bank deposits from South African government agencies. U.S. investment in South Africa dropped from $2.8 billion in 1983 to $1.3 billion in 1985, with 80 out of 350 U.S. companies operating there leaving by 1987. The economic pressure generated by American citizens helped to force the South African government to change its ways. Mandela was released from prison in February 1990 and was elected president of South Africa in 1994. The apartheid era was over.

Debt Relief

For many decades, the world's poorest countries spent billions of dollars to repay debts to wealthy nations and international institutions, often leaving little for development, health care, or education. These debts were incurred by past regimes mostly during the Cold War, when the United States, the Soviet Union, and international banks loaned billions of dollars to mostly corrupt and unaccountable governments. Current governments are saddled with these debts, siphoning off funds that otherwise could be used for investment or social services. Recognizing the debilitating effects of debt on poor countries, development agencies, trade unions, students, and churches came together in the 1990s to advocate for debt relief.

Debt relief activists recruited high-profile spokespeople, including Bono, the charismatic lead singer of the Irish rock group U2. By the time that world leaders met in 2005 for the annual G-8—the "Group of Eight" of the world's most powerful economies—summit meeting, debt relief was on the global agenda. In the lead-up to the summit, the anti-poverty organization ONE teamed with Bono, Bob Geldof, and the screenwriter Richard Curtis to plan rock concerts in each of the G-8 countries. Over one million people attended the concerts, with another 3.8 billion watching online or on television.

When the G-8 met in Scotland they agreed to 100 percent debt cancellation for eighteen of the world's poorest countries and significant increases in foreign assistance spending. Debt relief activists cite the rewards of their activism: When governments provided debt relief to Uganda, the country used the money that would have gone to debt payments to improve primary education and HIV/AIDS education and treatments; in Mozambique, half a million children were immunized; in Tanzania, school fees were eliminated; and in Benin, school fees for rural students were waived. Reduced or forgiven debt payments have helped these countries concentrate on the basics—raising the standard of living and ending extreme poverty.

Anti-Sweatshops

The modern effort to eliminate sweatshops and improve labor conditions for garment and footwear workers started to gain momentum during the early 1990s. As the debate over "globalization" heated up, increasing reports surfaced of abusive labor practices in the United States and abroad. By 1994, Secretary of Labor Robert Reich began a campaign to enforce the Fair Labor Standards Act in response to media reports of sweatshops in the United States. Consumer, human rights, and labor groups started coming together, targeting specific corporations with strikes, boy-cotts, and demonstrations. Labor rights advocates began operating across national borders in an effort to expose and shut down sweatshops internationally.

In 1996, a furor erupted over the working conditions at Honduran garment factories that produced clothing for the Kathie Lee line at Wal-Mart. In a good faith gesture, talk show host Kathie Lee Gifford allowed these factories to be inspected by local, independent human rights monitors to ensure conditions improved. She has since become active in the anti-sweatshop movement, helping keep national attention on the topic. Growing unease helped launch sweatshop-free enterprises, such as American Apparel, the popular clothing store that began in 1997. A year later, this national concern about domestic and offshore sweatshop conditions led to more factory inspections, labor and wage guidelines, labeling, and the creation of a White House task force by President Clinton. Once again, citizen activists had influenced U.S. policy.

HIV/AIDS

As HIV tore through Africa during the 1980s and 1990s, the epidemic far outstripped the resources dedicated to controlling it by the United States and other countries. It was not until 2003 that this began to change, when President Bush made the surprising decision to create an Emergency Plan for AIDS Relief, a major increase in HIV/AIDS funding, announced during his State of the Union Address.* Bush referred to this initiative as "a work of mercy beyond all current international efforts to help the

---

*In real terms, the results of these efforts are staggering. In 2003, the U.S. government's contribution to fighting HIV/AIDS was $840 million; two years later, that figure was $2.3 billion. In 2005, President Bush signed the United States Leadership Against HIV/AIDS, Tuberculosis, and Malaria Act into law and launched the President's Emergency Plan for AIDS Relief (PEPFAR). PEPFAR dedicates $15 billion over five years to support prevention efforts, provide ARV treatments, and care for HIV/AIDS patients in 15 of the worst afflicted countries in Africa and the Caribbean. It is still not enough, however.

people of Africa."* Why did an administration better known for its skeptical approach to foreign aid decide to confront the problem of HIV/AIDS in Africa? The answer lies in Bush's allusion to a "work of mercy," a religious reference designed to resonate with a surprising constituency of citizen activists who had been pressuring the government for action: evangelical Christians.

During the eighties and nineties evangelical Christian groups were better known for denouncing HIV/AIDS as a consequence of homosexuality and drug use than for efforts to prevent and treat the disease. However, Christian missionaries and aid agencies working throughout Africa witnessed firsthand the devastating consequences of the disease for that continent. They realized that no matter the politics of HIV/AIDS in America, it was their responsibility as Christians to mobilize their fellow believers to do something about the pandemic.

In February 2002, Rev. Franklin Graham, son of the legendary evangelist Billy Graham, and a close spiritual advisor to President Bush, brought together more than eight hundred Christian leaders and overseas missionaries to promote the involvement of conservative Christians in fighting HIV/AIDS. Throughout the following year, Rev. Graham and other Christian leaders quietly prodded the White House to get involved. Key White House advisors, including speechwriter Michael Gerson, were receptive, and so was Senate majority leader Bill Frist, who had personally worked as a medical volunteer with HIV/AIDS victims. By coupling the moral imperative of fighting deadly disease with data to demonstrate the effectiveness of prevention and treatment efforts, Christian leaders were able to convince the President to act on HIV/AIDS.†

---

*White House Press Release, "State of the Union," January 28, 2003.

†There is much disagreement about the appropriateness and effectiveness of the strategies used to fight HIV/AIDS. The conservative Christian approach promotes abstinence and is skeptical of many of the traditional strategies of other HIV/AIDS activists, such as comprehensive sex education and condom distribution. Some HIV/AIDS activists, including pastors in HIV/AIDS–ravaged countries in southern Africa, fear that focusing on abstinence and shunning condoms will lead to more unprotected sex and

---

There are some simple lessons to glean from each example of citizen action:

- Don't be afraid to be innovative.
- Reach out to groups beyond your normal alliances—like student groups befriending labor unions.
- Talk to both sides of the political aisle.
- Continue meeting and educating average citizens while lobbying key political leaders.
- Understand that to be successful these movements have to in some way be global in nature, so be prepared to connect with other like-minded individuals and groups outside the United States, in a larger coalition for change.
- When appealing to political leaders, use brains—not pure emotions—to convey your message.
- Most of all—don't be afraid to start small.

What Have We Learned?

Deadly disease, unforgiving debt burdens, horrific work conditions, and a segregationist policy that tried to deny equality and humanity to one group—these would seem to be overwhelming issues, certainly too large for one individual to take on. Yet in each instance one became many, and the many prevailed to support real change.

These lessons have also helped shape effective strategies in Sudan for the past decade. Before the genocide in Darfur began, the Sudanese government was engaged in other atrocities, including the decades-long war in southern Sudan. Through successful grassroots activists strategies, the United States and other governments became more involved in criticizing and sanctioning the

---

greater rates of HIV infection. These debates will continue, but the role of conservative Christian groups in engendering increased funding and attention to the issue from the U.S. government is undeniable.

Khartoum regime and eventually helping bring peace to that region of the country. These successes show that with enough insistence our government can act and that the Khartoum government is responsive to international pressure.

Pre-Darfur Activism in Sudan

Remember back to Chapter 3, where we told you about the war in southern Sudan that cost over 2 million southern Sudanese lives? During that time, a number of issues became important to a handful of committed American citizens and organizations. We want to tell you about a few of those before we talk about the current efforts regarding Darfur. The main reason for this is to demonstrate that U.S. government and citizen pressure does work in changing the behavior of the Sudanese regime. There were many important individuals involved in building a movement to end the war in southern Sudan, and none more so than John's good friend and mentor Roger Winter.

Roger is a longtime activist. In the early 1960s he was a part of the civil rights movement and got arrested a couple of times for his convictions. He was involved in urban anti-poverty campaigns in his earlier years. In the Carter administration, Roger was the director of refugee resettlement. At that point, this was a massive undertaking. The United States was accepting and resettling refugees from Vietnam, Cuba, Haiti, the Soviet Union, Afghanistan, and Ethiopia. Ethiopians were among the first refugees from Africa to be accepted into the United States. It was in this position that Roger crossed the domestic/Africa policy divide and became more interested in resolving the conflicts and humanitarian disasters in Africa that produced the refugees that he was meeting.

When the reports of atrocities committed by the Sudanese regime against southern residents of that country reached Roger's attention, he knew he had to visit. As you might have gathered from Chapter 3, southern Sudan was a tough place to travel in the 1980s. The southern SPLA rebels did not hold territory, but rather operated as a guerrilla movement in the zones in between government-held "garrison towns." In 1987, however, the SPLA took a town called Kapoeta and held it. Suddenly, visitors had a place to stay inside southern Sudan and learn about the SPLA and the government's war tactics. In one of his first trips to Sudan, John traveled with Roger in 1987 to Kapoeta, where the two met with Sudanese rebel leaders, internally displaced southerners, and hardy aid providers.

Roger, John, our friend Gayle Smith, and a few other activists had an idea to build a congressional constituency that cared about African humanitarian crises, and specifically about Sudan. In April of 1989, Roger helped Senator Gordon Humphrey, as well as Congressmen Frank Wolf and Gary Ackerman get to southern Sudan. They traveled by bumpy road to Torit, a town that the SPLA had just captured. This was the beginning of a long, continuous string of congressional visits to the region, often organized by Roger, and these visits were critical to building the constituency in Congress to support greater U.S. involvement in humanitarian programs and in ending the conflict.

The key to the growth and success of this constituency is that it has been durable and bipartisan. Congressional interest in Sudan has traditionally been driven not by partisan politics, but rather by a real sense of right and wrong. Two of the stalwarts on the issue are Democratic Representative Donald Payne of New Jersey and Republican Representative Frank Wolf of Virginia. Representatives Payne and Wolf have been outspoken defenders of human rights for the Sudanese (and other oppressed people around the world), and they have led the way in trying to impose stronger accountability measures on Khartoum for years of systematic crimes against humanity.

The clear moral issues at stake in Sudan became the basis not only for congressional action, but for broader interest and activism among ordinary American citizens. This was critical for activists that began to work on building grassroots support for U.S. involvement in Sudan.

In 1989, Roger, John, Gayle, and Brian D'Silva of the U.S.

Agency for International Development got together and created the Coalition for Peace in the Horn of Africa—an effort to try to raise awareness of the crises in northeastern Africa and push for greater U.S. support for solutions. They began to build a small constituency of people who were educated about the war that the government of Sudan was waging against its own people.

Nonprofit organizations like the U.S. Committee for Refugees, Bread for the World, Center of Concern, Amnesty International, and Human Rights Watch were critical in helping to build awareness. The National Association of Evangelicals and other Christian organizations also began paying attention to the crisis in Sudan. They did so in part because of the religious persecution and enslavement of Christians in the south, but also because the atrocities committed by the government were so heinous and so unrelenting that compassionate people of any religion simply could not ignore them.

Over the next several years, activists pushed members of Congress and the Clinton and Bush administrations to pay more attention to the situation in Sudan and to pass laws and implement policies aimed at isolating the Khartoum government, providing humanitarian relief to war-weary civilians, and—ultimately— ending the war. Milestones in these efforts included the Clinton administration's decision to place Sudan on the list of state sponsors of terrorism in 1993, U.S. diplomacy in the United Nations Security Council to pass multilateral sanctions on the government in 1996–1997, the Clinton administration's decision (backed by a bipartisan coalition in Congress) to impose comprehensive unilateral sanctions against the government of Sudan, the Bush administration's focus from the outset of its tenure on the peace process for southern Sudan, and President Bush's 2003 appointment of a special envoy, former Missouri senator John Danforth, to help negotiate a peace deal between the government and the southern SPLA rebels. It was not surprising that the most important behind-the-scenes actor working with Senator Danforth to secure the deal was Roger, without whose involvement there might have been no agreement.

So what did these early Sudan activists do? How did they raise the temperature high enough beneath the U.S. government to start punishing the Sudan government for their crimes and help end a twenty-one-year African civil war that killed more than 2 million people? Two stories illustrate how individual citizens became involved and made the difference.

Lost Boys of Sudan

As the war in the south heated up, thousands of young boys from southern Sudan were separated from their families. To avoid slavery, death, or forced induction into the Sudanese army, these boys walked hundreds of miles in the most hostile of terrains. More than 10,000 made it to refugee camps in Ethiopia, but thousands died along the way. When the Ethiopian government was overthrown in 1991, the boys lost their safe haven and were chased and bombed again, running back across the border into an unwelcoming Sudan. The fighting displaced more people, and the boys continued their trek farther south in Sudan, encountering further bombings and attacks. They were ultimately driven across the border into refugee camps in Kenya. Sixteen thousand Sudanese boys (and some girls) ended up in Kakuma refugee camp alone.

One of them, James Garang (no relation to the late SPLA leader John Garang), told us about his harrowing journey: "On our two treks, we covered hundreds of miles and faced gunfire, lion and crocodile attacks, disease, and starvation. We often had to eat leaves and, to some extent, carcasses of dead animals to survive."

Beginning in 2000, the U.S. government began bringing some of these "Lost Boys of Sudan" to this country. By 2001, 3,800 Lost Boys had come to America. Life in America was certainly an improvement on the horrors of existence in southern Sudan, but the transition was not always easy. According to James, "Grappling with language barriers, culture shock, foreign land and foods and establishing ethics punctuated our first few years in America. We had to work, go to school, and pay rent for the first time in our lives." Fortunately, the Lost Boys were not completely alone, and many Americans—especially church groups—embraced their cause and helped them adjust to a new way of life.

Since then, several news pieces, magazine articles, television shows, and a couple of documentary films have been made or are in production about the Lost Boys. Among the projects are a brilliant novel by award-winning author Dave Eggers called *What is the What*, the documentary *Lost Boys of Sudan* by Megan Mylan and Jon Shenk, and an episode of the popular television show *7th Heaven*.

Mylan and Shenk's film was shown to the Congressional Refugee and Human Rights Caucus staffs and to staff at the State Department. The filmmakers work with community groups to offer audience members concrete ways to get involved with the Lost Boys and with larger Sudanese issues. As a result, some people have become mentors, organized fund-raisers, and lobbied their representatives locally and nationally. In addition, a Lost Boys Education Fund, administered through the International Rescue Committee, was created to help all of the nearly four thousand Lost Boys and Girls resettled in the United States. James called the support of Americans for the Lost Boys and Girls "phenomenal, unprecedented, and a stroke of luck." He added, "Almost all of us felt welcomed and loved upon arriving at various cities across America, from San Jose to Salt Lake City to Grand Rapids in Michigan."

It was a 2001 *60 Minutes* episode on the Lost Boys that led John's close friend, the late Bobby Newmyer, the producer of such films as *sex, lies, and videotape, Training Day,* and *The Santa Clause* movies, to set out to produce his own "Lost Boys" feature film. Bobby explained, "I have always been politically active and aware, but never acted on it until now. I think I lost my way. I got married and had kids and was concerned with my business and making ends meet. One day, I woke up and felt this hollowness."

His goals for making such a film were social (to reinvigorate communication between families and friends of the Lost Boys), practical (to share information on employment and educational opportunities for the Lost Boys), and political (to unify the Lost

Boys in order to gain a political voice in Washington and translate needs into public policy). "The message is one of awareness," Bobby explained. "We want to spread awareness through the timeline of what has been going on, to expose this regime." Bobby's wife Debbie is picking up the mantle after her husband's untimely death and is pressing forward to make sure a movie about the Lost Boys gets made.

James Garang summed up for us just what all this support has meant to him and the other Lost Boys and Girls:

> All the public attention we received since arriving to the U.S. is encouraging, hospitable, and humane. This attention is both productive and educational—in the sense that most Americans came to learn from Lost Boys' accounts some basic knowledge on Sudan. Some went as far as pressurizing their congresspersons to push for legislation on Sudan. The American public and the Lost Boys of Sudan, through local activism, have indirectly contributed to the achievement of the peace agreement in southern Sudan.

Slavery's Ugly Resumption

In Chapter 3 we discussed the Sudanese government's support for slave raiding to terrorize civilians and depopulate areas of southern Sudan. Starting in the late 1980s, the government recruited and armed Arab militias called Murahaleen, offering them impunity to attack non-Arab villages, loot cattle, kill civilians, and enslave women and children. If these barbaric tactics sound familiar, it is because, with the exception of large-scale slave raiding, the government of Sudan has replicated them with the Janjaweed militias in Darfur.

The discovery during the 1990s that one of the most odious practices from American history was still going on in Sudan galvanized a groundswell of opposition to Khartoum. When John worked for the Clinton administration, there were people inside government, led by Susan Rice, who worked tirelessly to confront the Sudanese government on this issue. Susan coordinated with key members of Congress* to counter the atrocities being perpetrated by the Sudanese regime and, without the permission of the regime, traveled with John into rebel-controlled areas in southern Sudan to ensure U.S. government attention.

The efforts of government officials were reinforced by the grassroots activity on the issue, particularly the efforts of church groups, who focused on the forced conversion of slaves to Islam. This broad array of religious groups, ranging from evangelical missionary organizations to the Catholic Church to African-American churches, formed a network that engaged in letter-writing campaigns, demonstrations at the Sudanese embassy, and other citizen activism.

In 1998, Maria Sliwa had a prestigious job in Manhattan, but she was feeling empty until she met Richard Wurmbrand, a Christian pastor and founder of the Voice of the Martyrs, which aids persecuted Christians around the world. Wurmbrand asked Sliwa to help the children of Sudan. She resigned from her job and started Freedom Now Communications, maintaining an informational website, sending faxes and e-mails to thousands of people, routinely speaking about the abuses and slavery in the south, and writing articles for a variety of publications. "I believe that people can be groomed to care," she explains. "People should be socially responsible, and some of that is already beginning to happen."

An especially effective event was organized by a coalition of forty evangelical Christian churches in Midland, Texas, the hometown of President Bush. The churches brought Sudanese refugees to tell their congregations about the horrible consequences of the war, especially the slave trade, raised money for humanitarian aid,

---

*Again, bipartisan action was key. Illustratively, while working for the Clinton administration, John traveled with Congressman Tom Tancredo (R-CO), Senator Sam Brownback (R-KS), Congressman Don Payne (D-NJ), key congressional staffers from both sides of the aisle, and evangelical religious leaders, into rebel-controlled areas of southern Sudan, to highlight the resurgence of slavery and other atrocities.

and petitioned the White House to confront Khartoum. The Sudanese embassy in Washington, D.C., was so concerned by this surge of activity in "the town of George Bush" that the chief of mission of the embassy responded personally to the letter-writing campaign.

One particularly controversial tactic employed in the effort to stop slavery in Sudan was the practice of purchasing slaves back from Arab merchants in order to set them free. These efforts were undertaken by public schools, evangelical churches, and community groups in the United States, Canada, and Western Europe, and they raised hundreds of thousands of dollars for the buybacks. Christian Solidarity International was the most prolific organization involved in this effort, claiming to have freed about eight thousand slaves.

In February 1998, Barbara Vogel, a teacher in Aurora, Colorado, read an article to her fifth-grade class about Sudan, the human rights abuses in the south, and the efforts of Christian Solidarity International. Vogel was an associate at the American Anti-Slavery Group, an organization founded in 1994 by Dr. Charles Jacobs that works tirelessly to combat contemporary slavery around the world. Vogel's students were so affected by the tragedy of Sudan that they launched the Slavery That Oppresses People (S.T.O.P.) campaign, aiming to raise enough money to redeem one thousand slaves. One of the children asked, "Haven't we learned anything from the past?" They sold lemonade, T-shirts, and used toys and wrote a letter to the editor of the local paper, who commissioned a story on their campaign. The class's efforts eventually garnered the attention of the *CBS Evening News,* which, in turn, led to donations of over $50,000. The class also began an awareness campaign writing letters to national and international leaders urging an end to the slavery in Sudan. Other schools followed Vogel's class's example. "My goal is to show the power of children, to show that children want to help, and to show adults what children can do," says Vogel.

Rev. Gloria White-Hammond, a doctor who runs medical missions throughout Africa, first went to Sudan in July 2001. In the midst of the conflict, witnessing the physical pain and continued fighting, she felt "woefully inadequate and overwhelmed." Visiting a group of several hundred returning slaves, freed through a redemption program, she spoke with one woman covered in scars who was accompanied by her two children, one of whom was the result of a rape. The woman said, "I have suffered in the north, and I will suffer in the south. But in the south I will suffer among my own people. Thank you for returning me to the place where the soil is the color of my skin." White-Hammond understood that while she might not have enough medicine to heal all the wounds of the people she encountered, she could witness and tell their stories. She continues to do vocal advocacy work for the Save Darfur Coalition, and part of her focus is to encourage fellow African-Americans to "own" an African issue, such as Sudan, and advocate for Africans.

Buying back slaves was emotionally appealing and, when documented, such as in the vivid June 1996 series "Witness to Slavery" by two reporters from the *Baltimore Sun*, it verified the horrific reports of abuse and slavery that had been reported by NGOs and individuals but not necessarily believed by non-Sudanese for years. The story was actually unearthed in 1987 by John's friend and colleague Suliman Baldo, who with Ushari Mahmoud published a tract at that time that outlined the roots of the resurgence of this odious crime.

Over time, questions arose about the authenticity and effect of the buybacks, but the efforts undeniably raised awareness throughout America of the plight of the southern Sudanese. The real issue is that the tactic only addressed a symptom of the underlying conflict. Well-intended groups could free thousands of slaves, but without outside political pressure, the war would continue to create tens of thousands more, especially since the money paid for slaves was often being channeled back into the Khartoum regime and its slave-raiding militias.

Ultimately it was the wide-ranging and deeply committed network of activists, including government officials and human rights activists, members of Congress from across the political spectrum, and a broad range of religious organizations, that assembled the pressure necessary to shine the spotlight of international attention on the practice of slavery in Sudan. The creation of a U.S. Commission on International Religious Freedom, which labeled Khartoum the world's most egregious violator of the right to freedom of religion and belief, was exemplary of this campaign. These efforts helped to bring an end to the resurgence of slavery. While the difficult work of getting the enslaved people of southern Sudan free and back to their homes continues today, the widespread practices of slave raiding that marked the 1990s are over.

The Lesson

So what is the lesson from all these efforts? It's pretty simple. Unrelenting pressure from citizens on their elected officials helped generate the political will for the U.S. government to take stronger action to combat atrocities in Sudan and to end the civil war between the regime and the southern SPLA rebels. If we continue to ramp up citizen efforts through campaigns like ENOUGH, we can make an even bigger difference in Darfur, and in other places where mass atrocities have been perpetrated with impunity, such as Congo, northern Uganda, and Somalia.

DON:

"Because they know if we stand tall, we gonna have something called Black Power, y'all!" I'm posted up on the steps of the Grant Memorial in Washington, D.C., decked out in seventies finery, major afro and muttonchops rounding out my look, speechifying through a bullhorn to the small but committed crowd collected here to listen to Petey Greene, legendary Washington, D.C., personality, break it down to them like only he can. The crowd shows their enthusiasm, punctuating my rant with "That's right"

121

*and "Preach, brother!" I'd like to believe it's my
commanding presence that has them so captivated,
dedicated to the cause, but this being take ten at high noon
on a ninety-eight-degree, 90-percent-humidity day, it's much
more likely that it's this crowd's dedication to their
impending lunch and cool drinks that has them hanging on
my every word. Kasi Lemmons, the director of the film,
calls, "Cut," and that's a wrap for this location. It's my third
and last day in the city, and this being Saturday, my sister
has no second-graders to wrangle. So she's standing on the
sidelines waiting to spend whatever time I'm not being
Petey Green with me. Lucky Don.*

*The last three days here have been a steady flow of
activity, the filming of* Talk to Me *bringing to a close a trip
that found John and me not only on the Hill in the offices of
Senators Brownback, McCain, and Clinton (and one
impromptu, Heisman-esque, stiff-arm from the press
secretary of Kay Bailey Hutchinson), but also in the
company of erstwhile Darfur rebel leader Minni Minnawi
of the Sudan Liberation Movement (SLM).*

As soon as I knew Talk to Me *was headed to D.C., I
called John to pick his brain as to who would be the most
important senators to get in front of and plead our case. We
also wanted to get their recommendations on the best ways
to motivate the Bush administration to more strongly
confront the genocide in Darfur. We wanted to discuss
punitive measures against specific officials of the Sudanese
government, measures without which there would be no
remedy for the people of Darfur. John tested the waters and
came up with a list of the aforementioned senators as well
as Senator Barack Obama, a fellow soldier in this particular
fight, whose prior engagements unfortunately placed him
out of town that day.*

*We were looking to speak with those who had already
shown a proclivity to put Africa on their agendas and who*

most recently had spoken out on behalf of Darfurians. But just as important, we were looking for a representative with political clout who would have the ear of the president and could literally "walk-in" demands as an emissary from his/her constituency. High-reaching goals to be sure, but as my mother would say, "A closed mouth don't get fed." Our plan in place, we coordinated our schedules and confirmed the meetings.

And a funny thing happened on the way to D.C. For several months prior to this trip, one of my fellow producers on Crash, along with a group of producers, civic leaders, and the director Ted Braun, had been attempting to put together the financing for a documentary on activism as it relates to Darfur. A few weeks before I was scheduled to arrive in D.C., the money came through for the project, and it was decided that what John and I were doing might be good material. Several more schedules to coordinate and the crew would meet us there.

However, I got a jump on folks and took off for D.C. ahead of everybody so that I could spend my first night in town with my sister, whom I hadn't seen since I had been on the east coast some six months before. I call her as soon as I land and she comes over to meet me at my hotel. We spend the evening doing what we usually do when we see each other: not much; trying to make each other laugh, eating, talking about her gig, my gig, her nieces and nephews, Mom and Dad. At some point we get onto the subject of my other gig.

"So I guess this isn't just some fad for you, huh?" Cindy asks.

"I don't know what to call it exactly. 'Crusade' is too strong and 'job' is inaccurate, though it feels like one sometimes."

"I guess it's not important that you call it anything as long as you keep at it."

"True dat, do-dat-do-do-dat-dat-dat." A Tribe Called Quest jumping out of my mouth now.

The hotel I'm staying in is not swanky, but that's cool, neither are we. We're having fun in each other's company and finding nothing better to do than hang, Cindy and I order room service and watch bad TV until she has to take off to try and get some sleep before school the next day.

I'm also up at the crack of dawn to meet John, Ted, and the crew so we can go through our final touches before storming the Hill. Mindful of the brief amount of time each senator has afforded us, John and I identify very specific goals on which we want to focus their attention, namely the Three Ps: Protection, Punishment, and Peacemaking. We hope to be able to bring our documentary crew into the meetings but are aware of the fact that even though we've gotten prior approval, feelings often change when the actual rig shows up, the unblinking eye of the camera scrutinizing every gesture, microphones sucking up every word you say. We all understand the priorities here, documenting the event running distant second behind hopefully engaging the senators in an endeavor that might actually save lives. Everyone in agreement, we saddle up and ruck out.

Senator Brownback is our first meeting, and he couldn't be more affable, a quality I have always mistrusted in a politician. But if you look at his record on the subject in question, he has proven as committed an advocate as any on the senate floor, introducing the Senate's Darfur Peace and Accountability Act in July 2005. He's also cool with the cameras coming in. John and I go right into thanking the senator for seeing us and have time enough only to give him the slightest bit of our personal history when he jumps right in with "What is it you're asking of me?" Albeit abrupt and unexpected, it wasn't a rude cutoff. Brownback wanted to get down to business; damn the double-talk two-

step of many politicians when they have no intention of doing anything beyond making empty, constituency-appeasing promises.

John and I rolled out our three Ps plan. Senator Brownback listened intently, agreeing with our assessments and getting his staffers moving on drafting proposals. John and I then ask what we believe to be our most important question: would the senator be willing to walk this plan in to the president or enlist the help of someone who can as quickly as possible? It was a challenging prospect; the world, it seemed, had tilted on its axis that week, once again. We watched the Middle East for signs of the Great Conflagration—this time with the Hezbollah capture of Israeli soldiers along the Lebanese border, followed quickly by a bloody Israeli retaliation that had everyone on pins and needles. This new potential nightmare was pulling all focus. With regards to what we could expect in the way of a swift U.S. response on Darfur, "It's hard to act when the house is on fire," the senator said, surely referring to our country's close relationship with Israel, her fate inextricably linked, at least from a foreign policy standpoint, with ours. However inadvertent, the senator's metaphor was appropriate for the thousands of Darfurians literally, not figuratively, fleeing from fire, pursued by government and militia forces, burned out of their homes and livelihoods. Obstacles notwithstanding, Senator Brownback assured us he would get into the matter, and we assured him we'd follow up. After a brief outer-office confab, we moved on to our next meeting, with Senator Clinton.

Senator Clinton's outer outer office was abuzz with activity when we arrived. We were no more surprised when the senator whisked in and showed us to her office than we were when her press secretary (the root word of secretary, "secret," factoring heavily here) informed us that our camera would not be allowed into the meeting. No problem.

Again the most important aspect of these meetings was to rally the allies, not stress the photo op. And as allies go, Senator Clinton has similarly proven herself on this account, cosponsoring legislation urging deployment of UN peacekeepers, enforcement of the no-fly zone, engagement with NATO, and pursuit of targeted sanctions against Sudanese leaders and broader sanctions against Sudan. She also champions what we believe to be one of the most crucial aspects of our plan: the appointment of a U.S. envoy to Sudan to fill an untimely vacancy that left vital negotiations in a lurch from which they've yet to recover.

We waste no time here either, getting quickly into our plan, though with a wrinkle this time: we harbor no hopes that Senator Clinton will be the one to walk our work over to the White House, political divisions in this instance not solely reserved for parties in the Sudan. 'Nuff said. Like her Republican counterpart before her, the senator gives us her assurance that we can depend on her to move this issue forward, and we all leave the huge possibility that resides in her future unspoken.

We are early for our next meeting, so we mill around the halls of power with the documentary crew plotting what to do next. Turning a corner, I spy what looks to be a buffet table prettified with drinks and snacks at the end of the hall. The starving actor inside me (and every other actor, no matter how successful) is practically being pulled toward it. It is free food, after all. John steps up next to me trying to make out whom this party is for, eventually discovering that it is a gathering for the Republican Senator Kay Bailey Hutchinson. We must look like a splinter crew from a Michael Moore shoot, because it's not long before the senator's aide hustles down the hall in our direction and instructs us to turn off the camera and state our business. We do. He's unimpressed but assures us if we go through the proper channels in the future . . .

Browbeaten and snack-less, we amble our way to
Senator McCain's outer office, which today has the feeling
of a war room. It is very quiet here, and off to the side is a
small table, six men sitting around it dressed in dark-
colored clothes, their speech just a couple of clicks below
audible, only the occasional hard consonant breaking
through.

"It's a cabal," John offers.

"And the room is bugged, so you better shut up," I
counter. I've been told by many a lefty that they've seen "the
List" and I'm on it. I don't need any more attention. I'm
surprised I've been allowed in this far.

One of McCain's aides comes over and brings us into
his office. We ask about the camera crew and are told they
are welcome as well, and before we get settled the senator
breezes in announcing that he's brought along a special
guest.

"You all know Lindsey?" McCain offers. Lindsey
Graham, senator from South Carolina, is trailing close
behind.

"These folks don't give a damn about me, Senator
McCain," his fellow senator asserts. Senator McCain
traveled to Darfur, and he wrote an op-ed with former
Senator Bob Dole urging the U.S. to use its intelligence-
gathering capacities to collect evidence on senior officials in
the Sudan regime to build legal cases against them for war
crimes and crimes against humanity. His letter to the Save
Darfur Rally participants read in part, "We must act because
the situation in Darfur is a strategic threat. We must act
because our international credibility is at stake. But above
all we must act because Darfur is, at root, a moral issue.
The civilized countries of the world—the United States
among them—cannot stand idle in the face of genocide.
Should we do so, history will judge us harshly, as it should.
None of us has the strength to bear that shame again."

In a manner that has become a theme for today's meetings, the senator from Arizona eschews the small talk and asks us what it is we would like him to do. We've got the routine down by now and launch into our prepared Ps. Though Senator Graham appears skeptical, McCain is very attentive and his aide furiously makes notes while we pitch our plan. Senator McCain assures us that he will get into it, especially the matter of the special envoy. He and Senator Graham promise to raise the issue directly with President Bush and National Security Advisor Stephen Hadley. It's all over in less than twenty-five minutes. A small show-and-tell by Senator McCain of his photography (pretty good stuff) acts as a parting offer as we make for the door.

John and I compare notes as we walk toward our cars.

"So?" I want to hear his take. John's been in and out of the Beltway for years. "Was that all just some BS or did we accomplish anything today?"

"You know, Don, in a way that's as much up to us as to them. And by us I mean all of us. The general American public as a whole."

"What do you mean?"

"I mean we were just granted an audience with three very influential senators, and got Senator Graham as a bonus, all potential future leaders of the free world, all people who have publicly vowed to make the crisis in Darfur a part of their agenda. Who's to blame if we don't hold them to it? Believe it or not, there are people in the government who do care about these issues, but their hand is weakened when 'the People' don't propel the issue. We, the citizenry, bear or at least share some of the responsibility for our governments' inaction on Darfur. That's why we were up there and, no, it isn't just some BS."

I wonder if John is right. Would public outcry be persuasive in this instance or are there some issues that are simply insurmountable, no matter the amount of righteous indignation coming from "the People"? I knew one thing for sure; the situation in Darfur was rapidly deteriorating and the "news," in this country anyway, was completely preoccupied with political infighting, conflicts in the Middle East, and American Idol. It was as if once the word genocide had been uttered, all further responsibility, by all parties, was abdicated; the effort of conjuring the word was all the power the powerful could muster. Information about the river of pain in Sudan when it reached our shores was all but a small tributary. Perhaps John's theory would never be tested. How could "the People" voice their outrage about something they'd never even hear about?

"What do you think about it? BS?" John was looking for corroboration, but I couldn't offer any. I shrugged.

"We'll see."

7

The Upstanders

"Lo ta'amod al dam re'echa"
("Thou shall not stand idly by the shedding of the
blood of thy fellow man")

LEVITICUS 19:16

A True Citizens' Movement

It is difficult enough in the face of something like slavery to
fathom how one individual can affect positive change. In the face
of genocide or other mass atrocities, it can seem laughable—Don
Quixote challenging the windmills. But as the positive results
from the anti-apartheid and debt relief movements attest, the vocal few can become the defiant many. And as we have seen with
the successes in other areas of Sudan, the Khartoum government
is indeed responsive to persistent international pressure led by a
United States government pressed by its citizenry. And, on a twist
of chaos theory, the large shift begins with the flap of one butter-
fly's wings.

For some, the call to respond to the crisis in Darfur was
natural—maybe an extension of previous work in Sudan or a fa-
milial connection to the Holocaust. But many others had to learn
about events on the ground, to see interconnectedness between

---

◆

There are three interrelated forces at play in cultivating this fledgling movement:

- *The power of imagination. Despite a lack of pictures or consistent media coverage, citizens across the country have been able to envision the devastation, the pain, and the possibility of a positive solution in Darfur.*
- *The courage of our convictions. If we do nothing about it, the phrase "Never Again" will become a symbol of empty rhetoric that every politician dutifully mouths at relevant events. However, citizens and their elected representatives all over the United States are finally saying enough is enough, standing up and demanding more formidable action by the international community.*
- *The creation of a movement. Across the United States, we have steadily seen the development of a small movement of committed activists—many of them first-timers—organizing and pressing for a bolder U.S. response. They have organized events, held demonstrations, contacted members of Congress, and demanded that the U.S. government do more. We haven't witnessed anything like it since the anti-apartheid movement during the 1980s.*

---

themselves and those suffering in western Sudan and to realize the power of one person. "I confess that I was one that thought of change really only on a large scale (in numbers and size) and I feel like I've come into contact with the power of passion and the power of a few, and I believe that is what is going to change the world," says Robert Kang, co-pastor of The Church in Bethesda and a recent recruit to activism on Darfur.

Despite the obstacles and distance, people are getting involved. On college campuses, in churches and synagogues, and in cities and suburbs, individuals are spreading the word and working to bring an end to the large-scale deaths and devastation. From established organizations shifting their focus to Sudan or coming together to become more effective advocates, to college students mobilizing their peers and influencing their administrations, to individuals merely talking to friends, a true citizens' movement is building to confront the genocide in Sudan. With the launch of the ENOUGH campaign, this movement can be shaped into a permanent constituency fighting genocide and crimes against humanity wherever they occur.

Some of the most influential groups and individuals started early (but it's never too late!) and have been able to use a national or international platform to inform and encourage others.

Save Darfur Coalition

Out of a meeting of forty nonprofits in July 2004, hosted by the American Jewish World Service and the United States Holocaust Memorial Museum, came the most influential organization rallying for action in Darfur. After Gerry Martone of IRC and John addressed the group that day about what could be done to end the crisis, the attendees were pushed to action by the remarks of Holocaust survivor and Nobel Peace Prize winner Elie Wiesel (as discussed in Chapter 5). The Save Darfur Coalition is now an alliance of over 170 faith-based, humanitarian, and human rights organizations, representing 130 million people.

Its website acts as a clearinghouse of information and activism, including e-postcards to Congress and suggestions on how you can help in your local community, as well as ways to help fund educational (i.e., help buy ad space in newspapers or on television stations around the country to increase public awareness) and humanitarian efforts.

Jerry Fowler, staff director for the Committee on Conscience at the U.S. Holocaust Memorial Museum, was a key figure in the establishment of the Save Darfur Coalition. Jerry visited the refugee camps in eastern Chad in May 2004, where he met face-to-face with the survivors of Janjaweed atrocities. Upon his return to the United States, he gave a presentation on the situation to a group that included David Rubenstein, who had learned about Darfur from reading Nicholas Kristof's columns in the *New York*

Times. David was a consultant to nonprofit managers, and he had only recently developed an interest in international affairs. He became involved in aiding the developing world while he was reading Gandhi's autobiography, and "Gandhi said it was time for him to go serve his people; so I thought maybe it was time for me to go serve my people." Living as a middle-class Jewish person in Long Island, David thought it was best to go elsewhere to serve people in need. He took a five-month sabbatical in Guatemala and decided, "The rest of my career will be about helping people overseas and using the power and influence of the U.S. government." Darfur seemed to David like the most important work that needed to be done at the time. He attended the organizing meeting and helped draft the unity statement afterward for the coalition. He soon was asked to coordinate the coalition and helped lay the foundation for its rapid growth.

Ruth Messinger was also key to the establishment of the Save Darfur Coalition. Messinger serves as the executive director of the American Jewish World Service. This organization is modeled on the Peace Corps and works as an international development organization, running grassroots projects on the ground in developing countries. Additionally the organization responds to disasters. In March of 2004, the crisis in Darfur was brought to Ruth's attention. She knew it wasn't the type of disaster to which AJWS usually responded. Nonetheless, AJWS began visiting Darfur and providing humanitarian aid while also creating awareness in the United States. AJWS agreed to be a conduit for funders of the Save Darfur Coalition. Ruth took on this task with enthusiasm because, she notes, "Intervening to help save lives around the world is what I am devoting a part of my life to—whether the HIV/AIDS pandemic or the failure of crops or gross illiteracy or genocide—that's the work I do, and it's the work I've chosen to do, and I'm very moved by understanding the dimensions of these different types of crises. . . . I'm one of those people who always feels it's possible to make a difference rather than retreat to being overwhelmed." Additionally, after seeing *Hotel Rwanda* and remembering hearing about Rwanda in 1994 and not doing anything, Ruth wanted to "rectify that mistake."

In addition to organizing national days of prayer, on April 30, 2006, the Save Darfur Coalition planned the largest rally on Darfur to date in the United States. After months of advertising, organizing, and coordinating the resources of activist groups across the country, and a late but critical show of support from George Clooney, tens of thousands of people filled the National Mall in Washington, D.C., to remind the White House of their commitment to confronting the genocide in Darfur. Celebrities, politicians, human rights advocates, Darfurian refugees, and others demanded immediate action to end the crisis. The event was widely covered by national media and increased public knowledge of the situation. Nearly a million postcards from all around the nation were hauled onstage, all addressed to President Bush, urging him to fulfill an earlier pledge to support a stronger multinational force in the region and Congress to set aside the funds to do so. Shortly after the rally, the millionth and millionth-and-one postcards were signed by Senators Bill Frist and Hillary Clinton in a show of bipartisanship and then delivered to President Bush at the White House.

JOHN:

I had the privilege of speaking that day at the Save Darfur rally. I wanted to go up in a show of solidarity with two of my closest friends and allies in the world on these issues. So we arranged with the rally organizers to allow me to speak together with Gayle Smith and Samantha Power. Former marine captain and Darfur activist Brian Steidle introduced us as collectively having sixty years of experience combating genocide. Together we talked to the assembled about how to affect the political will of our elected officials. All three of us were floored by the size and commitment of the crowd, and saw that our collective long-held dream of a cohesive movement to end mass atrocity crimes had moved a little closer to reality.

On September 17, 2006, to coincide with the meeting of the United Nations General Assembly, Save Darfur coordinated another rally, this time in New York City. Musicians, former government officials, decision makers, celebrities, and faith leaders all joined in the effort. Again I had the privilege of speaking at the rally, and again I was joined by Samantha. Also speaking at the rally were former U.S. secretary of state Madeleine Albright and actress Mira Sorvino. This time roughly 30,000 people attended the meeting in Central Park, just one of many demonstrations taking place worldwide as part of an international "Day for Darfur."

Samantha and I talked beforehand about how alone we felt for years waging these struggles about forgotten or ignored crises. Staring out into the sea of people chanting for an end to Darfur's misery was an extraordinary feeling. Without question, the movement is growing, and along with it the possibility for positive change.

Students Taking Action Now: Darfur (STAND)

Students Taking Action Now: Darfur (STAND) is a movement present on over six hundred college, university, and high school campuses across the United States, with several more chapters in Canada and a growing membership overseas. Although they now represent a constituency of tens of thousands of students, STAND got its start through the commitment of a few determined individuals.

Nate Wright grew up in Blackfoot, Idaho, a very small, very conservative farming town where nearly everyone belongs to the Church of Jesus Christ of Latter-Day Saints (commonly known as the Mormon Church). As one of very few Catholic students, he was especially conscious of discrimination, as he was regularly harassed for wearing a cross to elementary school. While Nate escaped that environment by going to college at Georgetown, he didn't forget about how it felt to be the target of intolerance.

Wright was moved to act on behalf of others when he heard Sudanese bishop Macram Max Gassis speak at Georgetown during the summer of 2004. Bishop Gassis gave an impassioned speech about the plight of the people of Darfur, and at the end he challenged the students to respond. Wright, along with friends Martha Heinemann and Ben Bixby, decided to take up the challenge.

Upon returning to school in the fall of 2004, Bixby became the head of the Georgetown Jewish Students Association and was shortly thereafter contacted by Lisa Rogoff from the Holocaust Museum, who invited the school to participate in a symposium on Darfur at the museum. Bixby, Heinemann, and Wright organized a group of thirty students from Georgetown to attend. It was at that event that STAND was born, when the participating students realized the need to raise awareness among the college student community and tap their potential for mobilizing, as had been done by the anti-apartheid movement during the 1980s. Together, Wright, Bixby, Heinemann, and their friends worked to build an inclusive network of interested students, reaching out to a diverse coalition of student groups.

Wright came up with the idea of "STANDfast" as a symbolic gesture. They persuaded students to give up alcohol or another luxury good for the Thanksgiving weekend, and donate the money they would have spent to humanitarian efforts in Darfur. This was an effort to draw public attention to the conflict. The first STANDfast was held in November 2004. As Nate and his friends learned more about Darfur, they realized that a one-off event was not enough. As more people became involved, STAND grew into an organization that could rapidly expand to other universities. Wright knew that "We needed to be able to utilize the talents of individual schools while at the same time have a unifying voice to our efforts." STAND aimed to increase awareness, raise funds, and advocate for a political solution to the conflict.

Awareness-raising events would be replicated by STAND's growing number of chapters throughout North America. While the founders never expected STAND to grow the way it did, they were constantly contacted by students at other schools who wanted to use their organization as a model for efforts on their own campuses. Student groups have held scores of events on campuses to raise awareness and take political action. For example, in April of 2005, the George Washington University chapter of STAND organized a twenty-four-hour fast outside the State Department in an effort to shame officials there. The group also sponsored a National Lobbying Day to bring in students from other parts of the country to express their concerns over U.S. inaction in the face of genocide. At the Richard Stockton College of New Jersey, STAND members participated in a "die-in" in solidarity with the victims in Darfur that garnered so much attention that some students were asked to testify in front of the New Jersey legislature on behalf of a bill that would divest the state pension fund from the stocks of all companies doing business with Sudan. "Perhaps we were somewhat naive because we hoped not to be around as long as an organization," says Bixby, one of the cofounders. "After about a year, it became obvious that long-term planning was necessary."

Over the course of two years, through a series of national conferences and events held around the country, STAND groups gradually coordinated to form a national managing committee. This committee now helps to connect students around the world, design campaigns to unify student efforts and strengthen student lobbying power, and provide resources and support for campus organizing.

Genocide Intervention Network (GI-Net)

An Ecuadorian student who recently graduated from Swarthmore College and the grandson of four Holocaust survivors, Mark Hanis is no stranger to the concept of genocide. Embracing the slogan, "Never Again," Hanis's battle against genocide began early in his college career. After a seven-month internship in 2003 at the Special Court for Sierra Leone, he became interested in ways to respond to and prevent genocide. Upon his return to school in 2004, the lack of campus attention to the tenth anniversary of the genocide in Rwanda disturbed Hanis, so with a passionate group of students at school, he created a Genocide Awareness Month in April. The month included a screening of the documentary *Ghosts of Rwanda* and a special presentation by Joseph Sebarenzi, the former speaker of the Rwandan House of Parliament. As a result of this awareness month, students geared up to learn more about Rwanda and the crisis that was unfolding in Sudan. They created a Do It Yourself (DIY) kit to help students raise awareness and action for Darfur on campus. The students put the kit online, and the word began to spread to campuses across the country.

While news of the DIY kit and campus activism was spreading, Hanis and friend Andrew Sniderman devised a creative and unprecedented proposal: fund-raising for the African Union peacekeepers on the ground in Darfur, given that these forces were the only ones currently deployed to protect the people there. They also wanted to help create an anti-genocide constituency. Hanis and Sniderman knew that previously when Americans did get political around issues relating to genocide, the community of activists dissolved after the crisis. It is necessary to have a permanent anti-genocide constituency because "Darfur won't be the last genocide," Hanis explains. "Looking back at Rwanda, don't we wish someone had supported General Dallaire when he asked the United Nations for more civilian protection? Yes, of course."

Hanis and Sniderman concluded that if organizations could fund-raise for food, there was no reason they couldn't fund-raise for civilian protection. Convinced the idea was plausible, they asked for advice from Holocaust and Genocide Studies professors at various universities, and the positive feedback spurred them to begin pulling all-nighters, e-mailing former presidents, secretaries of state, and other high-level officials from past administrations to ask for support in fund-raising for the AU peacekeeping force.

The duo got Gayle Smith (now a senior fellow at the Center for American Progress) on board. Soon after, Howard Wolpe, the director of the Africa Program at the Woodrow Wilson Center; Anthony Lake, President Clinton's first national security advisor; James Smith, chief executive of the Aegis Trust; and John agreed to support the proposal. As support was building, Gayle felt confident in the efforts, and she made a trip to Ethiopia to negotiate a contract with the AU. The AU was "taken aback" but impressed with the students' unique approach. Swarthmore Sudan morphed into an international effort and took on a new name: the Genocide Intervention Fund (GIF).

The team pressed further and developed a new fund-raising initiative called "100 Days of Action," which began on April 6, 2005, the eleventh anniversary of the genocide in Rwanda. During those hundred days, GIF asked students, religious groups, and other organizations to hold events to both raise awareness and fund-raise to support the African Union, including a press event on Capitol Hill and a day of lobbying Congress. Hanis believes that the 100,000 letters that they solicited helped attract sixteen more sponsors on the Darfur legislation bills that were circulating.

Spurred by GIF, Mamaroneck High School in New York raised $5,000 with a benefit concert, "Jam for Sudan." A screening of *Hotel Rwanda* at Cornell University raised close to $3,000. Other schools sold bracelets and hosted a "Salsa for Sudan" fund-raiser. Overall, the "100 Days of Action" project raised a quarter of a million dollars, and the organization worked with the U.S. Treasury Department to get the requisite approvals to send the money to the African Union. Enthusiasm was building; GIF received a letter from one man who wrote, "Thank you for reviving my faith in humanity."

Stephanie Nyombayire, a Swarthmore student from Rwanda, had a very personal reason to become involved with GIF. Stephanie lost over one hundred family members and friends during the genocide in Rwanda in 1994, and she was determined to do everything in her power to avert a similar failure to act in Darfur. She became GIF's outreach director, and early in 2005 she took a trip to the Chad/Darfur border with Nate Wright of STAND and Andrew Karlsruher, a film student from Boston University. The three of them had received a grant from mtvU, a division of MTV, to be student correspondents and film a documentary about the plight of the refugees.

Stephanie remembered one of the first refugees she met, a fifteen-year-old girl who had lived in the camp for close to a year. The Janjaweed had killed the girl's parents during an attack and then raped her. She was thirteen and a half. "She had to walk for fifty days across the desert, where she survived by begging and eating dry leaves until she had reached the Chadian border," Stephanie recalled.

CNN and ABC interviewed Stephanie about her trip, and the connection between her personal experience with Rwanda and her firsthand look at genocide in Darfur resonated deeply with audiences. She focused attention on the state of impunity that allowed the Janjaweed to continue their killing spree unabated in Darfur. A similar impunity eleven years earlier had enabled the Interahamwe militias to kill 800,000 of her countrypersons in one hundred days.

During the summer of 2005, GIF pushed further, launching jointly with the Center for American Progress the "Be a Witness Campaign," an online campaign designed to pressure major media outlets to report on a current-day genocide.

Hanis and five other GIF members graduated, merged with STAND, and transitioned their student organization to a nongovernmental organization that focuses on constituency building, changing the name to the Genocide Intervention Network (GI-Net). Hanis says: "The change from Fund to Network was huge. For Darfur and future genocides, generating the political will to act is what's really important. You can raise money, but money is not the entire issue."

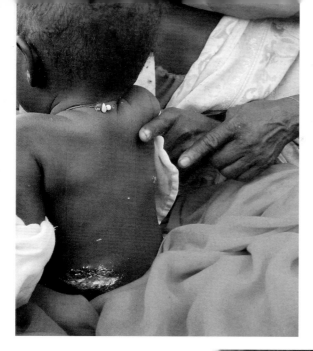

Helicopter gun ships and Janjaweed militia fighters attacked Mihad Hamid's village, Allieta, in October 2004. Mihad's mother picked her up and fled, but a bullet hit Mihad and punctured her lungs. Mihad's story is not uncommon. *(Brian Steidle)*

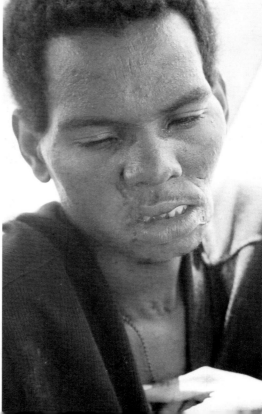

Hussein Bashir Abakr, 19, was shot in the neck and the mouth by the Janjaweed. His brother escaped but returned to bury the dead and found Hussein alive. He still cannot eat solid foods. *(Nick Kristof)*

Nijah Ahmed, 4, is carrying her little brother, Nibraz, who is 13 months old and mal-nourished. They fled from Darfur to the northern part of the Chad/Sudan border after their parents, uncle, and older brother were either killed or went missing when the Janjaweed attacked their village. Because so many men were killed and so many young women were carried off to be raped and killed, there are dozens of orphans in the area. *(Nick Kristof)*

This Janjaweed militiaman was shot and paralyzed when he attacked a village and the residents fought back. *(Nick Kristof)*

This Janjaweed militiaman was attacked and tied up by the people of the village he had raided in March 2006. He later told *New York Times* journalist Nick Kristof that he had been paid to participate in the attack. *(Nick Kristof)*

At a World Food Program (WFP) warehouse in Geneina, West Darfur, workers carry bags of food donated by the U.S. government. The United States has led the world in providing emergency assistance to displaced people and refugees, but humanitarian band-aids are inadequate to address the gaping human rights wounds in Darfur. *(Doug Mercado)*

This girl lives with other displaced people in Riyad Camp, West Darfur. Amidst all the violence and suffering, she remains hopeful that someday she and her family will return home. *(Doug Mercado)*

Most of the displaced people in Sisi Camp, West Darfur, were farmers or herders before the Janjaweed and Sudanese government forces drove them from their land. Now they rely on international donors and humanitarian organizations to stay alive. *(Doug Mercado)*

Displaced women return to their camp from collecting firewood. Hundreds of thousands of women in the displaced camps throughout Darfur face a Sophie's Choice: stay in the relative safety of the camps and starve with their families, or leave to forage for firewood for cooking and risk the probability of rape by Janjaweed militia. *(Doug Mercado)*

The situation in the camps for internally displaced people is desperate. These people in Riyad Camp, West Darfur, had not received plastic sheeting with which to construct temporary shelters, so they used whatever materials they could find. *(Doug Mercado)*

Fighters from the rebel Sudanese Liberation Army are battling the government of Sudan in Darfur. The movement came together in August 2001 and launched its rebellion in early 2003. (*Mark Brecke*)

The people who lived in this camp for displaced people had already been driven from their homes by government troops and Janjaweed, but the government of Sudan decided to attack them again. In the middle of the night, the government of Sudan bulldozed the camp to send a message to the residents. The message: non-Arabs are not welcome here. (*Brian Steidle*)

Don and Paul Rusesabagina met with diplomats in the Chadian capital, N'Djamena, before visiting Darfur refugee camps in eastern Chad. The making of the film *Hotel Rwanda*, based on Paul's heroic true story, was the beginning of Don's journey out of apathy. (*Rick Wilkinson*)

When Don and John traveled to eastern Chad in 2004 to film an episode of ABC's *Nightline*, they met the victims of the conflict. Most of the refugees in the camps are women and children. *(Rick Wilkinson)*

Don plays with the children in the refugee camps in eastern Chad. *(Rick Wilkinson)*

Activists in Washington, D.C., make a banner on September 9, 2006, the Global Day for Darfur. *(Lindsay Joiner)*

John speaks at a rally to support stronger U.S. action to resolve the crisis in Northern Uganda. John and his friend Betty Bigombe (left of John) have been directly involved in a peace process to end nearly 20 years of brutal civil war in Uganda. *(Keri Shay)*

After the Janjaweed attacked and chased the residents of Kokoba into the scorching desert, they burned the village to the ground. Hundreds of villages have been destroyed in three years of genocide. *(Brian Steidle)*

Academy Award-winning actor George Clooney, center, flanked by Sen. Barack Obama, D-Ill., right, and Sen. Sam Brownback, R-Kan., takes part in a news conference at the National Press Club in Washington on April 27, 2006, to raise awareness for Darfur. *(AP Photo/Mannie Garcia)*

On April 30, 2006, John, along with his friends and colleagues Samantha Power (center) and Gayle Smith (left) address the 50,000 people gathered on the National Mall in Washington, D.C., to demand greater U.S. action to end the genocide in Darfur. (*Save Darfur Coalition*)

John and Samantha Power speaking at the Voices to Stop Genocide Rally on September 17, 2006, in New York City's Central Park. Thirty thousand people attended the rally to press for a more robust peacekeeping force to protect civilians in Darfur. (*savedarfur.org*)

John gives more than 100 speeches a year to student groups around the United States, motivating them to get involved in the fight against genocide and mass atrocities. Don and Ryan Gosling, an Oscar-nominated actor (*The Notebook, Half Nelson*), join John at UCLA to speak and show their support. *(Bridget Smith)*

Don and John speaking about the Darfur genocide at UCLA. *(Bridget Smith)*

John travels frequently to eastern Chad and into Darfur to speak with the victims of the genocide. When you listen to the people most affected by these situations, you cannot help but want to take action. *(Sally Chin)*

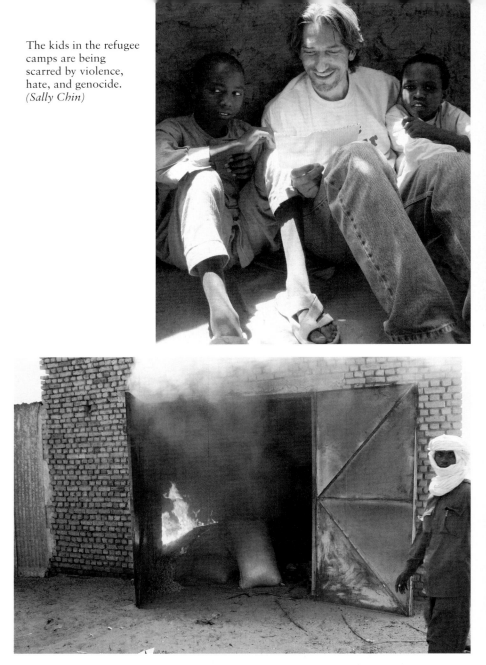

The kids in the refugee camps are being scarred by violence, hate, and genocide. *(Sally Chin)*

A government soldier burns the food surplus in a village called Marla. The residents of the village had fled, and burning the food is an effective way to prevent them from coming back. All across Darfur, government troops and Janjaweed destroyed food supplies and poisoned wells. *(Brian Steidle)*

Someone stole 15 animals from a group of Janjaweed, and they burned 15 non-Arab villages in retaliation. This is one of those villages. *(Brian Steidle)*

A Sudanese army helicopter looms over a village during an attack. The government has used air power to terrorize the people of Darfur. *(Brian Steidle)*

This is a genocide victim outside of a village called Adwa. Near the body, African Union military observers found a field 50 yards by 50 yards filled with human bones. Many of the mass graves in Darfur may never be found. *(Brian Steidle)*

Nick Kristof met this family of children traveling across the open desert. They fled their village after their father and brother were killed, and then the mother fell ill and could no longer walk. Sixteen-year-old Haiga Ibrahim is now head of the household. *(Nick Kristof)*

At a refugee camp in eastern Chad a child's finger dipped in ink verifies the receipt of a family's food ration, limited to one per day. *(Mark Brecke)*

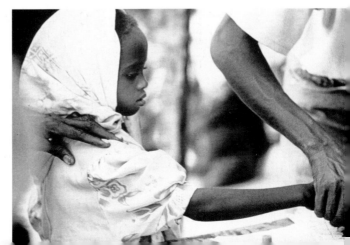

An exhausted Sudanese mother and her seven children arrive at a refugee camp in Eastern Chad. *(Mark Brecke)*

A tense SLA rebel stands guard following a Sudanese army ambush. *(Mark Brecke)*

This village in North Darfur is called Ankaa. A hundred families once lived here. In Darfur thousands of villages have been burned, crops destroyed, wells poisoned, and livestock killed. *(Mark Brecke)*

People walk for hours through the desert to take water from this well in North Darfur, which has not yet been poisoned or destroyed by the government or the Janjaweed. *(Mark Brecke)*

Nicholas Kristof

Many people have credited Nicholas Kristof, columnist for the *New York Times,* with introducing them to and putting several human faces on the Darfur genocide. Kristof himself was told of a growing number of refugees from Darfur in Chad by field workers with Doctors Without Borders and the International Rescue Committee. He agreed to do one story on the border area in March 2004. When he got there, though, he was "blown away." "I couldn't get those people out of my mind," he says. "The world simply wasn't paying attention to the atrocities in Darfur. . . . I had to go back and try, again and again, to drag it on to the agenda." Kristof has written dozens of columns (his op-eds on Darfur are consistently among the most forwarded articles on nytimes.com), traveled several times to the region, and with some success brought Darfur to national attention. He uses his columns to "try to force people to face up to this slaughter."

"I believe that once Americans pay attention, they'll get upset and the political process will work and politicians will respond," he says of his Pulitzer Prize–winning work. "This is not just a journalistic or literary exercise—I write the columns because I want to make a difference."

Professor Eric Reeves

For Eric Reeves, raising awareness has taken on a new meaning. A professor of English Language and Literature at Smith College, Reeves is the go-to man on up-to-date information from the field and for effective lobbying for increased efforts for the region. When the former executive director of the U.S. branch of Doctors Without Borders, Joelle Tanguy, told Reeves she thought Sudan needed a champion, she probably didn't expect it to be an English prof from Northampton, Massachusetts. He started before Darfur broke out, when it was southern Sudan that was the hot spot, with slavery, the Lost Boys, and a deadly civil war as backdrops.

Reeves began his work the way many other activists do: writing letters and op-eds. Then he began a weekly analysis of the country and a now popular website, www.sudanreeves.org, which acts as a resource center on the crises in Sudan. His e-mail list includes journalists, NGOs, policy groups, politicians, foreign diplomats, and concerned citizens. He also started a successful divestment campaign against Talisman Energy, and has been a catalyst for the current efforts across the country to get universities, cities, and states to divest all their stock holdings from companies doing business in or with Sudan. He has done all this while battling cancer. Reeves said, "Effective advocates must have a strong grasp of the issue, and people must be determined. . . . The more work I've done, the more apparent it has become to me that there is a lack of commitment on the part of the international community to stop genocide in Africa. I do not leave work unfinished and therefore will continue to do this work."

JOHN:

Calling my friend Eric Reeves a warrior is surely an understatement. Fighting cancer and frequently working from his hospital bed, he has waged an often lonely but always Herculean struggle to ensure that the American public is aware of what is happening to the people of Sudan—whether in Darfur, the south, or the Nuba Mountains. One night when I was working in the White House, there was a marathon Africa meeting at the State Department—we Africanists so rarely get a chance to speak in high-level policy meetings, so when we do, we often don't know when to shut up. It was about 9 P.M. on a Friday night, and I was down in the office of the then State Department Sudan desk officer, and rising star, Matt Harrington, just shooting the after-meeting breeze. The phone rang, and Matt just looked at it, looked up at me, and said, "Mother of God,

*it's gotta be Eric Reeves." There was genuine fear in his voice,
but fear tinged with respect and admiration. You can run
from Eric, but you surely can't hide.*

Paul Rusesabagina

As the "real-life hero" of the movie *Hotel Rwanda,* Paul Rusesabagina has unmatched credibility when it comes to responding
to genocide. Paul's experience with us in the Darfurian refugee
camps in eastern Chad reinforced his resolve to be active on Darfur. When Paul and our delegation arrived in the first refugee
camp in Chad, at least two thousand children were waiting to
greet us. Many of the children held drawings of Sudanese government helicopters destroying villages and killing people. But the
poster that touched Paul the most was one that read, simply,
"Welcome to our guests. But we need education." He immediately
thought of his own country, Rwanda, and the millions of displaced people growing up there without education, opportunity,
or hope for the future. Seeing this situation again in the dry expanse of eastern Chad and Darfur, and knowing that, as with
Rwanda, the world was failing to respond, reinforced Paul's determination to speak out about Darfur. And since early 2005, Paul
has given over two hundred speeches around the world to audiences of at least one or two thousand people. After all, this is a
man who stood up to those committing genocide in Rwanda and
helped protect over a thousand people from death.

Brian Steidle

Brian Steidle was a senior operations officer working in the Nuba
Mountains for a group called the Joint Military Commission. Initially, motivated by the money offered to work in Darfur, Steidle
got stationed as a U.S. representative to the African Union ob-
server mission. He immediately became a witness to the horrible
violence plaguing the region. After six months, monitoring the almost nonexistent cease-fire, Steidle realized "that nothing was

changing on the ground. And actually from when I got there in October to January things had even gotten worse. There'd been larger attacks and I did not see much media attention. I didn't see a lot of people who even cared. I would talk to people via e-mail and they would say we haven't heard anything about Darfur. Where is it? What's going on?"

He knew that he could have a larger impact by bringing the photographs that he had taken back to the United States and spreading the word as widely as possible about what was taking place in Darfur. "I can hopefully try to bring around at least awareness, if not some type of influence on the government and decision makers to actually do something to stop the genocide."

Steidle has made his photographs available through Nicholas Kristof's column, the Holocaust Memorial Museum, and other venues. He is currently working with the nonprofit organization Global Grassroots to raise awareness about Darfur by traveling and sharing his story. Steidle strongly believes in the power of the public voice. "The people move this government. . . . If we turn our eyes away from hundreds of thousands of people that are being killed . . . then we are lesser people for it."

mtvU

Stephen Friedman is the general manager of mtvU, MTV Networks' channel dedicated to college students. A powerful segment on Jim Lehrer's *NewsHour* ignited Friedman's interest in Darfur about three years ago. The segment covered a Holocaust survivor's college lecture tour, and how he had lost his entire family in concentration camps. The documentary highlighted the meeting of the lecturer and a young woman (Jacqueline Murekatete) he noticed crying at one of his events. The lecturer went to speak with the young woman, who told him, "Yes, the same thing happened to my family a few years ago in Rwanda." Moved by the documentary, Friedman recognized that genocide is still occurring. "Everyone said, 'Never Again,' but we had one eleven years ago. In Darfur we now have an example of a genocide in slow motion." Friedman wanted to talk with Jacqueline and tell her story. "The power of using someone's story gets under your skin. You dream about it, or have nightmares about it. Use the powerful, individual stories and hope that they resonate. The model of talking about numbers is too overwhelming, but you hear about one college student who is going campus to campus, and you realize that is something anybody can do." And once her story aired, it caught on and grew a life of its own.

At one point early on in mtvU's Sudan campaign, Friedman met Francis Bok, a Sudanese refugee who was enslaved in Sudan for ten years. Bok escaped, and his dream was to go to college. Featuring Bok in mtvU's PSAs helped make that dream a reality. Nate Wright, the cofounder of STAND, then approached Friedman about his STANDfast idea. Friedman decided to make the campaign national. "I wanted to shout about it on air, online." Eventually, over 170 schools committed to being a part of the campaign.

mtvU continued its involvement by giving major grants to student groups and doing commercial spots with Don. "College students are very pragmatic," notes Friedman. "They have also historically been the leaders of campaigns of change. Think about apartheid. They want to make change, and they want to do that through concrete action." Their efforts continued when mtvU sent three students to Darfur to create a documentary in March 2005. Friedman says that one of his greatest accomplishments on this campaign was "sending those students to Darfur. For a kid who may not know anything about it, it is a great, eye-opening experience. We did have Nate and Stephanie, but most important was Andrew Karlsruher, a student from Boston University. He was not an activist. Before he went, he said, 'All I knew about Africa was *The Lion King*.' But there was a willingness to explore in him, and you need to give that a chance."

In an ironic twist of innovation, Friedman learned that neo-Nazis are using video games to recruit new members, and he decided mtvU should do a video game against genocide. The game is called "Darfur Is Dying," developed by Susana Ruiz, Ashley York,

Mike Stein, Noah Keating, and Kellee Santiago of the University of Southern California. Anyone can play it for free on mtvU's website. mtvU's Alexis Hyder told us that the game has been played more than 2 million times, and tens of thousands have gone on to write letters to the White House, petition their representatives in Congress, or simply raise awareness by forwarding the game to a friend.

Friedman is inspired by a quote from Theodore Parker that Martin Luther King made famous: "The arc of the moral universe is long, but it bends towards justice." He says, "That's something that everyone at mtvU believes in our hearts. In the end, if you have compassion, knowing that you can make change, making change in small increments fires you up. It's the little things that get you to that point."

For all kinds of activist tips, go to the ENOUGH campaign website at www.enoughproject.org.

Darfur's Other Champions

DON:

Several years ago my old friend J. B. Schramm asked me to appear as a speaker at a Youth Conference convened by former President Bill Clinton at Georgetown University in Washington, D.C. J.B. is the mastermind behind an organization called College Summit, whose mission it is to help low-income high school juniors prepare for their college admissions via a four-day intensive writing program. College Summit's motto: working toward ensuring that every student who can make it into college makes it to college. Jeffrey Swartz, the president and CEO of the Timberland Company, is also scheduled to speak today and, like me, has found himself holed up in this small greenroom while we wait our turns, stressing over our speeches, confident that we will both undoubtedly be upstaged by President Clinton, also scheduled to appear.

"There's no way I'm going after him," Jeff tells me.

"Oh, don't worry. I'm sure he'll be batting cleanup."

In addition to his role at Timberland, Jeffrey also sits on the board of City Year, an organization dedicated to enriching the lives of young people by introducing them to civic strategies, specifically citizen service, civic leadership, and social entrepreneurship. Little did I know that this self-effacing "shoe guy" as he called himself would factor in what would become a mission of mine.

Jeffrey and I kept in touch over the next year or so, e-mailing back and forth whenever he would see me in something he loved, hated, or felt indifferent to. I always looked forward to reading his words whatever his opinion; he had a poetic turn of phrase and a unique insight, being both a social activist and CEO of a major multinational corporation. After viewing Hotel Rwanda, *Jeffrey wrote me a very long e-mail expressing how much it meant not only to him but also to his son, who convinced his junior high school to show the film and form discussion groups after the screening. I told Jeffrey about my learning of the Holocaust as a young man and wondered if our film would impact the students in the same way that the film* Night and Fog *had impacted me in my junior high school auditorium. Would we possibly one day see fruits from the influence of this modern depiction of genocide, many new activists joining the ranks in the not so distant future? Jeffrey assured me that he didn't need to be drafted; he wanted to get the call first thing when and if the battle cry went out for whatever dragon I needed aid in slaying. I e-mailed him my thanks and we both got back to our busy lives.*

Spring 2005, the movie Crash *is in theaters and the cast is making the rounds on all the television talk shows. Chris Bridges, Larenz Tate, and I do a turn on the BET program* 106 & Park. *In consideration of the company I'm keeping and the style of the show, I throw together a funky ensemble finished off at street level by my blue suede, seven-*

hole, Timberland boots. Crash, *it turns out, is a hit, and apparently so is the airing of this episode because not two days later, I receive an e-mail from Jeffrey, with a photo attached of me sitting on the couch talking with the cohosts of the show, AJ and Free, my legs crossed, and prominently featuring my footwear. Jeffrey wrote: "Great interview, footwear irrelevant. But I thought I would have gotten your design for a Darfur boot by now."*

I was shocked. Never had we spoken about the idea of doing something like that, but I was way into it. I wrote back immediately: "Watch my smoke" and grabbed a pencil and pad to sketch out some ideas. What an amazing opportunity this was. In my many discussions with John about outreach, ways to widen the circle of influence where Darfur was concerned, we had often broached the idea of "branding" activism, tying in the spirit of social justice with an easily recognizable and perhaps even popular outward symbol of such. At first blush, it may sound counterintuitive to combine the crisis of genocide in Darfur with the concept of being cool, but imagine the possibilities if such a marriage did exist. Remember the "Vote or Die!" campaign? Activism and fashion needn't be mutually exclusive, and in fact, if sporting a phat boot with a strong message can attract more young people and bring them into the fray, young people whose energy and drive this movement needs, young people who unfortunately may inherit this and other similar tragedies in years to come, why not take this opportunity to create a righteous blend? Besides, I've always rocked Timberlands and relished any excuse to stuff another pair into my shoe-heavy closet.

I played around with several boot ideas before shooting them off to Jeffrey, who put me in touch with his design team, which had already begun working on concepts. We went back and forth for the next couple of weeks tweaking our ideas for images and color. I wanted the boot to have a tread cut into its sole that left behind the message "Stomp Out Genocide" if the wearer were to walk on dry ground after traipsing through water, mud, or snow. Team Timberland was able to accommodate that, and every other design modification I requested. Shortly thereafter, they produced about one hundred pairs of boots that we subsequently delivered to humanitarian activists, policy makers, journalists, and entertainment professionals who had raised awareness of and championed change in Darfur. In addition to the boot, Jeffrey directed the company to produce T-shirts with the words "What Footprint Will You Leave?" emblazoned across the chest and "Save Darfur" boot tags. Both were available for purchase to the general public, with proceeds going to AmeriCares, a longstanding partner of Timberland, providing life-saving aid in the Sudan. I have since worn the boots and shirt on many occasions, from television appearances to red carpet arrivals to just general day-to-day errands. Almost every outing, without fail, I am asked about the design, often by young people, giving me a natural segue into talk about Darfur, affording me the opportunity to make a potential convert. I have Jeffrey Swartz to thank for this.

Hollywood and Hip-Hop Meet Darfur

A number of celebrities have used their platform to further the cause of Darfur and other crises marked by crimes against humanity:

- Angelina Jolie has traveled to refugee camps in Chad for the UN High Commissioner for Refugees. She and John went to Congo to document the human rights abuses being committed in the context of that conflict, particularly violence against women (see their photo exhibit online at www.ushmm.org/museum/exhibit/online/congojournal).

- George Clooney made a surprise visit with his father to Sudan and Chad in advance of the April 2006 Washington, D.C., rally in order to maximize his awareness-raising impact. He appeared on *Oprah* and did a press conference with Senators Barack Obama and Sam Brownback. Later Clooney addressed the UN Security Council with Elie Wiesel. Both appealed to the UN to do much more to protect the defenseless in Darfur and challenged the world body to not stand idly by while genocide was unfolding.
- Mia Farrow has also made two trips to Darfur with her son Ronan on behalf of UNICEF, and both have written moving op-eds in a variety of publications. Mia and John have teamed up to speak at venues throughout the East Coast. She also visited eastern Chad with David Rubinsteen in November 2006 and raised the alarm bell about Darfur's spillover effects in neighboring countries.
- Mira Sorvino went to Capitol Hill to raise awareness of the plight of women subjected to sexual violence in Darfur, and she worked with Amnesty International to organize a concert in the summer of 2006 to raise awareness and funds for the region.
- Ryan Gosling went to eastern Chad and raised funds for the camps, and he has further plans to make a movie about Uganda.
- Russell Simmons participated in the April 2006 Save Darfur Coalition rally in Washington, D.C., and has encouraged hip-hop artists to join the cause.
- Bradley Whitford is best known for portraying White House aide Josh Lyman on the television drama *The West Wing,* but when he was given the chance to get behind the camera and write an episode of the series, he used the opportunity to raise the issue of Darfur. Whitford learned about Darfur by reading about the efforts of Eric Reeves and attending a church where the genocide was discussed.

He decided to write an episode in which an activist visits the White House and urges the staff to do something about the region.

- Bradley's *West Wing* co-star Melissa Fitzgerald traveled to Uganda and has become an advocate for peace in northern Uganda. She spoke at a convocation sponsored by UGANDA-CAN and the Invisible Children project, which saw 700 students unleashed on Capitol Hill for two days of lobbying in October 2006.

- David Zabel is the executive producer and head writer of the hospital drama *ER*. He and his writers learned about Darfur by reading newspaper articles, looking for story ideas on issues related to health care in Africa. Because the show already had a character working for an aid organization on the continent, they decided to send this character to work in a camp in Darfur. The episode looked at the experience of displaced persons, showing their daily crisis of trying to stay alive and healthy. It showed this struggle and explored how aid groups combat tuberculosis, malnutrition, dehydration, and malaria. They were able to focus the attention of the show's 13–14 million viewers on the issue, and the episode coincided with the Save Darfur demonstration in Washington.

But you don't have to be a celebrity, have a newspaper column, work in television, or start a mass-based organization to have an impact. Every individual voice counts, as we shall see in the next chapter.

DON:

I got the call from my managers.
    "Don, I know we get a ton of these requests, but I think this is one you should really consider. The students from STAND, the ones you and John spoke with earlier this

year, are going to be participating in a rally this week at the UCLA campus with the Darfur Action Committee to try and get the University of California regents to consider divesting their interests from Sudan. They only need you to show up at the beginning. They have some media coming and want to maximize—"

"I got it. What time and where do I park?"

I was interested in helping these kids. John had talked them up a lot—how committed they were and how they had seeded a real movement that was already starting to make some real noise in colleges around the country. John and I had always remarked about how it consistently had been the students in most social movements, not only in this country but also around the globe, that ultimately made a difference. Even though the best outcome we could hope for today would be the regents voting to simply "consider" the question of divestment, with the much larger decision to do it or not occurring later, I was honored that I had been asked to lend my voice. What was bumming me out about the whole thing was my leg. I had undergone knee surgery earlier that year, and though my rehab was coming along, I couldn't always swing spending extended periods of time on my feet. But given that they'd only need me for the beginning of the event, for a rousing kickoff speech and some face time for the cameras, I figured I could pull it off, no problem.

Traffic in LA is a buzz-kill, and sitting in this smog soup on rally day is grinding away at my enthusiasm. I am supposed to show up at 11 A.M., but from where I am now, crawling along on Wilshire Boulevard, it doesn't seem possible. I call my manager and ask that she let the folks know that I am doing the best I can to get there but have fallen victim to the vicissitudes of an LA commute, everybody scrambling, getting nowhere fast. When I finally arrive, I am more than a half an hour late and my head is throbbing in sympathy with my knee. Damned activism. I am met at the garage by a bright-eyed, young DAC rep, and her enthusiasm momentarily quiets my aches and pains— momentarily, that is, until she explains that we need to walk a short way to get to the hall where the press conference will be held.

"Short way?" I ask.

"Yes sir-ee!"

Boy, she's chipper.

I quickly do an age and projected health scan of my guide; eighteen to twenty years old, svelte, able-bodied . . . There's no way she and I have the same definition of a "short way." But I didn't come out here to fold, so off we go.

When we arrive at our destination—a bum knee–challenging ten blocks away, uphill of course—I am shocked at how few people have assembled.

"Where is everybody? I thought there was going to be a rally."

"There is. The press conference is first. I did expect there'd be more people here too, though."

The licks may be a little different, but the main song is the same; where Darfur is concerned, it is difficult to draw a crowd. There are only about fifteen people in the seats in this small hall. I am waved up to the dais and take my seat next to Adam Sterling, student activist and ringleader for this event. He thanks me, I deflect it, make a small speech, the ABC cameras roll, and before you know it the press portion of the program draws to a close. I feel altogether unsatisfied. I know that there is probably some value to me showing my face here today, and the possibility of news coverage is nothing to sneeze at, especially for a subject as underreported as this. But still . . .

I have stepped outside to do a one-on-one follow-up interview with the local anchor and start my good-byes, when one of the DAC students asks if I wouldn't mind coming over with her to Meyerhoff Park, a small area on the campus where their group has set up to marshal participants for the rally. If my knee could talk, it would be cursing at me for even considering her request, but my spirit wins the fight.

"I'll follow you."

"Great. It's only a little ways from here."

Four blocks later (don't kill her, Don) we round the bend, coming upon a table full of fliers and a lawn full of grass, and little else. Again, there are only a handful of people here listening to the impassioned speaker booming over the PA, "Divest now! Divest now!" The curious passersby eating their lunches far outnumber those collected out of real interest for the cause, but it does nothing to diminish the enthusiasm of these speakers, almost hoarse now from shouting over the microphone. When I come into view, they all turn to me almost simultaneously, and Jenny Wood, the Undergraduate Students Association Council president, asks if I wouldn't mind saying a few words. I nod in agreement and she turns back to the mike.

"And now please join me in welcoming a tireless ally in the fight for Darfur and actor in such films as Hotel Rwanda, Boogie Nights, *and* Ocean's Eleven *and* Twelve. . . ."

I'm sure she said my name next, but all that's ringing in my ears is those last two titles, their juxtaposition to what I am doing right now discordant as hell. But more heads do turn and more bodies do begin to collect. It is a perfect— yet to me often strange—example of the power of "celebrity." I probably know less than Jenny about whence I speak, and possess maybe a quarter of her energy, and yet the uninitiated and heretofore uninterested are now beginning to pool to hear what Basher Tarr of Ocean's eleven/twelve/etc. has to say. Fine then. It shouldn't be all sunglasses and autographs anyway. I have been blessed with

*the rare opportunity to draw focus for however long it lasts,
and I am happy to have something to talk about other than
Brad Pitt's favorite food or what Catherine Zeta-Jones is
really like in person (tacos and lovely, respectively).*

*I jump right into it, telling the students that history is on
their side as far as their being the catalysts for change. The
youth have always possessed the vision and energy to
address the ills of lethargic, outmoded policies and to
transform them for good. I implore those gathered to not
allow their legacy to be that of those who stood by and
watched the genocide happen, a genocide in part funded by
the California university system's investments in Sudanese
companies. The rally starts to take on the feel of . . . well, a
rally, as our numbers slowly swell over the next hour,
different speakers stepping up to the podium to add their
perspectives and insight. The DAC students pass out signs
to those gathered, about thirty strong now, and Jenny lets
me know that it is time to march over to James West
Alumni Center for the regents meeting, where they will be
taking up the divestment issue.*

"I'm sorry, did you say march?"

*"Parade, strut, whatever. We've got to get more people
out here for this, old school, sixties style. March and chant
all the way, you know? That'll draw 'em." She's full of vim
and vigor, inspired by our growing numbers. I'm full of
apprehension.*

"March. Right. How far away is it?" I ask.

"Oh, it's not that far."

*It wouldn't be right to kick her in her enthusi-ass-im,
but my knee is begging me to, as its last, dying act. The
thing about it is, though, she's right. As we make our way
to the meeting, chanting as we go, students begin to
gravitate toward the processional to investigate. Our
numbers increase if for no other reason than many who
have joined us want to see a confrontation between*

*students and the "establishment." These tough, young
college kids are wrapped around an adolescent's high-
school, gooey center, playing back their old tapes now,
following the underdog to the fight behind the gym, hoping
the bully will finally get his ass kicked. But even those with
strictly voyeuristic interests at first are seemingly being won
over by the information the DAC and those previously
converted are reporting. No one in the periphery, it turns
out, is a fan of genocide, and if an increase in numbers and
a strong showing of solidarity among the students could
possibly mean results for the Darfurian people, then
everybody here now wants to be counted as agents of
change. Hallelujah.*

*When we arrive at the center many hours after this all
began, in numbers much greater than we could have
imagined, though I know I will be limping tomorrow, I'm
standing tall now, heartened by how the perseverance of the
few can rally the support of the many.*

*We pour into the Alumni Center's lobby that sits
adjacent to the conference room where the regents
meeting—already in session—is being held. It's a nice, large
area, and that's a good thing as our numbers have now
dramatically increased to near one hundred students, one
reporter/cameraman team, and one one-legged actor
scrambling to the bench for a much-needed sit. From what
I've been told, I won't be sitting long, as the question of
divestment is the first issue scheduled on the docket for
discussion in the meeting. But as the minutes begin to click
off the clock, it becomes clear that there is no real hurry to
get to us. No one is dissuaded, however, quite the opposite
in fact. If this is a gauntlet thrown down by the
"establishment," you know these students are down to pick
it up.*

*After about an hour or so an official-looking woman
sticks her head out of the door and asks that we wait*

outside; one hundred people talking even at just a normal volume can cause a small din. When we ask about when we might gain admittance to the meeting, we are told that there has been a schedule change and that they are currently in a closed session and it is unclear as to when they will get to us. Were we misinformed, mistaken, or are they trying to cool us off? No matter now, the crowd happily complies, moving to the steps just outside the building and drawing an even larger crowd. Nearly an hour later, light beginning to fade on the day, this "drive-by" is now approaching five hours for me, but there's no way I'm leaving now. Adam and his team dig into their pockets and pool enough money to buy everybody Taco Bell while they wait it out. The students keep one another's spirits strong, making impromptu speeches and singing songs, doing their best imitations of Berkeley in the sixties, and it's fantastic to watch. And all the while our numbers have only increased. Finally, the security guard steps outside and invites us in.

We file into the room, taking up all the seats and every other bit of free space in the room—over a hundred students standing silently, arms linked, holding pictures displaying the Janjaweed's dirty work and the international community's apathy, imploring the men and women collected there to divest their support from those supporting these horrors. One by one, Adam and his team make their impassioned, intelligent speeches to the board, pulling me in at the end to wrap it up. I try to get a read on the faces there, for some indication as to their leanings. Everyone seems to be on board, and sure enough, when the vote is called for, the proposal passes unanimously. Our celebration is loud and immediate, with everyone feeling the power of the collective. It makes me very hopeful that what has worked on this small scale could be a microcosm for what might possibly be applied in a larger framework, with even bigger results.

We pour outside congratulating one another and saying good-byes, promising to offer support once again and ever again if the need arises. Hobbling to my car, I'm almost sad the day has come to an end. Never before or since have I seen such movement in so short a time.

Sore as I am, my battery has been recharged. What's next?

8

◆

Strategies for Effective Change

*"We as Sudanese know that the peace in southern
Sudan was the effort of the American government.
Regardless of the political agenda, we deeply appreciate
that. The killing of civilians there has stopped. The
media and advocacy groups in the United States could
do the same in Darfur. Do not lose hope."*
SUAD MANSOUR, A DARFURI WOMAN AND PEACE ACTIVIST

Y ou have the power to make a difference.

This is not just rah-rah, cheerleading pablum. The cold
truth is that there is little appetite on the part of any government,
including the United States, to confront the Sudanese regime or
other merchants of death and to take the necessary actions to
bring these tragedies to an end. Therefore, the only means by
which U.S. policy can change, and thus the only way genocide and
other mass atrocities can be stopped, much like slavery and violence in southern Sudan, is if U.S. citizens raise their voices loud
enough to get the attention of the White House and force their
government to change its policy.

Effective activism needs strong leadership, direction, intelligence, and commitment. A broad strategy for moving forward
must focus on both the short-term goal of halting atrocities in Su-

dan, Congo, and northern Uganda, and the long-term goals of ensuring that the U.S. government has the tools to respond to mass atrocities in the future, and creating a constituency that will hold policy makers accountable for failing to act.

To help you find your voice, we offer six strategies for effective change:

- Raise Awareness
- Raise Funds
- Write a Letter
- Call for Divestment
- Join an Organization
- Lobby the Government.

Strategy One

SOW THE SEEDS — RAISE AWARENESS

Each year, the nightly newscasts of ABC, CBS, and NBC devote a total of roughly 25,000 minutes to news. Nonetheless, for the entire year of 2004, as genocide was ramping up in Darfur, the three main networks' nightly newscasts dedicated only 26 minutes to the conflict, according to the Tyndall Report Year in Review.

During June 2005, a full two years into the Darfur crisis, NBC aired a mere five segments on the genocide, and CBS had none, according to a study by the Be A Witness campaign.* It analyzed network and cable news coverage of the Darfur crisis and revealed what many Americans had long suspected about modern corporate media—it is sensationalistic and obsessed with the trivial at the expense of serious news developments like genocide. During that same June 2005 period, NBC and CBS each aired well over

---

*www.BeAWitness.org.

three hundred reports on Tom Cruise's romantic relationship with actress Katie Holmes and well over five hundred stories on the Michael Jackson trial. FOX News had forty-one pieces on Sudan, but an astounding 1,753 stories dedicated to the dethroned King of Pop, Mr. Jackson. In all, the top television news teams aired sixty-five times more segments on what amounts to celebrity gossip than on the genocide in Sudan. The Be A Witness campaign encouraged viewers to send letters and petition ABC, NBC, CBS, and FOX News to further cover the unfolding genocide in Darfur. The networks need to be treated much the same as politicians; they need to hear from their constituents (viewers) in order to make something a priority.

People cannot be expected to care about or act upon something they are unaware of. As these numbers attest, it is not enough to assume the mainstream news media will reach the greatest number of citizens or that they will convey the urgency of a situation. From the smallest gestures, such as talking with a friend, to larger-scale efforts, such as sponsoring a public forum, raising awareness is the key to ending the crisis. It is the first, critical step to affecting change.

And not everyone can be an Eric Reeves, dropping everything to dedicate his every waking moment (and probably a large portion of his agitated dreams) to the people of Sudan. Postcards, green wristbands, banners, op-eds in local papers, flyers, and speaking with friends about events in Sudan are all effective means of getting the word out and activism up. Remember: even small gestures can have great significance. For instance, Eleanor Kumin, a seventeen-year-old living in the Washington, D.C., area, convinced her family to buy Save Darfur wristbands and information cards and hand them out at their annual December party. "The family felt so good about what they were doing that they have been handing out bracelets to friends at every opportunity since," Eleanor explained.

Sometimes, those small actions inspire larger movements.

Action Begins at Home

Larissa Peltola demonstrates perfectly that you don't need a Ph.D., an influential post in the White House, or even to have finished elementary school to make a difference. This ten-year-old Los Angeles resident has been an advocate for Darfur and other human rights issues for the past five years. Larissa is growing up with the unusual after-school playground of Amnesty International's offices, where her mother, our friend Bonnie Abaunza, works as director of Artists for Amnesty. Bonnie was responsible for our meeting at a premiere of *Hotel Rwanda*. When she first overheard her mom working tirelessly on human rights cases, Larissa was scared and upset, but she thought, *Wow, I need to tell everyone about this so we can make a difference*. Larissa has been creatively working to "make a difference," from writing her papers at school on Darfur and reading them in front of her class, to holding garage sales and selling her massive Barbie collection to raise money for Darfurian refugees. With the wisdom of optimism, Larissa says, "You just have to stand up for what is right and fight for what you believe in. No matter how young you are or old you are, you can make a difference if you put your heart into it."

When Beverly Collins received a severance notice from her former employer several years ago, her first thoughts were not of how to find a new job, but of her passion for painting pictures, especially of women. It was this same passion that compelled her to paint images of Darfuri women. "As I looked at their faces when I was beginning to paint them, I saw the hurt and the atrocities put upon them," she says. Having only seen images of the brutality occurring in Darfur sporadically through newspapers and media, Collins felt an urge to tell people about what was going on. She now shows her exhibit, "The Invisible Women of Darfur," hoping to "inspire viewers to help with the cause."

For Melinda Koster of Pomona College in Claremont, California, it began with bread and a simple note. Stunned at the lack of discussion about Sudan on her campus, she and fellow student Ellie Winkelman began "Challah for Hunger," a weekly fund-raiser selling home-baked challah bread for the price of writing a letter about Darfur to a government official. The success of "Challah" led to similar groups forming at the other five Claremont colleges. This, in turn, led to a T-shirt campaign. More than 25,000 shirts have been sold nationally online already. Since late 2004, students at the Claremont Colleges have sold over two thousand shirts on campus—raising more than $8,000 for refugees in Darfur. Not satisfied with just motivating her fellow students, Koster coordinated with four other friends a "Road Trip for Sudan" to raise awareness among high school students and average citizens, to gather signatures for a petition, and to fund-raise throughout California. The "Road Trip" has inspired efforts at other universities across the country.

Colleen Connors decided to take the message to commuters. She had followed the situation in Sudan for some time, but at first felt that "such a big issue can make people feel so small. I wanted to do something but couldn't figure out what that was." It was on a drive near her home in Bethesda, Maryland, that she realized how she could help. When she saw a banner outside a synagogue that read "Save Darfur," she says, "I almost crashed my car." It was at that moment that she decided that "every house of worship should have that banner. Anyone from a mom in a minivan to our congressional representatives works and lives in the area. It could reach a lot of people," she notes. Her logic—when someone sees the banner but doesn't know what or where Darfur is, they will try to find out. Her initial goal was modest: get a banner up in as many synagogues and churches in the D.C. area as possible. Through the Internet, interest outside the Beltway grew. Now she is working with several organizations, including Save Darfur, selling hundreds of banners across the country that read, "A call to your conscience: Save Darfur."

In October 2005 when a group of students heard that the government of Sudan had hired Robert Cabelly, from the lobbying firm C/R International, for $530,000, they decided to take action. One Sunday afternoon they visited the neighborhood where Ca-

Seven Deadly Sins of Human Rights Advocates

Beware of the Seven Deadly Sins of would-be human rights advocates like us. We can get pretty sanctimonious, long-winded, and overzealous. So here are some things to avoid when you are trying to make your case, whether to a politician or to a group of people you are trying to educate.

1. *Don't be too boring!* Advocacy is not like an academic conference. We need to think through how to make our presentations stand out. Tell a story, tell a joke, make what you have to say interesting. Don't paint in black-and-white; paint in color!

2. *Don't be too long-winded!* Most of us who get involved in advocacy could hardly be accused of being shy. We often tend to drone on just a little too long about the issues that fire us up. Zero in on the main points and be concise!

3. *Don't be too unilateral!* We often just make long presentations or speeches at our meetings and events. We need to focus on interaction with our interlocutors or audiences. After initial presentations, engage people by asking questions. Be interactive!

4. *Don't be too complex!* We often overload our message by telling everything of interest about our subject in all its glorious complexity. Pick the highlights. Make a few simple points!

5. *Don't be too unstructured!* There's often so much to be said about our topics that we have the temptation to just blurt it all out in a stream of consciousness, sort of like hurling mud (or any other similar substance) against a wall and hoping it sticks. Instead, it is important to make a tight situation report and then present a focused set of recommendations. Make it flow!

6. *Don't be too random!* To a U.S. government policy maker or an American audience, we need to remain focused somewhat on what the United States can do. So make sure you focus your audience or interlocutor on the two or three most important things the American government can do, and how that person or group can help make it happen. Be focused!

7. *Don't be too touchy-feely!* We have to match our advocacy agenda to the big picture. We can't just rely on the "because it's the right thing to do" argument, or simply hope that for

humanitarian reasons people will respond. We also have to connect
our issues to larger national interests and what politicians and
Americans care about. For example, if our longer-term
counterterrorism agenda is being undermined by the way in which
the United States pursues this agenda in the short term, we need
to shout that from the rooftops. If our promotion of freedom is
going to be a central objective, then we need to demonstrate how
these freedoms are being undermined and not promoted by our
counterterrorism policies. Be relevant!

belly lives and went from house to house leaving flyers for Cabelly's neighbors letting them know whom their neighbor was
representing. A month later, students held a bake sale outside his
office to help raise money for C/R International and Cabelly so
they would no longer have to represent the government of Sudan
to earn a living. While the students did not quite raise $530,000
with their baked goods, shortly after the bake sale Cabelly
stopped representing the Sudanese government.

Many Sudanese have played a significant role in raising Americans' awareness and understanding of the crisis in Darfur. John's
friend Omer Ismail is a human rights activist from Darfur. He has
cofounded two organizations—the Sudan Democratic Forum and
Darfur Peace and Development (http://www.darfurpeaceand
development.org/home.php)—which encourage dialogue and action on democracy, peace, and human rights in Sudan. When the
situation in Darfur began to deteriorate in 2003, Omer went into
overdrive. He devoted himself for two full years to raising awareness and testifying about the atrocities being perpetrated in Darfur for panels, student organizations, the United Nations, and the
U.S. government.

Another activist from Darfur is Dr. Ali Ali-Dinar, the outreach
director for the African Studies Center at the University of Pennsylvania and the president of the Sudan Studies Association. Dr.
Francis Deng, a former representative of the UN Secretary-

General on internally displaced persons and Ambassador from Sudan to the United States, is also a powerful voice for ending conflict in Sudan. Like Omer, they have worked tirelessly to draw attention to the brewing crisis in Darfur through public speaking, conferences, and the media.

Simon Deng knows how harsh life in Sudan can be. Simon was nine years old when slave raiders supported by the government captured him in southern Sudan and gave him to a family in the north. Simon was a slave for three and a half years. The family forced him to perform grueling physical labor, beat him regularly, and forced him to sleep with their farm animals. Having lived through these horrors, Simon was not surprised when he learned about the genocide in Darfur. And he was determined to do something about it.

Simon was already well known in the early part of this decade for speaking out about southern Sudan as a strong advocate for the rights of the Sudanese people. "I have spoken at rallies in front of the United Nations, in Washington in front of members of Congress, and at events all across the U.S.," he told us, "yet the problems facing Sudan continue. It is for this reason that I decided that something out of the ordinary is needed to really raise awareness." Simon decided to lead the Sudan Freedom Walk, a three-hundred-mile march from New York City to Washington, D.C. He began in New York City on March 15, 2006, and many people walked with him as he made his way down the East Coast. He stopped in towns and cities along the way to speak about the crisis in Darfur, and local newspapers ran stories about his trek. When he arrived in Washington in April, Senators Sam Brownback and Hillary Clinton, along with Representatives Donald Payne and Betty McCollum, joined him in a rally outside the Capitol.

One person really can make a difference.

Bill Andress helped found Sudan Advocacy Action Forum, and he spends about six hours a day working on Sudan-related issues. Andress became involved in Sudan when he heard a pastor from

Sudan, Ezekiel Kutjok, who was touring and talking about the situation in southern Sudan. Andress realized someone had to do something, and he partnered with bobbie frances mcdonald to start an advocacy group. Their group has about twenty-five hundred members, half of whom are Presbyterian. Monthly they release a situation report, and once every six weeks they ask their group to do something active such as sending letters to congresspeople or the president. Andress explains, "Our strategy is very simple: pray, act, and give."

Andress is motivated to devote his life to this because of his religious beliefs. "After hearing about Sudan, I woke up at 3 A.M. day after day after day, worrying about nobody doing anything about it. That was ignorance speaking. I thought nobody was doing anything about it, but I was certainly not doing anything. I can imagine facing St. Peter and him saying, 'You didn't do such and such,' and me responding, 'I didn't know,' but not 'Yeah, I didn't want to.'" Andress believes the atrocities in Sudan are relevant to all. "Even if you're not Christian, if you have a faith at all, I think every faith requires a level of humanity. This is not just a Christian issue, it is more broadly a humanitarian issue, and this country needs to stand for what's humanitarian."

The American Islamic Congress (AIC) was also motivated by religious beliefs to help the people in Darfur. "Protecting and defending human rights are the foundation of Islam," explains Jana El-Horr, DC program director of AIC. "This message is not true only for Arabs or Muslims, but for all of humanity. That is why it is important to have interfaith dialogues and understanding." To foster such communication, AIC asked interfaith communities to lead a fast in October (during Ramadan) and break the fast together to raise funds for and awareness of Darfur. AIC also forwards newsletters from different Darfur-related organizations to its four-thousand-person database, and in conjunction with the al-Khoei Foundation, AIC is trying to meet with all Muslim or Arab ambassadors to the UN to press for more action in Darfur. "We are impartial politically. We are looking at the human rights issues. There are people dying for over three years, and no one is doing anything."

Interfaith Action

As a way of encouraging awareness, many Christian, Jewish, Muslim, and other religious organizations have organized prayer sessions or incorporated Darfur and the refugees into their services. Through meditation and/or prayer, you can deepen compassion for others, and that compassion can help bear witness to and end the suffering of others. As the Dalai Lama said, "The true expression of nonviolence is compassion. Some people seem to think that compassion is just a passive emotional response instead of rational stimulus to action. To experience genuine compassion is to develop a feeling of closeness to others combined with a sense of responsibility for their welfare."

In the Darfur campaign, prayer and meditation have been exceptional tools for reaching out to large numbers of people. These are mostly carried out within congregations, but much more could be done to promote interfaith efforts and alliances. One weekend in July 2005, through the advocacy efforts of the Save Darfur Coalition, the United States Congress recognized a National Weekend of Prayer and Reflection for Darfur. Across the country 350 communities of faith focused their prayers on those suffering in Sudan. In April 2006, Save Darfur helped organize a "Week of Prayer and Action for Darfur" for communities of faith, where over eight hundred religious institutions participated.* The organization offered suggestions for incorporating Darfur into a sermon, homily, D'var Torah (which is a brief explanation of the weekly Torah reading), or Jumuah Khutbah (the Muslim Friday prayers) and provided sample prayers on its website for institutions that participated in the effort, such as the following:

---

*The Save Darfur Coalition (www.savedarfur.org) has a congressional network that you can sign up to be a part of that will send updates about how the religious community can be involved in education and advocacy efforts.

A PRAYER FOR OVERCOMING INDIFFERENCE

I watch the news, God. I observe it all from a comfortable distance. I see people suffering, and I don't lift a finger to help them. I condemn injustice but I do nothing to fight against it. I am pained by the faces of starving children, but I am not moved enough to try to save them. I step over homeless people in the street, I walk past outstretched hands, I avert my eyes, I close my heart.

Forgive me, God, for remaining aloof while others are in need of my assistance.

Wake me up, God; ignite my passion, fill me with outrage. Remind me that I am responsible for Your world. Don't allow me to stand idly by. Inspire me to act. Teach me to believe that I can repair some corner of this world.

When I despair, fill me with hope. When I doubt my strength, fill me with faith. When I am weary, renew my spirit. When I lose direction, show me the way back to meaning, back to compassion, back to You. Amen.

Naomi Levy

Amy Butler, the senior pastor at Calvary Baptist Church, not only got her D.C. congregation to hang up Save Darfur banners, she also committed to mentioning Darfur in her service every Sunday one fall. She sees intentionally praying for the people in Sudan and empowering her congregation to take action through donation, letter writing, or prayer as worth pushing the comfort zone of many Baptists who have a strong belief in the separation of church and state. "All of us can agree that this is something that we never want to see happen again. We all need to raise our voices and say this is wrong."

Robert Kang of The Church in Bethesda and his copastor April Vega were feeling overwhelmed by what they read about Darfur. It really hit home for them when they read a *Washington Post* article about a fourteen-year-old Darfurian girl who was raped. Learning about the plight of raped women in Darfur—the cultural implications of a raped woman being seen as a damaged or dirty woman—was overwhelming. "I remember being so struck by that that I actually took it to church and gave a talk on Sunday regarding it. I don't know what the exact point of the talk was, but I just wanted to make the story heard and known. I knew if this had happened to my neighbor in this city, people would have been all over it, but here was a distant woman and no one was doing anything about it. What can we do?" he wondered. "This little insignificant church?" Then he heard of five outdoor prayer services being held by his old church, Cedar Ridge Community Church, where Brian McLaren is the pastor. Inspired, Kang and Vega joined these efforts hoping that it would bring attention, media coverage, and people to join in prayer. For the services they partnered with Rabbi David Saperstein, director at the Religious Action Center, and in this way were able to bring together a large interfaith community to discuss the situation in Darfur. More important than large numbers of participants were the stories shared, the passion of the people there, and the link of interfaith unity that was created.

Kang says, "Just personally, I've been really challenged in my limited view and faith. Being a part of this five weeks of worship for Sudan and Darfur has made a significant impact on my spirit and what I value as action, and I hope and pray that it continues to grow. I confess that I was one that thought of change really only on a large scale (in numbers and size), and I feel like I've come into contact with the power of passion and the power of a few, and I believe that is what is going to change the world. People who are passionate, and devoted, and will fight to change the world. In a small way, I feel completely blessed by this."

Raise Awareness: Actions You Can Take

1. Educate yourself about Darfur and the world's other most urgent crises at www.enoughproject.org.

2. Talk to your family, friends, and colleagues about these crises and what we can do to help end them.

3. Host a screening of a documentary about Darfur such as Paul Freedman's *Sand and Sorrow* (www.sandandsorrow.org), *Darfur Diaries* by Aisha Bain, Jen Marlowe, and Adam Shapiro (www.darfurdiaries.org), or Brian Steidle's story captured in Annie Sundberg's film "The Devil Came on Horseback" (www.thedevil cameonhorseback.com).

4. Write a letter to your newspaper or local TV news asking for more coverage of Darfur and other areas that need our help.

5. If you are a blogger, blog to end genocide on leading blog sites!

6. Invite a speaker to your house of worship to talk about Darfur and what must be done to end genocide and mass atrocities worldwide.

7. Join/start prayer groups or promote interfaith events.

8. Organize a vigil, fast, or protest to support stronger action to stop crimes against humanity.

9. Wear the cause: purchase T-shirts or green wristbands and give them as gifts.

Strategy Two

UNDERWRITING CHANGE—RAISE FUNDS

The organizations operating on the ground in Darfur and neighboring Chad, where many refugees have fled, are in constant need of money to meet operating costs. For instance, nearly 3 million people in Darfur and on the border with Chad depend on food aid. However, in May 2006, the United Nations World Food Program (WFP), the largest humanitarian organization operating in the field, announced that it was cutting its daily rations for the refugees and internally displaced (IDPs) because of a severe funding shortfall. That meant that the food ration would be less than the minimum required to stave off malnutrition, rates of which were already on the rise in Sudan.

It should not have come to that. According to WFP, throughout Sudan, more than 6 million people depend on food aid for basic nutrition at a cost of $746 million. Nicholas Kristof said about WFP in one his columns, "Without the World Food Program organizing food shipments to Sudan and Chad, hundreds of thousands more people would have died. Those U.N. field workers are heroic." But as of June 2006, barely half the aid requirements were funded. The United States had given nearly $200 million, the EU $60 million, and the UK $90 million—that left a marked shortfall. One of Kristof's readers contacted him to find out to which organization he should donate a $1 million cash dividend from Microsoft. But you need not be a millionaire to have a direct financial impact. You can contribute money or you can write letters and advocate for more U.S. funding. In this case, the latter activity led to a surge in governmental contributions to the relief effort around the world and to an increase in the WFP rations.

Much has been written about whether donated funds really get to the people for whom they are intended. The emphasis on improved efficiency over the last two decades has resulted in much better targeting of resources to the truly needy, and much less waste and overhead. *Money* magazine ranks these aid agencies according to how efficient they are at ensuring their money goes to the intended beneficiaries, and this has helped spark a real effort in the aid industry to make sure that each dollar that is contributed goes to helping people on the ground. The track record has improved enormously during these last twenty years. Today, your money will make a difference in saving lives, more than it ever has before.

You can also raise money for organizations that get at the root causes of the violence, so that endless appeals for food and medicine become unnecessary. Organizations like the International Crisis Group (www.crisisgroup.org) and campaigns like ENOUGH aim to end the conflicts and atrocities that produce extreme human deprivation.

Groups and individuals around the country have been doing creative things in the way of fund-raising for Darfur's victims of violence. Traditional fund-raising methods (e.g., bake sales, T-shirt sales, dinners) and nonconventional ideas (e.g., CD sales, birthday party fund-raisers, etc.) are part of a widespread effort to assist humanitarian projects in Darfur, and even to help advocacy groups who try to get at the root causes of the violence. College groups have thrown parties at clubs and bars to raise money for Darfur relief. Many colleges have used money raised to support a project of the Darfurian-run Darfur Peace and Development organization, which sets up schools in Darfur and Chad for children who are IDPs and refugees. Others have organized benefit concerts, like fifteen-year-old Spencer Wiesner from upstate New York, who raised $20,000.

Rachel Karetzky, a thirteen-year-old activist living in Philadelphia, Pennsylvania, learned about Sudan while on vacation and started a fund-raising campaign to benefit the victims of Darfur as part of her Bat Mitzvah community service project. "I saw genocide on the news and thought, *Why doesn't the world do anything?*" she asked. "Everyone knows what happened to the Jews in the Holocaust, and I learned about it for so long in Hebrew school, etc. Then you realize the consequences afterwards, and that it shouldn't happen again. And now it's happening again and it's wrong." With some initial guidance from the American Jewish World Service, she started her campaign. In six months, she raised almost $15,000 to benefit the victims in Darfur.

She initiated "Cans for Darfur"—collection cans in salons, bakeries, and shops for people to make donations. To raise additional funds, she held a raffle with donated prizes, sold green Save Darfur bracelets that said "Not on our watch: Save Darfur," and on the Jewish New Year, Rosh Hashanah, she handed out flyers and asked people to make donations. She also spoke at her own synagogue, Beth El, and the Society Hill Synagogue along with Ruth Messinger, president of the American Jewish World Service. Aside from talking about her own project and how meaningful it was to her, Rachel spoke about what other Bar and Bat Mitzvahs should do to also get involved and make a difference. Rachel's efforts did not just target her Jewish peers at her school. She also chose to do a curriculum project comparing Darfur to the Holocaust and was able to share her research at a fair and collect donations. Her hard work and efforts paid off, as she appeared on *Nick News* on Nickelodeon describing the comparison between the Holocaust and Darfur. She also got signatures for a petition that was sent to the president.

After raising all that money, Rachel says, "I felt overjoyed, happy and excited. I felt like I was really making a difference, so I continued. At times it got hard, but I like to speak in front of people." The advice she would give someone who wants to get involved would be to "always think that you're making a difference. Keep on trying and raising money even if you pass the Bar Mitzvah. Don't stop your campaign, because you are making a difference."

When Miles Forma, an eighteen-year-old student from New Jersey who has cerebral palsy, saw the movie *Hotel Rwanda,* he was so moved that he started a fund-raising campaign for a special school program in Rwanda. He organized an African dance workshop and then gave a PowerPoint presentation on the Rwandan genocide. Miles had family members who perished in the Holocaust, and he kept asking himself how the world could turn its back. Only the idea that he would make a difference was comforting to him.

Speaking through his DynaVox, Miles said the movie made him feel "sad and angry and inspired." In his presentation he paraphrased the philosopher George Santayana, "People who ignore the lessons of history are doomed to repeat them." And he explained to the audience that one of the lessons of what happened in Rwanda is not to turn our backs when a country needs our help. About thirty-five to forty friends, students from Crotched Mountain, a center for people with disabilities, and individuals from the community came to Miles's event. His goal was to raise $1,000, but he has raised almost $2,500 to date.

Miles followed that with a fund-raising campaign for Darfur in November 2006. He researched the issues and interviewed a young man from the region who works at his school. He also put together another PowerPoint presentation and had a chance to meet Paul Rusesabagina as well.

Rebecca Bernstein is an investment counselor at a money management firm in San Francisco who in March 2005 organized a benefit event at a bar to help increase awareness of what was going on in Darfur. Rebecca had been reading a lot about the crisis there but felt that little was being done about it, that the atrocities were simply being "swept under the rug." After getting an e-mail from her sister that said how important it is to speak up when no one does, she decided to organize an event to try to get people involved. Aside from collecting donations at the door, Rebecca also sold raffle tickets for donated restaurant gift certificates. A speaker came from the American Jewish World Service, and Rebecca put up photos and distributed literature about the crisis. After raising nearly $2,700, she said, "I would do it again and it wasn't that hard to organize. If anything, I would hope to do a better job and raise more money next time."

Jesse Brenner had the benefit of an internship with Afropop Worldwide, a radio program, website, and database that help to raise awareness about music produced by the African Diaspora. Afropop works to ensure that the benefits return to the artists and their home countries. While updating Afropop's website, Brenner learned about the developments in Darfur. Appalled by the lack of mainstream media coverage of the genocide, he and fellow "co-conspirator" Eric Herman founded a production company and record company called Modiba Productions to help raise awareness. Brenner cites his Jewish heritage and horror at past genocides as his motivation. He recalls watching the killing unfold in Rwanda and "feeling very angry. I remember screaming at the

---

Raising Funds: Actions You Can Take

1. **Make an individual or family donation to humanitarian, human rights, or advocacy organizations. (You can find a list of these organizations on the ENOUGH website—www.enoughproject .org)**

   2. **Urge your employer to make a contribution to one or more of these organizations, or place one of these organizations on its United Way designated charities.**

   3. **Organize a fund-raiser in your community by hosting a dinner, a concert, an auction, a fun run, or a fast.**

   4. **Link to the organizations you support from your personal home page or your blog.**

TV." Seeing genocide in Darfur a decade later, Brenner felt impulsively, "I need to do something. Genocide is man-made. There is a moral imperative to act. We can't stand idly by."

Through Modiba, he and Herman released the *Afrobeat Sudan Aid Project* (ASAP) to benefit the internally displaced in Darfur. They talked with Ben Cohen of Ben & Jerry's, and through him, they were sponsored by Truemajority.org, a grassroots education and advocacy project. They also teamed up with iTunes. As we went to press, Modiba had sold over 8,500 copies, raising more than $135,000 for Save the Children in Darfur. As Brenner puts it, "People should use whatever talents they have to take action. They should realize the fate of these people [in Sudan] is tied up with their own fate as fellow citizens of the globe."

Strategy Three
WRITE A LETTER—SAVE A LIFE

It is worth reminding ourselves what Senator Paul Simon said back in 1994 about the Rwandan genocide: how a mere one hundred letters to each member of Congress could have changed the outcome.

Our democracy is taken for granted. We forget that our congresspersons are our representatives—not unreachable decision makers. Often it is as simple as clicking on an e-postcard already prepared by an organization devoted to Darfur. But e-postcards are not nearly as effective an advocacy tool as an impassioned, personal letter addressed to your local, state, and national representatives, or even to the president of the United States. A personal letter tells elected officials that you care about the issue enough to take fifteen minutes out of your busy day to put your thoughts on paper. Indeed, Amnesty International has shown through the decades the success of impartial letter-writing campaigns in freeing political prisoners. As Professor Eric Reeves emphasizes, "People don't realize it, but members of Congress are very responsive."

However you choose to do it—fax, e-mail, phone, postcard, letter—the few minutes it takes to write and send a message could mean the difference between collective action and continued atrocities. Personal, impassioned letters are more effective, ultimately, than clicking on a website, if you are willing to take the extra few minutes. That is what makes politicians take notice: constituents taking time out of their day to write letters themselves.

Here is an example of what a letter might look like. Be aware we are writing this in early December 2006. You will need to update your letter by going to www.enoughproject.org.

Dear Representative/Senator _____:
I am a taxpaying and voting constituent and am writing to appeal to you as my elected representative to do more to help end the genocide in Sudan. As you may be aware, since 2003 the Sudanese government has orchestrated and waged a deliberate campaign of murder, rape, and displacement against the people of the Darfur region. More than 400,000 people have died, thousands of women have been systematically raped, and

more than two million people have been displaced and forced to live in squalid refugee camps. I appreciate your leadership and ask you to do more to help end the crisis in Darfur.

First, Congress must continue to support measures designed to protect the civilians in Darfur. The United States provides significant humanitarian assistance to Darfur, but that is not enough. Congress must urge the Bush Administration to rally more UN Member States for a stronger, more robust international peacekeeping force. It is also critical that Congress continue to adequately fund an international peacekeeping force in Darfur until the perpetrators of these crimes are brought to justice and the civilians can return to their lives in peace.

Secondly, the United States must play a stronger role in finding a political solution to the conflict. The Presidential Special Envoy to Sudan must continue to engage directly with the relevant parties, including the rebel groups who have not signed the Darfur Peace Agreement, the African Union, the major stakeholder groups, and the Sudanese Government of National Unity to reconvene talks on how to make the Darfur Peace Agreement more inclusive. The Darfur Peace Agreement resulted in part from United States engagement, but we have failed to secure the level of inclusiveness required for a peace agreement to succeed.

Lastly, the United States should impose targeted sanctions on National Congress Party officials responsible for crimes against humanity in Darfur. The orchestrators and perpetrators of genocide must be held accountable and there must be pressure on the ruling National Congress Party until the genocide is brought to an end. I urge you to ask President Bush to ensure that the U.S. government cooperates with the investiga-

---

♦

Write a Letter: Actions You Can Take

1. Write letters to urge your representatives to take specific actions for Darfur and other crises.

2. Ask your family, friends, and colleagues to write letters to their elected officials. And hound them until they do so.

3. Sign or start a petition calling for greater accountability for those responsible for genocide and other crimes against humanity. And present it to your local congressperson.

4. Think big! Start a letter-writing campaign at your high school, university, house of worship, or office.

5. Write a letter to the editor of your local paper and support specific policies while targeting specific elected officials.

---

tion of the International Criminal Court into crimes against humanity in Darfur. Punishing those responsible for atrocities is necessary to achieve justice for the victims and prevent similar crimes from occurring in the future.

Thank you so much for your time and I look forward to your response.

Sincerely,

The Golden Gate Community helps rebuild lives of at-risk youth in San Francisco. Despite their local focus, the community created and distributed postcards on Darfur for Congress, handed out informative bookmarks at book fairs, and held a benefit concert that informed attendees about the crisis, raised funds, and offered petitions for people to send to President Bush.

Josh Gleis, a graduate student at Tufts University in Boston, started a "pen campaign," sending letters to policy makers with pens, urging them to sign strong legislation to help end genocide in Darfur. The pen avoided any excuses about not being able to vote or sign a bill into law. He says, "One may collect ten thousand signatures for a petition and mail it to the president. But that is one envelope with ten thousand signatures. If you send ten thousand individual letters, that's even better. If you send ten thousand individual letters with a pen in each one, it is not something to be ignored."

Strategy Four
STOP FUNDING THE GENOCIDE — CALL FOR DIVESTMENT

Not since South Africa's brutal and repressive apartheid system of racial segregation has an African tragedy generated such outrage within segments of the American public. Through the 1980s and the early 1990s, citizen-driven divestment from companies doing business with the racist government in Pretoria helped free Nelson Mandela and end apartheid. And as with the anti-apartheid movement, a nascent divestment effort has begun with Darfur activists. Traditionally, Khartoum responds to the stick, not the carrot, and foreign direct investment is a lifeline that helps keep its war machine afloat.

Anti-genocide activists are now calling for the removal from school, state, and personal pension and mutual funds of assets that are tied to the Sudanese government. The objective of many advocates is targeted divestment, which focuses on companies providing revenues for the government. Such targeting allows the penalty to be focused directly on the perpetrators, not indirectly on the Sudanese victims. By depriving the Khartoum government of investment from abroad, particularly in the oil and energy sector, these activists are helping cut off the funding for the genocidal campaign in Darfur.

The push for divestment from Sudan began before the conflict in Darfur. Despite a restriction on conducting business in Sudan, non-U.S. oil companies were hampering the boycott by continuing to operate there. A growing number of grassroots organizations began pushing for divestment from these companies, including Canada's largest private oil company, Talisman Energy. Since

1995, Canadian NGOs and student groups had pressed Talisman shareholders to sell their shares in protest and demanded that Talisman (and earlier its predecessor Arakis) pull out of Sudan.

As a direct result of this pressure, Citizen's Bank of Canada sold its Talisman holdings and the Ontario Teachers Federation said it would divest its $184 million (Canadian) of Talisman stock. In the United States, pressure from activists, spearheaded by Professor Eric Reeves, led to the divestment of more than $100 million by ten major shareholders and additional divestments by New York City's pension fund, Teacher Retirement System of Texas, the California Public Employees' Retirement System (Cal PERS), and the Vanguard Group. As a result of the divestments, Talisman announced in 2000 that it would have to buy back $300 million of its own shares to buoy the share price, which had dropped by 35 percent. Because of economics and public relations, the company was soon forced to seek a buyer for its oil concession holdings in southern Sudan and leave the country.

Universities, private investment firms, and public retirement systems should make it a priority to review their portfolios and divest themselves of any holdings in companies that act as patrons to human rights violators and war criminals. The divestment should also be made public, to generate media coverage and send a clear message that the actions of perpetrators of mass atrocities and the companies that support them are intolerable.

In October 2004, a couple of students at Harvard University, Ben Collins and Manav Kumar Bhatnagar, read an article in the school paper that compelled them to act. The article, "Endowment Tied to Sudan," by staff writers Daniel Hemel and Zachary Seward, described how the university was heavily invested in the Chinese parastatal oil company PetroChina, a major player in the Sudanese oil sector. The article outlined how oil revenue funds Khartoum's killing machine and how Chinese support at the United Nations helped deflect stronger international action to end the slaughter. Collins and Kumar decided to start a movement to call on Harvard to sell its stock in PetroChina and four other oil companies operating in Sudan. They paid $10 for a domain name and started an online petition. They e-mailed students and professors asking for support, and within a week they had a thousand signatures.

As the genocide in Darfur worsened, press coverage increased and a student activist group—the Darfur Action Group—formed and began holding rallies to urge Harvard to divest. Harvard President Lawrence Summers, who students felt was sympathetic to the cause, helped convene a special session of the university's Advisory Board on Shareholder Responsibility. Collins and Kumar spoke at the meeting, and the advisory board submitted a report recommending that the university divest from PetroChina. On April 4, 2005, following intense pressure from students, the Harvard Corporation voted to sell its stock in PetroChina only. Harvard students kept pushing, and eventually the university divested from another Chinese oil company, Sinopec.

Following Harvard's April 2005 decision to divest from PetroChina, Stanford University's Board of Trustees voted unanimously to divest from PetroChina and three additional companies: Sinopec, Tatneft, and ABB. Since then, more than two dozen universities and colleges, including Yale, Brown, Brandeis, University of Vermont, and the University of California system, have enacted divestment programs. Another almost three dozen, including the Massachusetts Institute of Technology, Northwestern University, the University of Illinois, and the University of Washington, have ongoing divestment campaigns. Daniel Millenson of the Sudan Divestment Task Force, which now helps to generate and coordinate divestment efforts on campuses and in cities and states nationwide, says, "I think that one of the best ways of encapsulating the strength of the movement is by comparing it to South African divestment. There, a decades-long campaign yielded investment decisions from about fifty-five universities." During the Darfur campaign, thirty-one schools divested during the first year and a half, with more student groups pressing their schools each day.

Having first learned about Darfur from reading Nicholas Kristof's articles (yet another example of the power of the pen, particularly Nick's pen), Adam Sterling and Jason Miller joined the Darfur Action Committee on their campus of the University of California at Los Angeles. It was here that they developed a divestment proposal that eventually turned into the University of California Divestment Taskforce, a student activist organization that is pushing the UC system to divest from companies that do business with Sudan. In March, the University of California Regents voted to divest all UC shares of the following nine companies with business in Sudan: Bharat Heavy Electricals, Sinopec, Nam Fatt Co., Oil & Natural Gas Co., PECD Bhd., PetroChina, Sudatel, Tatneft, and Videocon Industries.

In terms of private investments, one campaign targets Warren Buffett's Berkshire Hathaway, which holds $1.9 million shares of PetroChina. Tools for those investors who want to avoid Sudanese holdings are being developed by Northern Trust, Barclays Global Investors, and State Street Global Advisors.

Backed by Congressman Donald Payne and Governor Jon Corzine, Joe Madison, a radio host in Washington, D.C., helped start up a campaign for New Jersey to divest its pension fund from companies doing business in Sudan. Joe gathered information about companies investing in Sudan and joined with former congressman and cofounder of the Congressional Black Caucus Rev. Walter Fauntroy to begin to push for divestment. In part as a result of their combined efforts, New Jersey formally divested in June 2005. They continue to push other states for formal divestment.

In September 2006, Congress passed the Darfur Peace and Accountability Act, which urges the president to prohibit Sudanese oil tankers from entering U.S. ports. It also freezes and blocks assets of individuals involved in the genocide. In October, President Bush signed it into law and issued an executive order "blocking property of and prohibiting transactions with the Government of Sudan."

However, a key amendment, which received bipartisan support, was dropped due to corporate pressures. The National Foreign Trade Council (NFTC), representing more than three hundred multinational companies, led the campaign against the provision that would protect states' rights to pass divestment laws. NFTC says the amendment would have encouraged states to develop their own foreign policy. Senate Foreign Relations Committee Chairman Richard Lugar agreed, arguing that with said clause the bill was unlikely to pass. Despite the setback, states and municipalities have continued to pass or debate their own divestment schemes.

The state legislatures of New Jersey, Illinois, Oregon, Maine, Connecticut, and California have all approved divestment plans. Nonbinding divestment resolutions have passed in Ohio and Vermont. North Carolina's state treasury independently divested a selection of Sudan-related holdings. Several states, including Missouri, Louisiana, Tennessee, Pennsylvania, and Arizona, have passed or are considering rules requiring regular reports on how state funds are linked to terrorist states, including Sudan (some of which are nonbinding). Many of these states have left open the option of subsequent divestment. Finally, over a dozen states have active divestment movements with varying levels of involvement from state officials. Cities have begun consideration of divestment as well: San Francisco, Providence, New Haven, and Philadelphia have passed measures prohibiting certain Sudan investments while the fiduciaries of Los Angeles; Newton, Massachusetts; and some other smaller cities are considering the issue.

"The genocide in Cambodia happened under Carter's watch. The genocide in Rwanda happened under Clinton's watch," notes Jason Miller. A president will not necessarily act alone to do the right thing. In fact, failure to act is the rule, not the exception. But if citizens, through their actions, show that they support stronger U.S. action to end genocide, our leaders will be more confident to take those actions.

Senator Sam Brownback took matters into his own hands. In

November 2006 the senator's family decided to divest their holdings of mutual funds whose investments include companies that the Sudan Divestment Task Force identified as the "worst offenders." Any citizen can follow his example. All you have to do is get your mutual fund's annual prospectus or call them and find out whether they own any of the stocks listed by the Sudan Divestment Task Force. If they do, then sell the shares, inform the mutual fund why you sold them, and buy one of the growing number of Sudan-free funds.*

Divestment is a concrete action that citizens and institutions can take to say "NO" to crimes against humanity, but most universities will not take on this task without encouragement from students. At Stanford and Harvard and many other universities around the country, student pressure was instrumental, and student-led activist groups such as STAND and GI-Net have made their voices heard throughout the country.

University administrations, mutual fund company heads, and state government officials need to hear directly from students, alumni, and average citizens that investments in companies who are in partnership with genocidal governments are unacceptable and that investors who fail to take the simple step of reviewing their portfolios have chosen to be bystanders to crimes against humanity.

DON:

I never slow-play aces. Let me explain. Over the last couple of years or so I have become a big fan—not unlike thousands of others—of no-limit poker. It is a seven card stud game where each player is dealt two facedown cards and then sees five more community cards dealt

---

*You can also go to the Sudan Divestment Task Force website—www.sudandivestment.org—and use their screening tool. This simple web-based tool allows you to enter in the name of U.S. mutual funds and quickly learn whether or not the fund is invested in a targeted list of offending companies.

faceup on the table. Each player then uses these cards to make the best five-card poker hand possible. I love the game and find myself looking for excuses to play all the time: "The casino's only thirty minutes away, honey" (if I drive ninety mph the whole way). Or "I'm much happier when I come home, aren't I?" (if I've won, that is). So shooting the latest Ocean's *flick in Las Vegas, it's a surefire bet that I will find myself at almost any off-camera hour sitting at the no-limit table at the Bellagio. Today is no different. I've been on a little card rush (when the cards dealt to you are winners) over the last hour, and right now I'm looking at pocket rockets, American Airlines, aces in the hole, the best hand you can have before the other cards hit the board (table). But though the hand is the strongest at this point, the cards that are about to come could spoil it all for me, so when it's my turn to bet, I push all in— committing all of my chips to the pot, putting the pressure on the other players to call my bet. And I do immediately get a caller, but it's not the one I was expecting. It is Theodore Braun, the director of the Darfur activism documentary that I am producing,* An Indifferent World, *calling me on the cell to let me know that two very important bills currently sitting on the governor's desk concerning California's divestment from Sudanese companies might get vetoed within hours.*

Bills AB 2179 and 2941, authored by Republican Assemblyman Tim Leslie of Tahoe City and Democratic Assemblyman Paul Koretz respectively, direct two major California retirement funds (CalPERS and CalSTRS) as well as the University of California schools' regents from investing funds in companies with active business operations in Sudan. The bills were solid and had been specifically modified to address problems that had occurred with similar divestment legislation passed and pending in other states. But we knew that the bills' veto was a definite possibility, a probability even (this information coming from a source inside of the governor's advisory circle), so Ted's news wasn't a complete shock. It still had me pretty pissed, though. Just one month earlier I had stood shoulder to shoulder with Adam Sterling, executive director of the student-led UC Sudan Divestment Taskforce, one of the subjects in our documentary and a man with whom I shared the spotlight at the UCLA Darfur rally, as well as Assemblyman Paul Koretz, author of AB 2941, and several other civic leaders on the steps of Los Angeles City Hall, holding a press conference concerning the bills. We then walked (an unfortunate theme for my knee) the over four thousand signed postcards in support of our request to the governor's office. Governor Schwarzenegger did not meet us that day, but someone from his office collected the postcards and dutifully thanked us for our efforts. We all felt we had just received the high-class brush-off and left much less than enthused. Knowing that George Clooney and the governor had worked together in the past, I had called George earlier that week to see if he would put in a call on our behalf; a request he obliged, but he had yet to receive a return call. Given all this, I had all but written off the bills as dead. But Ted's call, albeit poorly timed for my poker game, put a blip back in the flat line.

"Don, we may have some daylight. Governor Schwarzenegger is going to be calling for George and you any minute now to talk about the bills."

Sure, I'm happy, but . . .

"Now? I'm all in, here, Ted!"

"Damn right! Me too. What number should I give him?"

I forgo clarifying things, give him the number to George's bungalow, and hang up. Everybody at the table here recognizes my huge raise for what it is and folds his hand, giving me just enough time to stack my chips and break for the exit, making a call to George on the way.

"George, it's Don. Mr. Freeze is going to be calling us in your room in a minute about these bills. You ready?"

"Yeah. Could you come by, though, and we'll go over everything first?"

"Already moving."

Some backstory: This last calendar year has seen George Clooney join in our fight for Darfur in a very robust and demonstrative way, from going to the huge D.C. rally held on April 30, to speaking to the UN Security Council, to actually traveling to the region with his father Nick, a journalist, in tow, to see and chronicle the horrors for himself. His participation has given a great lift to our efforts, and we are incredibly grateful. But this particular issue today is somewhat outside of George's purview, so now I'm sprinting to the business center at the hotel to print up some bullet points on the bills and then on to the bungalows to get George up to speed before the phone call comes in.

When I arrive at his room, the door is cracked so I let myself in, finding George kicked back on the couch.

"Yo."

"Yo," he shoots back. "How's it going?"

"Good. Check this out."

I hand George the bills' descriptions, and we break them down to their most salient points, going over what exactly it is George should say to the governor and, if a handoff is necessary, how I'll chime in. Minutiae aside, our request is simple: we want the governor to lead the way in divesting by signing the bills into law, and if he is going to veto these bills, we want to let the governor know that we intend to voice our displeasure publicly, loud and clear.

We don't have long to review before the phone rings. When he answers, George's salutation is surprising yet definitely appropriate.

"Hello, Mr. Governor."

Not Arnie or Arnold or Big Freezie or A Swizz? How diplomatic. This guy really should run for office. I grab our prepared document and start circling bullet points for George's easy viewing but quickly surmise from George's side of the conversation ("Oh. . . . Okay, that's great. . . . We had heard that. . . . Great.") that our convincing offensive may not be necessary. The governor instructs George that he was always going to sign the bills into law and doesn't know where the idea came from that he wasn't. I don't know either and frankly don't care; we're about to "move the chains." George thanks the governor for his very necessary leadership and support and hangs up.

"Wow."

"Yeah." I'm surprised too. "That was easier than I thought."

"Wonder what happened." George pondering now. "Maybe he heard the cavalry coming and backed down?"

Our inner circle "source" had told us without equivocation that the bills were indeed in jeopardy. The source had repeated this to us on more than one occasion over the last week, every time we had called in to check on the bills' progress, in fact. Was George right? Had we just seen our unwavering determination in the face of adversity overcome an obstacle, or had we simply been misinformed of the gov's intentions?

"I don't know, but I'm not looking this gift horse in the mouth."

"That's probably best," George agrees.

I thank Mr. Danny "Batman" Ocean-Clooney, we BS for a beat, and I take off back for the poker tables to feed the monster, finding the necessary excuse for such activity now by telling myself that I deserve it after all the "hard work" I've just done. I know, people, I got problems.

As I'm boarding the plane back to LA, my phone chimes. It's a text message from George informing me that

Call for Divestment: Actions You Can Take

1. **Educate yourself about divestment and the targeted companies at the Sudan Divestment Task Force website at www.sudandivestment.org and the ENOUGH website at www.enoughproject.org.**

2. Research your investement portfolio to see if you have investments in companies that are targeted for divestment, and then pull your assets out of any fund that does. And tell them you did!

3. Join a group that is pushing for divestment at your university (or alma mater), your municipality, and your state.

4. Write to your pension fund manager and demand that your pension fund be free of the targeted companies.

5. Encourage your family, friends, and colleagues to make sure that their investment portfolios are free of those companies.

the governor would like for George and me to attend the bill signing ceremony, an invitation George very willingly will accept. I text back that I am of the same mind and will see him early Monday morning to stand with Adam, Assemblyman Koretz, and George behind the governor in a bipartisan display of hope for a better future for Darfur. And I left Vegas $250 up too. Not bad.

Strategy Five

CREATING COMMUNITIES OF INFLUENCE — JOIN AN
ORGANIZATION

Volunteering with an existing nonprofit or ad hoc organization can be an incredibly effective and rewarding way of getting involved. Creating a new organization may seem intimidating, but keep in mind many groups started small but focused. Often all it takes is the persistence of one person; sometimes friends or colleagues coming together for a single task can develop into a fuller community. Activist associations have often grown to have tremendous influence, usually by working in coordination with similar groups. Through such efforts, momentum is built, people see that they are not alone in caring, and powerful networks are created.

Tim Nonn, a stay-at-home editor who was busy raising his five-year-old son, found it difficult to face the suffering of the children in Darfur, Sudan. Instead, he avoided dealing with the issue for several years. One night Nonn was watching *The Charlie Rose Show* and John was on talking about Sudan along with Samantha Power. They told a story about a mother in Darfur walking across the desert for several days with her children after their village was destroyed. Nonn thought, "God, some days it feels hard to walk with my son through the grocery store." This finally got him motivated to get involved.

He went to his church in Petaluma, California, and gave a sermon on Sudan. After the sermon, Nonn spearheaded an initiative called the "Dear Sudan" campaign from his church to raise awareness about Sudan. The idea was simple: raise enough funds to feed the same number of refugees in Sudan as people in Petaluma (roughly 55,000). By putting it in these terms, Nonn wanted to show people in his congregation what it takes to feed their own community and how hard it would be to feed the millions displaced in Darfur and Chad. "We, in a way, try to put it in terms that people in that community can recognize, so they realize what it takes to feed their own community for a day." Nonn believes, "As individuals, we have a certain level of influence, but as communities we have more influence with our congressional representatives, and as a network of communities we have even more power to not only raise money for the refugees but help create the political will to end the genocide."

The campaign raised over $10,000, more than enough money to feed a displaced community in Sudan the size of Petaluma for one day. With the encouragement of Susan Sanders at the National Office of the United Church of Christ, Dear Sudan quickly became a national movement, endorsed and funded by many denominations. Its goals have expanded beyond raising money for Darfurian displaced persons and refugees to include ending the genocide and educating the public about the crisis in Sudan. For example, Nonn hosted an essay contest with junior high and high school students asking why they should help the hungry. Congressman Frank Wolf, a longtime and dedicated Sudan advocate, gave them congressional certificates to honor their efforts.

Nonn hopes to have five thousand Dear Sudan communities eventually. "Our hope is to reach that critical mass point when there are so many communities who are organizing that the movement cannot be ignored any longer and there will be not only a massive relief effort but also a political response. We must find ways to work together; it's happening on a lot of levels—parents, religious communities—and it's growing."

Online organizing has been key in bringing people together as well as spreading the message to a diverse audience. Perhaps the most unusual group to emerge has been the Harry Potter Alliance. Created by Andrew Slack of the Late Night Players, the Harry Potter Alliance seeks to motivate Harry Potter fans to take a stand against tyranny, genocide, global warming, and more, using parallels to the book series. Inept political leaders become the Minister and Ministry of Magic, while the oppressive and tyrannical are depicted as Voldemort and the Deatheaters. In May 2005, Slack and his friend, and fellow Harry Potter fan, Justin Oberman created a site, myspace.com/hpalliance, dedicated to discussing the parallels between Harry Potter and social justice. The site took off immediately, so Slack created the Harry Potter Alliance, made up of Potter fans and activists for social justice. With nearly six thousand members, the group has been able to bring the crisis in Darfur to a larger audience. Through concerts, comedy shows, and even a formal dance, they raised money and informed people through the myth of Potter. "I'm aware of how tragic the crisis in Darfur is and how something must be done. We want to connect the apathy around Voldemort's return to our government's apathy to the genocide in Darfur," said Andrew. "When I spoke about this parallel at one of our shows, people in the audience screamed, 'I want to fight for Dumbledore! Thank you for bringing up Darfur!'"

Andrea Strong, a New York City–based food writer, was provoked by Samantha Power's article about Darfur in *The New Yorker* and—again—Kristof's columns to do something positive. She originally planned a single large event, using her connections as a critic, to benefit the International Rescue Committee's work in Sudan. As two to three restaurants a day were contacting Strong to participate, Dining for Darfur transformed from one event into a nascent organization. At the first event in April 2006, more than sixty restaurants in New York, California, Hawaii, Massachusetts, Miami, and even Tokyo donated 5 percent of their gross sales (over $29,619) to IRC's humanitarian efforts in Darfur and on the border with Chad. A Dining for Darfur event in New York in August 2006 raised another $30,000 for IRC, and some restaurants participated in the organization's "Wine Out"— during the entire month of August profits from specific wines went to IRC. "People often feel paralyzed and unable to do something when these situations occur. This whole thing has shown me that it's possible to help and that it feels good in a personal way, even if that's selfish."

Janice Kamenir-Reznik, a fifty-three-year-old mom and former lawyer, is the chair of Jewish World Watch, a Los Angeles–based coalition of synagogues working together to mobilize other synagogues, their schools, their members, and the broader community to combat genocide and other egregious violations of human rights around the world.

Jewish World Watch began when Rabbi Harold Schulweis gave a sermon at Valley Beth Shalom in Los Angeles, where he stressed the need to globalize how the congregation thought of themselves as Jews. The words "Never Again" are used as a Jewish mantra, but it must really mean "no genocide" and be applied to all of humanity, not just to Jews. There have been several genocides since the Holocaust, and Rabbi Schulweis felt that his community did not do everything it could in the face of those horrific events. Therefore, he challenged his congregation to form an organization to educate and act on behalf of Darfur. He proposed the project and asked Kamenir-Reznik to chair the organization. Since it was launched in October 2004, Jewish World Watch has mobilized the Valley Beth Shalom community as well as twenty-four other synagogues and reaches nearly 100,000 people, more than half under the age of seventeen.

The organization focuses on activities in three areas: providing public education, advocacy, and refugee relief work. It provides a curriculum to teachers in Catholic, Jewish, and public schools in addition to sending guest speakers, putting on community events, and making presentations. Through petitions, letters, and postcards, Jewish World Watch works to influence policy makers. The organization has raised up to $150,000 for the International Medical Corps and its work in Darfur. Every $50,000 will stock medical clinics in Chad for refugees from Darfur. JWW funded two medical clinics that can service four hundred patients a day. Another $50,000 funded the building of ten water wells. This money was mainly raised by children in schools in the LA area. To achieve its goals, JWW has collaborated with Stop Genocide Now, Camp Ramah (a Jewish summer camp), and other religious organizations of different faiths.

Kamenir-Reznik says, "At the end of each day, I think about another eighty or so people we've touched or who read the article we got in the paper, and I can say today, this is what I did to force an agenda. If I do enough for a long enough period of time, I can influence public policy. 'Do unto your neighbor as you would have them do unto you.' I am taking words of the Torah to the road and applying them."

Perhaps the greatest challenge in creating a community of influence on issues like Darfur is sustaining energy and activism that can lead to lasting change. We've experienced periodic spurts of activism on Africa and atrocities, but not a sustainable long-term movement to hold politicians accountable for responding to and, ultimately, preventing mass violence against civilians wherever it occurs. Early in 2007, ENOUGH launched with the goal of building such a movement.

ENOUGH is a collaborative effort between John's employer, the International Crisis Group, and the organization Gayle Smith works for, the Center for American Progress (CAP). The campaign emerged out of a couple meetings that brought together a number of individuals from disparate backgrounds, united in their motivation to do more about Darfur and other crises.

Gayle and John have been friends for twenty years and were colleagues in the Clinton White House. As activists, they always dreamed of making atrocities prevention mean something to more Americans. As Gayle told us, "When I was in government, there was not a united constituency that pushed the U.S. to lead on these issues. There is a low level of understanding, a high level of indifference, and a sense of intractability about conflict and atrocities in Africa."

John and Gayle developed ENOUGH with support from Humanity United, an initiative started by Pam Omidyar in 2005 to help end mass atrocities, human trafficking, and slavery. Pam hosted a seminal meeting* in Las Vegas, bringing human rights advocates from around the world to brainstorm on how to build a wider and deeper movement to confront and prevent mass atrocities. Political strategist Tom Sheridan, Pam, and Randy Newcomb, a member of Pam's team who traveled with us to northern Uganda in 2005, helped devise the strategy for ENOUGH. The focus of the organization is to provide training, strategic support, and field-based policy recommendations to the diverse groups all over the country that are the building blocks for action on the issue of genocide and crimes against humanity, while working with others

---

*The other key meeting in the creation of ENOUGH was the meeting we both attended in New York that Don writes about at the end of Chapter Nine.

Join an Organization: Actions You Can Take

1. **Learn about ENOUGH (www.enoughproject.org) and the other organizations working for change.**
2. **Volunteer and attend meetings of organizations that have chapters in your area.**
3. **Encourage your family, friends, and colleagues to make the same commitment.**
4. **Start your own organization.**
5. **Coordinate with other groups to amplify your efforts.**

---

to build more cohesion and unity of purpose around the goal of creating a bigger, more effective movement over time.

"Right now it is not clear where the responsibility lies in the U.S. government for failing to respond to atrocities," Gayle told us. "What we need is more than incidental responses by activists. We need sustained pressure to change policy at a structural level and to invest more resources in fighting the conditions that give rise to crimes against humanity in the first place."

Indeed, enough is ENOUGH!

Strategy Six
"KEEP PUSHING AND PUSHING"—LOBBY THE GOVERNMENT

Beyond writing a letter or signing a petition, meeting with and personally talking with elected officials at the local, state, and national level is a way to give a face to the anti-genocide movement and to have a greater impact on the discussion. It may seem daunting at first, but making an appointment by yourself or with a local group to meet with your elected officials when they are visiting their home district offices can be a fruitful endeavor. These officials are there to listen to *you* as a voter and constituent; you have a *right* to meet with them and tell them what you think they should be doing. That is the way our political system works. If you don't use it, you lose the ability to influence it.

In 2005, a joint International Crisis Group and Zogby poll of likely voters found that the majority believe that ending the killing in Sudan is a U.S. responsibility. Most say more can be done diplomatically, and seven out of ten would back the creation of a U.S.-enforced no-fly zone to prevent Sudanese planes from bombing civilians. However, most politicians in Washington are probably unaware of these voters' personal opinions and are thus less likely to vote for or introduce what might be considered politically risky legislation without constituent pressure.

"I remember one instance, in Smith Center, Kansas, which has about five thousand people and is in the center-west of my state, during a town hall meeting, a lady came up to me after my speech, passionately asking about what are we doing about Sudan. There is a real grassroots movement of people who care about what we are doing," notes Senator Sam Brownback. Now imagine, if one woman in a small town can make an impression on a senator in Washington, what kind of impact could hundreds of thousands of citizens united in their outrage make on Washington policy makers?

An independent filmmaker and photographer, Mark Brecke, has documented events in Cambodia, Rwanda, Kosovo, and Iraq, as well as Sudan. He spent five weeks with the Sudanese Liberation Army (SLA) in Darfur. In 2004, Senator Brownback invited Mark to give a presentation to members of Congress. Rather than fly from his home in San Francisco to Washington, Brecke took the train and spent the three-day trip showing his photos of Darfur to other passengers. "Out of twenty-four interviews, only one person knew about what was going on in Darfur," Brecke told us. Many people wanted to know what the U.S. government and the UN were doing to stop the genocide. They wanted to know why the media wasn't covering such a massive human tragedy.

Brecke shot footage of the interviews and created a feature-length documentary called *They Turned Our Desert into Fire*.

Senator Brownback asked to hang Brecke's photographs on the walls of the Senate. Brecke, who continues to show his photographs around the country, explains, "These shows leave a greater impact and influence people to contact their member of Congress. I come from an experimental fine arts culture, and I'm an artist who has become a witness to history."

Richard Cizik is the vice president for public policy for the National Association of Evangelicals, which represents fifty-two denominations and 45,000 churches in the United States. In 2004, the NAE called on President Bush to authorize massive humanitarian aid to Darfur and "active exploration of all available intervention options—including sending troops to Darfur." While the current administration has yet to make all these moves, senior officials are concerned about the opinion expressed by evangelicals who represent a key segment of Bush's Christian support base. Previously, evangelicals' activism efforts have pushed the president to support efforts to fight AIDS and the trafficking of women, as well as to lead peace talks with southern Sudanese rebels. Evangelicals have come together with other faith-based groups and human rights organizations. This diverse coalition has brought important pressure on the Bush administration, though not yet enough to secure meaningful policy change.

Beth Riley is a stay-at-home mom with three kids in Fort Wayne, Indiana. She first heard about Darfur through news reports. She thought the situation was horrible but "didn't know what to do." Then, when talking with her friends in her mothers of preschoolers group about how to help victims of the tsunami, she brought up Darfur. She typed up a couple of information sheets and brought them, along with a letter that she found on the Internet, from a Darfurian refugee who questioned how the world could respond to the tragedy of the tsunami and not the tragedy in Sudan, and she met with her pastor, asking what the church could do. She then developed a bulletin insert and a petition for people to sign at Sunday services. Riley made copies of the signed

Lobby the Government: Actions You Can Take

1. Find out your representative's record on Darfur. Visit www.darfurscores.org to learn about each member of Congress's individual voting record.

2. Make an appointment to see your national representatives when they are in your area, or get a group together and travel to Washington, D.C., for a lobby day. Making an appointment to meet with Congress isn't as tough as it sounds. You voted for them and you have a right to tell them exactly how you feel about the issues that matter to you.

3. Visit city council members and state representatives and encourage them to divest and pass a resolution urging stronger action to end genocide in Darfur and atrocities wherever they occur.

4. Urge your elected officials to speak publicly about Darfur.

5. Keep sending those personal letters to Congress, the president, and key officials like the secretary of state, secretary of defense, and national security advisor.

petition and sent them to her representative and two senators, as well as Secretary of State Condoleezza Rice. She also faxed the petition to members of the House International Relations and Senate Foreign Relations Committees. Her pastor mailed the bulletin inserts to congressional representatives and other Methodist churches in Fort Wayne to encourage a similar effort. Since then, she has begun writing op-eds, calling the local news outlets, and circulating more petitions through additional churches, one of which she hand-delivered to Senator Richard Lugar's office.

You have the power to affect real change—change that can save and improve thousands of lives. Through seemingly simple gestures, and large coordinated efforts, you can use the strategies discussed to demand a better, more secure future for those suffering in Darfur and beyond.

Few public officials have spoken as forcefully about the need for greater citizen action to end the genocide than Mukesh Kapila, the upstanding former UN humanitarian coordinator for Sudan we told you about in Chapter 4. In July 2006 he offered these inspiring words:

> People can show solidarity by not forgetting. One of the most terrible and depressing things when you are a refugee or an internally displaced person from a war like this is you feel completely forgotten. You feel that you are stuck there somewhere in a camp in the middle of nowhere and the world has simply passed you by. And that, more than anything else, takes everything away from you. So help; don't forget; and bring pressure on the authorities to do what must be done.

DON:

"*Y*ou *knew Petey Green, huh?*"
     This cabbie is sixty-plus at least, old enough to remember Petey Green well. His next statement is icing on the cake.

     "*Knew his daddy too. My daddy and him used to run together,*" *he adds, turning left on K Street. "He was a bad mother too, man. Dangerous.*"

     I wish I could drive around with him all day, but I'm late for my meeting with John, the crew, and Minni Minnawi, the SLA rebel leader from Darfur.

     The cabbie pulls up at the hotel and drops me off. I thank him for the history lesson and turn right into the lens of a camera.

     "*Oh, right, we're making a documentary.*" *I step off to the right so Sus can mike me while I scan the general area looking for my partner in crime. Ted (director Theodore Braun) reads my mind.*

     "*He's not here yet.*"

     "*Good thing I rushed.*"

"But there's Minni over there."

Ted points across the walk to a little table just off to the side that is surrounded by many African men in suits. They are very animated, each man interrupting the other, speech in high gear, gestures sharp, cutting through the air and whatever last argument was just brought up. Ted's quick on the uptake.

"Dark gray suit."

"Got it."

I sit down at the little table on our side of the walkway staring at this rebel leader. He's a rebel leader? Minni Minnawi looks very statesmanlike. They all do. Sitting at the table under the umbrella sipping coffee, these men don't remotely conjure images of freedom fighters storming through the desert sands firing automatic weapons at an invading army. They look more like a delegation of politicians or group of lawyers debating some contentious ruling.

Ted catches Minni's eye and he comes over, cell phone pressed to his ear.

"I'm going up," he reports and turns on his heel, several of the men following him. I see the soldiers in them now, men dutifully guarding their leader's flank as he advances, five or so hanging back to secure the rear, all flowing like clockwork. As I sit staring, trying to guess each of their ranks, John comes casually strolling up the sidewalk believing he's the first one here. I tell the cameras to swing around, wanting to document the moment, a safeguard against future "tardiness" denials.

"Buddy." It's his regular salutation.

"You're late" is becoming mine. "I'm going to get you a watch."

"Got one. See?" He shows me his BlackBerry.

"Do you know how the clock thingie works?"

This goes back and forth for a couple of beats while

*John gets miked up, and then we're headed upstairs with
our crew to interview Minni.*

*I'm slightly nervous about this one. From everything I've
learned about the situation in Darfur as of late, it is a
crumbling house of cards. Minni is in a particularly difficult
position, having signed a peace agreement with the
Sudanese government that none of the other rebel parties
have agreed to, citing its lack of enforceable protections.
The treaty has been largely criticized for leaving the
responsibility for disarming the Janjaweed up to the
government of Sudan—the same government that armed
the militia in the first place. Without the oversight of an independent UN peacekeeping force, few people believe the
agreement could have real teeth. This inexorable division
has resulted in such intense infighting between the rebel
factions and has become so widespread that thousands
more Darfurians are being displaced, and the zones where
people felt even a remote sense of security are shrinking
rapidly. What we're seeing is the employment of a classic
tactic of those in power, one it seems that almost never
fails: divide and conquer. With the rebels splintered and
Minni's faction of the SLA potentially coopted, the
Khartoum regime can more easily suffocate the
insurrection, much of its dirty work handled by the very
people originally opposing the government for its violent
and unlawful practices. How do you broach such touchy
subject matter? Are we about to be interviewing a man
caught desperately between a rock and a hard place, a
freedom fighter only doing what he believes to be right,
facing down incredible odds for the betterment of his
people? Or is this man a turncoat aligning himself with
those who promised to fill his coffers in payment for terrible
deeds exacted on defenseless Darfurians? Only two things I
am sure of: (1) I do not know the answer, and (2) I am
anxious, apprehensive even, to hear his reply.*

We ride up in the elevator strategizing. We want to ask questions that we can get answers to. However, we are well aware that if our fears of Minni's about-face are true, this may be a go-nowhere, learn-nothing conversation filled with doublespeak and subterfuge. John is particularly keen to ask Minni about reports from his own field staff and from Amnesty International about various human rights violations in the displaced camps, perpetrated by Minni's faction of fighters, the most egregious being the rape of several indigenous aid workers. I hope this soldier ain't packing today.

When we enter Minni's hotel room, it is immediately evident that if the Khartoum government is paying him, it is a paltry sum. The cramped room can barely fit the two double beds and armoire, let alone the two of us, our small camera, sound guy, and Ted. As our interview begins, Ted in fact has to retreat to the closet to give us sufficient room.

We ask softball questions at first: "How are things in the region now?" "What is the condition of your fighters?" etc. We get the expected softball answers, then slowly segue to more substantive matters. When asked about the peace accord, Minni takes pains to tell us that we must remember that his is not the only signature that appears on the agreement, citing the AU, EU, Germany, Great Britain, and the Arab League as signatories as well, demanding of us that we hold all parties accountable for the success or failure of the peace.

"Speaking of accountability . . ."

Uh-oh, here we go. John sits forward in his chair.

"What do you have to say about reports coming out of Darfur of your men colluding with the Sudanese army and committing human rights violations, rape specifically?"

For the first time, Minni's voice rises, strenuously denying the accusations, calling them "lies and propaganda" fabricated by those who oppose him. I'm an all right poker player but can no more tell if he's speaking honestly or lying through his teeth. Minni definitely appears upset, but that could be the result either of being caught or of his rank and file being wrongly accused. But the door has been thrown open, so I venture in and ask:

"Given the fact that you are basically under siege, fighting on two fronts at once, what do you believe the future holds?"

There's a pause as he considers it; his answer is as universal a truth as any stated today.

"I don't know."

There's little else to add, so John and I wrap it up and say our good-byes.

John is mumbling to himself as we walk down the hall.

"You don't believe a word he said, do you?" I ask him.

"That report isn't wrong. He's on the other side now. He's becoming a government lackey, which will end up just killing more Darfurians."

We walk in silence as the true depth of the instability sinks in.

Months later, after John returns from Sudan for a 60 Minutes piece on the crisis in Darfur, he leaves me a voice mail.

"Hey. Just got back. You sitting down? Minni Minnawi and his people are now basically acting as one of the wings of the Sudanese army. They're preparing to mount an offensive at the end of this month. Tell you more about it when I see you."

And the hits just keep on coming.

9

Stop Mass Atrocities Now:
An Agenda for Change

*In Germany they came first for the Communists, and I
didn't speak up because I wasn't a Communist. Then
they came for the Jews, and I didn't speak up because I
wasn't a Jew. Then they came for the trade unionists,
and I didn't speak up because I wasn't a trade unionist.
Then they came for the Catholics, and I didn't speak
up because I was a Protestant. Then they came for me,
and by that time, no one was left to speak up.*
—PASTOR MARTIN NIEMOLLER

Darfur and other crises marked by mass atrocities can seem
overwhelmingly complex and insoluble. But the truth is that
they can be ended. If the United States and other governments—
working directly and through the United Nations—have sufficient
political will, they can work with concerned African governments
to make a difference in conflict-plagued countries. How we influence political will was the subject of Chapters 6, 7, and 8. What
needs to happen once we have the political will to act is the subject
of this chapter.

It is not an exaggeration to say that a modern-day holocaust is
well under way in Congo, northern Uganda, Somalia, and Sudan,

with well over 6 million freshly dug graves over the last two decades. Unless the world responds more urgently, the death toll will continue to mount.

These four cases represent the four deadliest, most brutal conflicts in Africa, and arguably the world, over the last decade or so. They certainly represent some of the most heinous atrocities seen during the last century of warfare. They are also the biggest generators of human displacement globally.

We've already covered Darfur in detail. The following is a short introduction to what at the time of writing are the other three most destructive conflicts in Africa: Congo, northern Uganda, and Somalia. None of them can be defined as genocidal, but the crimes against humanity committed are at times just as deadly as Darfur's violence has been. We provide more information in the ENOUGH campaign website (www.enoughproject. org) for those of you who want to learn—or do—more about these crises. We hope that will include YOU!

Congo, 1996–Present

Imagine if the entire population of the city of Los Angeles was slowly wiped out, community by community. The media would be transfixed, and we would all surely know who was suffering, where it was happening, and why. Yet since 1996 some 4 million people have lost their lives in the lush rain-forest landscapes of the Democratic Republic of the Congo, and how many of us have heard of places like Goma, Bukavu, or Bunia?

The current conflict in the Congo has many of its roots in the rolling hills of neighboring Rwanda, where hundreds of thousands of souls are laid to rest. Eleven years after genocide tore through Rwanda, many of those killers washed up in neighboring Congo, where the blood still flows. When Rwanda and Uganda invaded the Congo for the second time in 1998 (having done so in 1996 to overthrow the dictator Mobutu Sese Seko), the assault sparked a regional conflict that many people dubbed Africa's First

World War. Men and children with guns flooded into Congo, and militia thugs killed and displaced civilians on a massive scale.

A peace deal was struck in 2003 that established a power-sharing arrangement between rival warring factions, but the violence in eastern Congo continued. Levels of sexual assault in eastern Congo rival any in the world. Amid increased reports of kidnappings and sexual slavery, soldiers and other armed men continue to tax, harass, loot, and rape local populations. Humanitarian-aid delivery is a monumental challenge. The constant cycles of displacement experienced by Congolese civilians have left most communities on the knife edge of survival, and the predatory presence of the armed groups ensures that unacceptable mortality rates, with people denied the medical help they need, will remain among the highest in the world.

Northern Uganda, 1986–Present

In early 2005, we traveled together to northern Uganda with a television crew from ABC's *Nightline*. Around the world, children face all manner of depredations, but the stories we heard in northern Uganda may be among the most horrific ever told.

For nearly twenty years, the Ugandan government has been involved in armed conflict with the rebel group called the Lord's Resistance Army (LRA). As we discussed in Chapter 3, the LRA, which is on the U.S. government's list of terrorist organizations, was primarily supported for over a decade by the Sudanese government, to terrorize the southern Sudanese. The LRA's pattern of widespread atrocities sparked the first investigation into crimes against humanity by the International Criminal Court (ICC). In July 2005, the ICC issued warrants for the arrest of LRA leader Joseph Kony and four of his top lieutenants.

John has traveled many times to northern Uganda and spoken directly with LRA commanders. They tell John that Joseph Kony is rooted in a grotesquely distorted view of the Old Testament. He thinks of himself as a modern-day Moses, imposing the Ten

Commandments on people who refuse to obey him. Kony's "philosophy," if you can call it that, is eye-for-an-eye. In seeking revenge against the Ugandan government for past transgressions against northerners, Kony believes that he is instructed by God to attack and punish civilians who collaborate with the government.

The LRA's extreme brutality has displaced 1.6 million Ugandans, and its attacks on civilians continue. As Don told *Nightline,* "The LRA has a particularly ugly way of replenishing its ranks, kidnapping. Their targets are children between the ages of eight and fourteen. Rebels raid villages, stealing what they need and burning the rest. According to UN estimates, more than thirty thousand children have been forced into the service of the LRA since 1994."

In 2005, the LRA expanded into eastern Congo, further adding to that tortured country's many problems. Without more international support for a credible peace process and a mechanism to effectively protect civilians from the predators that lurk in the night, the children of northern Uganda, eastern Congo, and southern Sudan will be condemned to a living nightmare of abduction, torture, rape, and murder.

A renewed peace process that began in July 2006 offers a glimmer of hope for long-suffering northern Ugandans, but the United States has been absent from the negotiating table. The government of southern Sudan, a semi-autonomous entity created by the north-south peace deal in Sudan, is leading the mediation efforts, but the mediators need support from the international community. The United States could have demonstrated its commitment to end this conflict by sending a senior diplomat to support the process. If the talks don't succeed, the United States will regret not having made the effort to bring this nightmare to a peaceful end.

Somalia, 1991–Present

John has traveled to Somalia regularly for the past two decades and witnessed that country's free fall into anarchy and human suffering. His first trip was in the 1980s, before the disastrous military intervention that led to the infamous "Black Hawk Down" battle in 1993 in which eighteen American servicemen were killed. Back then, the U.S. government was still propping up a warlord dictator to support Cold War interests and ignoring widespread human rights abuses. As a young activist, John was appalled that his government would allow defenseless Somali civilians to be cannon fodder in a strategic battle with the Soviets.

Following the collapse of the Soviet Union, the Somali government imploded in 1991, and efforts to create a new government have consistently collapsed into new bouts of bloodletting. After the Black Hawk Down battle, the U.S. and UN troops withdrew over the following year, and largely absented themselves from concerted efforts at rebuilding a functioning central authority. Somalia is the very definition of a failed state, the only country in the world without a government, and millions of Somalis deal with chronic drought and hunger without the safety net of a functioning polity.

After September 11, 2001, the U.S. government feared that this failed state would become a safe haven for al-Qaeda terrorists, and there are some terror suspects living in Somalia. Al-Qaeda operatives have used Somalia as a base from which to plan and launch devastating terrorist attacks in the Horn of Africa. These attacks include the bombings of U.S. embassies in Kenya and Tanzania, the bombing of a hotel on the Kenya coast, an attempt to shoot down an Israeli passenger jet with a surface-to-air missile in Kenya, and a foiled attempt to crash a plane into the new U.S. embassy in Kenya.

Somalis have appealed to the U.S. government for assistance in building a functioning state, but U.S. policy has focused exclusively on capturing or killing terrorists. During John's most recent trips to Somalia, he saw evidence of covert U.S. support for warlords—some of the same warlords responsible for killing U.S. Army Rangers in 1993—in hopes that they will capture terrorist suspects. Unfortunately for Somalis, the United States and its allies in the global war on terror have not even tried to develop solutions to the statelessness, poverty, and despair that have allowed violent extremism to take root. The United States should be doing everything in its power to crack down on terrorist networks in Somalia, but the current policy approach has turned ordinary Somalis against the United States and increased the power of Islamic extremists.

In 2006, the weakness of U.S. strategy was exposed when militias loyal to a loose network of Islamic courts routed the warlord allies of the Bush administration. The Islamists, some of them associated with al-Qaeda, captured control of much of southern Somalia and threatened a holy war against Somalia's neighbor, and longtime enemy, Ethiopia, which in turn invaded and overthrew the Islamist authority. Catastrophic conflict looms, violent ideology spreads, and terrorist networks infiltrate Somalia, where men and boys with guns act as judges, juries, and executioners for ordinary Somalis trying to survive.

Root Causes

The roots of these four conflicts (Sudan, Congo, northern Uganda, and Somalia) are similar to those of other wars all over the world, whether in Chechnya, the former Yugoslavia, Colombia, Cambodia, or the Middle East.

The first reason for violent conflict is political exclusion. Wars don't usually start without a cause. That cause is usually rooted in a particular ethnic, regional, religious, or political group that feels excluded or marginalized from power. For example, Darfurians and southern Sudanese certainly rebelled because of deep-seated grievances that drove thousands of people in both these places to pick up a gun and fight for their rights.

The second reason for violent conflict is greed. In conflicts around the world, those in power control the access to resources—whether natural or state—and they are often not inclined to share. It should come as no surprise then that these economic disparities are a driver for conflict. In some cases, wars begin for bigger principles but slowly transform into predatory warlordism, where armed groups take advantage of conflict and chaos as much as they possibly can. Some of the greatest predators in the world in the last century hail from this region: the Janjaweed militias in Darfur, other militias in eastern Congo and Somalia, and the Lord's Resistance Army rebels from northern Uganda.

The third reason for violent conflict is impunity. In so many countries stricken by conflict, there is no accountability, no rule of law. Governments or rebels, or even militias, without a cause commit unspeakable crimes against humanity, with no penalty, no sanction. The message is clear: you can kill as many people as you want, and there will be no consequence.

The Three Ps of Confronting Mass Atrocities

Earlier in the book we talked about the haunting similarities in how and why genocides and mass atrocities are committed and what the international community does (or does not do) in response. However, there is one critical difference between past genocides in Rwanda and Bosnia and the crises unfolding today in Sudan, Congo, northern Uganda, and Somalia: THERE IS STILL TIME TO ACT TO END THE SUFFERING.

Despite the almost ritualistic pledge of "Never Again," no coherent international system or process is in place for responding to genocide and other atrocities. What does exist is chaotic and marked by futile finger-pointing, while the slaughter continues. Passing resolutions in the UN Security Council that have no teeth (e.g., no punitive measures focused on accountability for the commission of mass atrocities) will certainly not influence the calculations of mass murderers. Left uninfluenced, the Sudanese government's killing will not end in Darfur, and any African Union troops that might remain there will continue to have front-row seats for the slaughter.

The real lesson of the past decade and a half dealing with the regime in Khartoum is that trying to gently persuade and offer incentives to mass murderers doesn't work. It is a pragmatic government; it will do what it must in order to survive. Only when Sudan has been the target of serious punitive pressure aimed at stopping the atrocities will the regime modify its behavior. UN Security

Council sanctions led by the United States in the 1990s proved that; Khartoum renounced its ties with al-Qaeda and other terrorist organizations as a direct result. The lesson couldn't be clearer, but it has been completely ignored in the context of Darfur.

Ultimately, those committing mass atrocities must understand that punitive action will be avoided or removed only if they stop killing people and obstructing peace.

As the ENOUGH campaign has stressed, we need to *make them pay* for their crimes.

The genocide in Rwanda took one hundred days to exterminate 800,000 lives. Darfur and these other cases are Rwandas in slow motion. In Darfur, up to 400,000 lives have been extinguished in three years. There is a clear path out of this quagmire of death and destruction. The killing could stop tomorrow if the United States led the world in pressing forward the agenda encapsulated in the Three Ps of genocide prevention: Protection, Punishment, and Peacemaking. The United States has the ability and capacity to lead the world in responding in these three arenas. It is only a question of political will as to whether that will happen. We the people have a say in this. The Three Ps:

1. Protecting the People

The inability to protect human life when it is threatened en masse is the most significant failure of the international community. In Darfur and elsewhere, the world usually defers to the state authority to carry out that protection function in the context of the international legal principle of state sovereignty. But it is often the states themselves that are perpetrating the mass atrocities, or at least encouraging them or standing idly by while they happen.

It is like the fox guarding the hen house, and in many cases the fox happens to be rabid.

Sometimes, protection of civilians can be achieved without the use of force. The presence of human rights monitors and protection officers from humanitarian agencies can, in some cases, provide limited protection to potential victims. The deployment of international officials and their strong protection advocacy with the relevant authorities can have a deterrent effect on would-be attackers. A word of caution, though: in most cases where mass atrocities are being perpetrated, protection by presence is inadequate and only provides an alibi for those governments and institutions that don't want to do more.

Many of us peace and human rights advocates are rightly reluctant about the use of force. We need to get over it. There is such a thing as evil in this world, and sometimes the only way to confront evil is through the judicious use of military force. As long as the use of that force is accountable, multilateral, and focused on stopping the further suffering of victims, then we advocates of peace and justice need to be prepared to support the legitimate and discriminate use of force. Another word of caution: force needs to be deployed very carefully, or it has the capacity to make matters worse. Every situation is different. Sometimes the use of force—undertaken at the wrong time or in the wrong manner—can further inflame a crisis. A strong knowledge and understanding of the local context is critical to the successful application of external military force to protect people.

The key to protecting civilians from atrocities is supporting international institutions to enhance their capacity to do so *and* building the political will in the international community to take the necessary action. In cases like Darfur and Congo:

- IF we want to protect women from the ongoing scourge of mass rape,
- IF we want to protect villages from being attacked and burned, and
- IF we want to help millions of people return to their homes someday,
- THEN peacekeeping operations have to be capable, well trained, able to operate together, well equipped, and given a mandate specifically to protect civilian life. Strong U.S. diplomatic leadership is necessary to achieve this.

The Challenge to Protect Civilians in Darfur

At the outset of the Darfur crisis, only the African Union volunteered to send troops to Darfur to help end the fighting. Two years into their deployment, it was clear that the job was too big for this fledgling organization to handle. Given the Sudanese government's stated opposition to a UN transition, by mid-2006 the African Union reached a significant fork in the road for its Darfur deployment and the future of the organization. Either it would take control of its own destiny or continue to allow itself to be manipulated by the Sudanese regime, losing credibility with each passing week.

The AU had been a perpetual supplicant up until then, having to beg every month for assistance even to pay its troops. International donors, including the United States, had promised to fully fund the mission but simply didn't deliver. By continuing a halfhearted, under-resourced, and insufficiently mandated deployment with too few troops to make a difference, the AU was just providing an excuse for inaction by the UN Security Council, without doing enough to be able to protect a critical mass of civilians.

At the end of 2006, faced with the prospect of a crushing failure in its first major test as an organization, the AU had to make a decision, to decide whether to announce a date for handover to the UN or to withdraw its forces altogether from Sudan. Instead, it simply extended the mission for another six months, missing an opportunity to act boldly and regain some leverage that it had lost as the mission drifted and Darfur continued to burn.

As an AU officer expressed to John, "When you are walking and not going anywhere, it is time to stop. The time for the UN to come in is now. I am African, but I have to admit that we cannot do that job with the existing resources and mandate."

The organization will be increasingly necessary to prevent and confront atrocities across the continent. However, it could become a scapegoat for what has been a truly international failure in Darfur. The regime in Khartoum has taken the AU for a ride. It used the AU for its counterinsurgency and peace-breaking purposes. It divided Africa and the international community by forwarding the fantasy that only the AU could do the job. An AU officer told John, "The government of Sudan wants to keep a weak AU."

The AU has to stand up and decline to be anyone's tool anymore, and just as importantly the UN Security Council has to take up its core agenda to address great threats to international peace and security. The UN should provide the foundation of any response to mass atrocities wherever they occur on the face of the earth. Africa cannot be an exception. The capacity of the AU should indeed be developed, but it should occur under the umbrella of the UN. Any other approach once again makes Africa the exception to the rule, and subject to the whims of donors and politicians everywhere.

2. Punishing the Perpetrators

For sixty years, the international community has struggled to find the means to punish the perpetrators of genocide, war crimes, and crimes against humanity. Until now, efforts have been ad hoc, from Nuremberg to the international tribunals in Rwanda and Yugoslavia, to the special courts in Sierra Leone and Cambodia. But now we have a historic opportunity to chart a new legal course through the newly created International Criminal Court (ICC). The ICC's first three cases, not surprisingly, are the Congo, northern Uganda, and Darfur—the three deadliest conflicts in the world.

The ICC issued its first indictments for the top five rebel leaders of the rebel Lord's Resistance Army (LRA), responsible for the highest child abduction rate in the world over the last decade. The ICC issued its first indictment in Congo for a warlord who has destabilized the northeast part of that country for years as he plundered the region's natural resource wealth. In addition, in March 2005, the ICC had a case referred to it for the first time by the United Nations Security Council; it regarded Darfur.

The best post-Nuremberg chance at institutionalizing accountability is at stake in these, the ICC's first three cases: northern Uganda, Congo, and Darfur. Failure in these three will ensure that impunity reigns supreme, that warlords like those in Somalia and elsewhere will feel no deterrence, and that international justice will have little meaning. The direct effect that would have on peace processes and implementation of peace agreements would be catastrophic.

Though it has not ratified the international treaty in support of the ICC, the United States could still provide valuable information and intelligence to the ICC about specific targets for prosecution. The United States has the best intelligence in the world, and sharing some of it with the ICC would help accelerate efforts to indict the most heinous war criminals. It is simply unacceptable that the United States acts as a bystander while this historic attempt at justice slowly moves forward.

The only chance we have for U.S. participation and cooperation is through concerted, coordinated citizen action. Making our voices heard to our members of Congress and to the president is vital. It is a political decision whether the United States shares information and intelligence with the ICC or not. We need to raise the political cost of noncompliance. We need to shame the U.S. government until it provides help to the ICC.

In addition to the ICC, two other tools of punishment are key to ensuring that would-be future war criminals are deterred from their atrocities: targeted sanctions and divestment.

The UN Security Council can impose sanctions that are targeted on specific individuals accused of war crimes. This usually involves freezing assets and banning travel, the equivalent of an international scarlet letter that has variable impacts depending on how much the targeted individual cares about such penalties. Divestment is covered in Chapters 7 and 8; it involves campaigning to convince institutions, governments, and mutual funds to divest themselves of all stock holding in companies doing business with governments committing mass atrocities. Sudan is currently being targeted, much as apartheid South Africa was in the 1980s and early 1990s.

Again, at a minimum, we must make them pay for their crimes.

3. Promoting the Peace

U.S. influence and diplomacy can have profoundly positive consequences in resolving deadly conflict, and the most cost-effective
initiative the United States could undertake in the entire arena of
foreign policy worldwide would be to put a few more seasoned
peacemakers in action in conflicts around the globe. The United
States and its allies put extraordinary energy and money into
cleaning up the messes caused by war and atrocities—literally billions of dollars in humanitarian and other aid—but in many of
these places the international community barely lifts a finger to
try to address the causes.

In this regard, there is not much difference between what the
United States does locally and what it does abroad.

However, successful examples of peacemaking abound.

JOHN:

*When I worked for President Clinton, I had the honor
of working with the president's special envoys
working to end Africa's wars. One of the things I liked most
about the former president was that he was special
envoy–crazy in the best of ways. He wanted the United
States to promote peace wherever it could.*

*Former national security advisor Tony Lake was asked
by the president to be one of these special envoys, and he
volunteered two years of his life to negotiate between
Ethiopia and Eritrea. The war between them was the
world's deadliest between 1998 and 2000. Through Lake's
determination, backed by U.S. leverage, we got a deal. The
guns went silent immediately, and have remained so right
up until the time of this writing. I served on Lake's team
during the entire process, along with Gayle Smith, Susan
Rice, and Lt. Col. Mike Bailey.*

*I learned a lot about what the United States can
accomplish when it commits to an honorable objective.
With Lake's gravitas and connections, we were able to*

increase our intelligence-gathering capacities and diplomatic energy in support of the peace process. We would begin every negotiating session with an authoritative military briefing that let everyone know that we knew as much as they did and that we wouldn't be snookered by the usual BS slung in the context of negotiations processes. We worked very closely with partners from the African Union (formerly the Organization of African Unity) and the European Union, so there was total unanimity within the international community. U.S. leadership, in close partnership with Africa, ended that war, and the cost to the United States was negligible.

Nelson Mandela acted as an African envoy in support of conflict resolution in the tiny, violence-wracked nation of Burundi. President Clinton named former congressman Howard Wolpe as his special envoy for the region. Howard worked closely with President Mandela and the European Union special envoy, Aldo Ajello. We worked closely on strategy and brought leverage to the table. Mandela successfully brokered a peace deal that has largely held up for years.

I have some amazing memories of traveling with Howard in support of the negotiations process in both Burundi and Congo. We had to regularly consult with President Mandela, or "Madiba" as he is fondly known in South Africa. At his home during these consultations, he would insist on serving us tea himself despite the toll the years and his imprisonment had taken on his body. He is the most gracious and infectiously friendly person I have ever been in the presence of, but his smile belies a steely interior when it comes to negotiating. In the sessions at his home, his phone would ring incessantly, with world leaders asking for his advice or his blessing on a dizzying array of issues, about which he always had an opinion.

When the United States seriously partners with its

African colleagues, we can make a huge difference in promoting peace throughout the continent. We have talented diplomats and other dignitaries who would gladly serve in the capacity of envoys of the president and the American people in the search for peace in Africa.

I've also had the opportunity to work on peace processes with African colleagues as a private citizen. In 1999, in between my time at the National Security Council and the State Department, I traveled with my former White House colleague Shawn McCormick and the imam of Sankore Mosque in Timbuktu, Abass Haidara, on a multi-country mission aimed at securing the signature of the final holdout Congolese rebel group for the Congo peace deal. After a week of flying around by private jet to meet the heads of state throughout the region, we spent a day with the rebel leadership in eastern Congo, gaming out their options and presenting arguments as to why they should move forward and sign. Coincidence or not, they signed the next day.

Another private-sector peace initative I was involved with was the effort to initiate a legitimate peace process for northern Uganda. I worked closely during 2004–2006 with Uganda's unofficial mediator, Betty Bigombe, who hails from the north of the country and is trusted by both sides like no one else on the planet. We came up with the first set of comprehensive peace proposals that had been generated in the nearly two-decade war. We didn't succeed, but we helped lay the groundwork for the efforts of the government of southern Sudan as it took the mantle and initiated the first state-sponsored peace process between the LRA and the government in nineteen years.

In both Sierra Leone and Liberia, the Economic Community of West African States (the west African regional organization) tried alone to address these two interlinked crises and failed. However, when the broader international community—led by the United States and the United Kingdom—joined more closely in partnership with ECOWAS, both ugly wars were brought to an end.

In southern Sudan, the United States and Europe worked closely for a decade with the east African regional organization IGAD (Inter-Governmental Authority on Development) to broker a peace deal ending the two-decade-long civil war there. President Bush overrode objections within his administration to name a special envoy and chose former senator Jack Danforth, who helped bring the leverage of the White House to the process. It cost the U.S. taxpayers almost nothing and brought tremendous results for the people of southern Sudan.

As of mid-2006, President Bush's advisors continued to resist naming special envoys for the crises in Congo, Somalia, and northern Uganda, but were divided on Darfur. In response to enormous pressure from Congress and key American constituency groups, the president finally named Andrew Natsios as his special envoy for Sudan. The resistance to naming envoys for these conflicts seemed to come from the officials in the administration who would feel diminished by such appointments, and by an attitude among many that Africans should solve their own problems. Of course we are not going to unilaterally solve these crises, but the United States can help facilitate dialogue leading to solutions, for pennies of the cost of humanitarian or military cleanup operations.

Diplomats can also do more to prevent atrocities by making use of the incredible amount of information available at their fingertips and engaging in preventive diplomacy. In 1994, policy makers clung to the line that they "didn't have enough information" to prevent or respond quickly to the Rwandan genocide. If it was difficult to imagine that in 1994, then it is completely preposterous today. The United States and other nations knew exactly what was happening in Darfur in 2003, yet, for a number of reasons (the counterterrorism partnership between the United States and the Sudanese regime foremost among them), they failed to take the necessary steps to put diplomatic pressure on the government of Sudan to end the killing, and continued to do so for the following three years.

U.S. influence, creativity, leverage, and direct involvement, when utilized for good, can have profoundly positive consequences in resolving deadly conflict.

Where You Fit In

In response to a major advocacy push in the spring of 2005, we had our first three victories in the campaign to confront genocide in Darfur, after two years of policy gridlock. The Security Council finally authorized targeted sanctions on those committing atrocities in the region and referred the case of Darfur to the International Criminal Court for investigation into crimes against humanity. And in April 2005, Harvard University became the first university to divest all of its stock holdings in companies doing business with Sudan. It set off a slow but steady chain reaction all over the country, from universities to state pension funds.

Those were the first baby steps. All three happened because a growing chorus of voices in the United States was demanding more substantial action. However, as time went on, implementing those measures proved difficult. The Security Council didn't have the courage to impose the sanctions it had authorized on any significant official in Khartoum, and the United States didn't share information and intelligence with the ICC to help accelerate the process of gathering evidence necessary for indictments. Without creating a cost for the killing, it proved hugely challenging to convince these same killers in Khartoum to allow a United Nations force into Darfur to protect the civilian targets.

The strategic counterterrorism relationship between the United States and Sudan is probably the largest, though unspoken, factor in why there has not been a more robust global response to Darfur. As during the Cold War, the United States puts short-term strategic advance at the expense of long-term solutions. However, there is grass roots political pressure on the Bush administration to do something about Darfur, so the administration in Washington seems to want to do the minimal necessary to appear to be doing something effective. This cannot be allowed to stand. Only greater pressure on our elected officials will produce the kind of policy change necessary to stop the killing in Sudan.

In May 2005, the International Crisis Group and the Zogby International polling firm teamed up to conduct a public opinion survey of one thousand Americans, to ascertain public attitudes toward Darfur and what the United States response should be. The participants represented diverse political views, religious beliefs, incomes, and ethnic backgrounds. Yet American public opinion is more united on halting genocide in Darfur—and preventing mass atrocities wherever they occur—than on many other foreign policy issues. An overwhelming 84 percent of respondents said the United States shouldn't tolerate an extremist government like that in Sudan committing such attacks, and should use its military assets, short of committing United States combat troops, to help bring them to a halt. Eighty-one percent supported tough sanctions on Sudanese officials who control the Janjaweed militias, 80 percent supported establishing a no-fly zone over Darfur to prevent the deadly bombing raids by the Sudanese air force, and 91 percent said the United States should work with the International Criminal Court to help bring to justice those accused of crimes against humanity.

Clearly, there is a strong constituency throughout the United States for doing more, which could be tapped and expanded. We are not alone.

After the April 30, 2006, Rally to Stop Genocide in Washington, D.C., President Bush dispatched his deputy secretary of state Robert Zoellick to Nigeria to work on the Darfur peace talks. After two years, the peace process was often drifting, but in less than a week Zoellick was able to help strike a deal between the government of Sudan and one of the three Darfurian rebel factions. He presented letters from President Bush to the rebel leaders, urging them to sign the deal. Although the deal was incomplete and ultimately inadequate, this episode demonstrated that when the United States chooses to really engage, we can make a huge difference. Unfortunately, in this case, the engagement was not sustained. Thus, the inadequacies of the deal were not addressed and the two non-signatory rebel groups didn't come on board. Sustaining peace efforts is as important as launching them, as this example so aptly demonstrates, since the truncated and incomplete effort actually made matters worse in Darfur.

We need to build a network focused on practical, country-specific responses. It must be framed by a collective embrace of the international "responsibility to protect" and of the imperative to prevent and resolve conflicts. The concept of "responsibility to protect" demands more assertive action—including, when necessary, military intervention—in situations marked by mass atrocities. Instead of putting the onus of responsibility on outsiders to intervene, this new concept focuses on the importance of authorities to protect those who are being victimized, and if local actors cannot or choose not to do so, *then* external action is legitimized. Actions can include economic, diplomatic, or military measures. Though many governments accept this concept in principle, when actually confronted with a situation in real time, like Darfur, most come up with excuses or reasons why the activation of this responsibility to protect must be delayed. And the longer action is delayed, the more people die.

As Samantha Power writes, we need to create a political cost for ignoring these issues. Without that cost, people being victimized by mass atrocities will be totally subject to the will of politicians, which, absent strong support from constituents, almost always leads to nice speeches but no action.

We can use the Six Strategies for Effective Change: Raise Awareness, Raise Funds, Write a Letter, Call for Divestment, Join an Organization, and Lobby the Government. With these tools, we can build the network, increase pressure on the United States and other governments to act quickly and appropriately, and ensure that the political costs for inaction will always be too great.

DON:

Tomorrow is November 29, my birthday, and it is shaping up to be unlike any other. Starting today, I've traveled to the Big Apple to attend an International Crisis Group awards lunch at the University Club on Fifty-fourth Street in Manhattan. They are honoring Paul Rusesabagina with one of the countless awards he has received since the movie's release. Crisis Group is John's baby and he is chuffed beyond words to have the two of us attending. When I arrive, he thanks me profusely, but I tell him not to sweat it; I'm honored to be the one handing the beautifully engraved chunk of crystal to Paul.

The lunch goes off without a hitch, and Paul is his usual eloquent, erudite self, speaking as only he can about his experiences in Rwanda in April 1994. At the end of the ceremony, Paul is swamped by the guests, all wanting to have just a small audience with the man who has given so much inspiration and hope. I don't blame them. In fact, I encourage them to crowd him, it gives me the opportunity to duck out of there and get back to the apartment my friend has been so generous to offer me while he is out of town. I'm on a writing deadline for a television version of the movie Crash *and have a lot of work to do before tomorrow.*

In the cab on the way back, I start running over all the Darfur-related events that have cropped up for me as of late. It is amazing what happens when you open yourself up to things. It's similar to thinking of a band you like and then suddenly hearing their music everywhere you go, on the radio, in elevators and stores. Saying "Yes" to Darfur was very much the same for me. People from all over and from many different walks of life began to come into my sightline, all concerned about what was happening, all looking for solutions to a problem spiraling out of control by the hour, hundreds of them writing to me on my website, looking for insight. We were all passionate, ready to throw our energies into whatever proposed plan could prove beneficial or effective, but our methods were often disparate and unconnected from one another's. We were like-minded individuals, yet each of us was doing his or her own thing. I wanted more cohesion. My dream was to put together as many folks as possible that I had come in contact with over the last year or so, to see if we could form a collective to create an ideological wedge and then drive it into the Darfur problem rather than attacking it scattershot. Though my wife and kids might disagree, I thought it very fitting that the only date that all parties I contacted could converge would be my birthday. The New York location also made it a tricky "family pass" to acquire, but everyone agreed that the opportunity to be productive on Darfur should not be squandered. The cake and special cards my daughters made would hold until I returned.

I wake up on the couch still in my clothes, the screen saver on the computer in front of me now scrolling through my photo album. It's almost 11A.M., and I haven't slept in this late since before I had kids. No matter now. I've got to hustle if I'm going to make it to this meeting on time.

Everything about this apartment rivals a hotel for its amenities, but right now I could use a doorman and his whistle. Even though Matt's place is in a very cool neighborhood near the NYU campus, and Giuliani's "sting" on racist cabbies in the city has garnered some success, I've still been posted up on this street corner for twenty minutes, in a suit mind you, very unsuccessfully trying to hail a taxi. I'm really not trying to be late today. After about the sixth cab passes me, I step off the curb, taking my life into my hands, and wave my arms like a madman at the next rusty-looking yellow dart zooming by. The tires make a reluctant sound, and the nose of the vehicle dips low as it screeches to a halt.

"Are you crazy?" the cabbie blurts out as I throw open the back door.

"No. Are you? Or is there some other reason you weren't going to stop? Twenty-fourth Street and Madison Avenue."

Now, I'm sure there was something more appropriate, more productive to say in this moment, but I'm pissed that it had to come to this, my risking life and limb for a ride, especially when it's mostly brown people I'm getting dissed by. I know that it is a ridiculous assumption to make, but I am always looking for a greater measure of solidarity between we of the darker hues, no matter the original region from whence we came. Maybe it's this kind of misguided belief that gives me the desire to help people in a land far away and has me hoping against hope that the people I'm meeting with today can actually realize progress where little has been made. But at this moment, ruminating on the potential promise this day holds, I'm feeling a little petty, headed to our peace summit front-loaded with animosity. A couple blocks into our trek I try to strike up some small talk to smooth things over.

"You been doing this long?"

It doesn't work. My man isn't in the mood.

"I didn't see you, OK? I would have stopped. I stop for everybody, my friend. I am not a racist!"

The remainder of our ride is nice and quiet save for the sounds of the city and the cabbies' dispatcher breaking in over the radio every now and then.

Fifteen minutes later the taxi pulls up to Eleven Madison Park. Guilt guides my hand, and as I hop out, I reach into my wallet for the fare and a tip much more than fair. I add stupidly, "Great ride," really overboarding it now. The man barely nods, just pulls away in a hurry. I hope this little diplomacy bobble is not indicative of how the day will go.

Up ahead, Gayle Smith is standing next to John on the steps.

"You been waiting long?"

"Nope. You're good. This is Gayle."

"Hi, Gayle."

"Hello. And happy birthday."

We do a quick pleased-to-meet-you and head inside.

John, as usual, was the first person I called when this brainstorm hit. I wanted to make sure that the people we were inviting not only had the ability but also the will to make noise in their respective fields and keep the light shining on Darfur. We're fortunate to attract a pretty impressive group first time out. Present at the gathering, in addition to John, Gayle (now a senior fellow at the Center for American Progress with twenty-five years' experience in Africa), and myself were Jeff Swartz, social activist and CEO/president of Timberland, along with his personal assistant Carolyn Casey; David Rubenstein from the Save Darfur Coalition; Nick Kristof, Pulitzer–Prize winning columnist from the New York Times*; Samantha Power, Pulitzer Prize–winning author of* A Problem from Hell: America and the Age of Genocide*; Tom Sheridan, political strategist; and rounding out the crew, Senator Joe Biden and his assistant Norm Kurz.*

We don't have a ton of time today—only about two hours—everyone's schedule is tight, so we get right to it, permission given and liberties taken to throw everything out on the table no matter how ridiculous or radical, in search of steps toward solutions for Darfur. Some suggest American boots on the ground to back up or perhaps even replace the African Union. Others scoff at that idea, believing the presence of U.S. troops to be a detriment to the region, further exacerbating the problem and potentially pulling us into yet another dangerous conflict with no end in sight. Gayle suggests we bring the mountain to Mohammed and sponsor trips for refugees, specifically refugee women, to the United States to interface with influential politicians on the Hill, giving them the opportunity to personally tell their stories to a captive audience. Multiple suggestions, multiple debates focused on creating a movement in the U.S. to confront genocide and other mass atrocities such as those happening in Darfur, culminated in the creation of the ENOUGH campaign. Oh, and birthday cake too.

We all leave cautiously optimistic, knowing better than to celebrate a victory. This was but a small step on a long journey against a ticking clock. How much time do we have to put this campaign into effect? Will there be anything to protect if we wait too long? In what state will Darfur be when you read these words? Caution is certainly warranted. John and I make tentative plans to meet up later, and I head back downtown. If I had the discipline, I think, I would write a book about it. I imagine many people looking for a way to move on this would be comforted to know that they are not alone. Perhaps our exploration of methods could inspire others to seek their own, providing a jumping off point for multiple movements. Nice dream.

The remainder of the day passes uneventfully, and soon the hour creeps up on me where, were I at home, I would be surrounded by family and friends, blowing out candles and hugging my kids. Matt's beautiful apartment now feels like an enormous gilded cage. My daughter's protests are hitting home. How could I have allowed myself to be in New York, alone, on my birthday? Gone are the days when I could just pick up the phone and put New York on notice.

"It's Don. Birthday. Tonight. Do yourself a favor, holla at your boy."

Nope. That's Jay-Z who's juiced up like that. Whenever I spent an extended amount of time in this city in the past, I

*was a theater geek, preparing a role and then performing it
eight times a week. I never went out. I know about four
people here now, but only have two of their numbers. First I
call Miles.*

*"Yo . . ." My caller ID's not blocked; he'll recognize the
number.*

"D. What's up? You in town?"

"Yep and it's my birthday. What are you up to?"

"Shoot, hangin' with you."

"Word 'em."

*We kick around a couple ideas but are really content to
just go listen to some good music and have a very chill
night, which leads me to my next call.*

"Maestro."

"Mr. Cheadle."

"What's up, Wynton."

*"It's you, man." Mr. Marsalis's voice even sounds like
jazz.*

*"Hey, check it out, it's my birthday tonight and I wanted
to know if there was anything happening at your spot."*

*"It's your birthday? Ah, man. I wish I'd have known. I
would have put something together. You know what? Give
me an hour."*

*I didn't want him to go to any trouble; I was honestly
just hoping for a cool little hang, but he was gone before I
could stop him. Almost an hour to the minute and Wynton
calls back.*

"Hey, man, come on through the club at nine."

*I call John and Miles to give them the info. Maybe this
night won't suck after all. Even "actor-vists" should get to
celebrate their birthday.*

*When we arrive at Dizzy's, a club in Jazz at Lincoln
Center, I see a table down front with my name on it and the
five other people I know in New York: Courtney Vance,
Jamal Joseph and his wife, Gayle, Terry George and his*

*wife, all of them called by my managers back home. It's a
great impromptu surprise. Wynton sidles up to me. "Cool?"*

"Are you serious? This is the shizzit!"

"Cool."

*Wynton joins his band onstage, and after a Louisiana
second-line-style rendition of "Happy Birthday" I'll never
forget, his band goes on to play a blistering set until about
one in the morning. That would have been enough right
there, but the basketball degenerate in all of us takes us
next door after the show, revealing the true depth of
Wynton's addiction: a portable hoop sits off to the side of a
practice room currently set up to host a donor's banquet.
Fifteen tables, fully appointed with tablecloths and place
settings, surrounded by chairs, sit carefully positioned
about the room. Within minutes the whole shebang is
unceremoniously dragged to the side, and dressed as we
are—linen shirts, slacks, Gucci shoes, and all—we pick
teams and play three on three until three o'clock in the
morning. It will go down as one of the greatest birthday
celebrations I've ever had.*

*Walking down the boulevard to catch a cab, steam
coming off our overheated heads in wispy plumes, John
throws a fastball.*

*"Buddy, buddy, buddy . . . what do you think about a
book?"*

Conclusion: Never Again

You get from the world what you give to the world.
OPRAH WINFREY*

I*t sounds silly, almost Pollyannaish: send a letter, stop a genocide. But it is true.*

You have heard lots of bad news in this book: genocide, crimes
against humanity, famine, mass rape. In Congo, the deadliest war
in the world since World War II continues to unfold. In Somalia,
the legacy of Black Hawk Down and CIA support for the warlords continues to fuel civil conflict and conditions of anarchy. In
northern Uganda, the highest child abduction rate in the world
creates legacies of violence and trauma that will take generations
to unpack. In Darfur, the Genocide Convention was officially invoked by the Bush administration, with no effect but to desecrate
the very intentions of the Convention.

The good news is that all this can be changed.

We believe the only way that our government will move toward a
more constructive position is if the political will to do so is increased. The only way that political will can be increased is through

---

*Oxygen Media Press Release, "New Series from Oprah Winfrey," February 6, 2001.

citizen action. All of us are capable of writing letters and making phone calls to our elected officials.

The most frustrating aspect of this work is seeing that it wouldn't take much more effort for the United States to play a much larger role in confronting mass atrocities, especially in Africa. *The keys are the Three Ps for Preventing Atrocities and the Six Strategies for Change.* In punishing the perpetrators, we could provide information to and cooperation with the ICC and move their indictments forward dramatically. In promoting the peace, we could name special envoys to help resolve the conflicts in Congo, northern Uganda, and Somalia in a much more focused way than current efforts allow. And in protecting the people, we could ensure that peacekeeping missions have at their centerpiece civilian protection in word and deed.

The failure to act effectively to end the carnage in Sudan, Somalia, northern Uganda, and Congo highlights how little progress the world has made since the genocide in Rwanda in 1994. These debacles also remind us that the world body charged with leading the response to crises of this kind—the UN Security Council— remains largely unwilling to confront the perpetrators of mass atrocities in the world's peripheral zones. Divisions within the Security Council over whether to act remain huge, and the divisions themselves become an excuse for inaction.

But we must remember that the UN Security Council is not some bureaucratic entity. It is composed of fifteen governments, five of which are permanent members with disproportionate power: China, Russia, France, the United Kingdom, and the United States. So when someone says the UN isn't doing anything, it is these five governments that should have to answer *why*.

U.S. leadership is often the key variable in whether genocide or other crimes against humanity are prevented or stopped. (Often the other members of the Security Council wait to see what the United States will do, and if we are silent or disinterested, the matter is closed.) Any past, present, or future U.S. president is unlikely to take the risk of acting in these situations unless he or she is pressured by Congress. Congress won't hammer the president unless constituents back in home districts throughout the country are turning the heat up on their members.

JOHN:

I have worked in the White House, State Department, Congress, and the UN. I've seen firsthand this continuum of pressure and its results. When citizens write letters and press their agendas in a coordinated way, Congress responds. And when Congress presses the president to act on a foreign policy issue, the president responds. When citizens are silent in the face of the world's horrors, as they were during the Rwandan genocide, it is almost certain that the president will not act. It was incredibly frustrating when I worked in government to see so little noise being made outside in support of vigorous U.S. action in reaction to major crises in Africa. And it remains frustrating now that I'm on the outside to watch my government stand idly by in the face of monstrous atrocities because we still can't make enough noise. This has to change. This is why I'm working with Don on this book and on the ENOUGH campaign. This is why I do what I do with my life.

Change in policy will come only if every one of you who reads this book, and everyone you can bring with you, makes this the beginning of a personal commitment, not the end.

If we stand idly by, the responsibility for the continuation of these tragedies will be all of ours. So there it is. Write a letter, stop a genocide.

Not all of us have to be human rights or peace activists who risk their lives in harrowing trips to the field to get the truth out. But it is important that we tip our caps to those who are, so that we can learn that truth. The work that human rights and peace activists do can be very difficult

*and dangerous. For example, the conflict prevention organi-
zation I work for, the International Crisis Group, and other
human rights groups, have undercover personnel in conflict
zones who risk their lives every day.*

*This danger was brought home again in 2005 when my
dearest friend in Somalia, Abdulkadir Yahya, was gunned
down in front of his family after the publication of a Crisis
Group report on the scope of the terrorist threat in that
country. His main counterpart and great friend, Matt
Bryden, had to move all the way to South Africa because of
direct threats against him by those who had been exposed
in the report. Yahya's passing symbolizes the remarkable
commitment of many activists on the front lines in Africa
and around the world, people who risk their lives every day
to stand up for human rights and peace.*

*On one of my plane rides crisscrossing the country to
speak to audiences about these issues, I sat next to a man
who was really into his movies, which he was playing on his
DVD player. At one point, though, during a particularly
boring scene from an unmentioned movie, the guy began to
check out what I was reading out of the corner of his eye.
He finally broke and said, "How do you take it? Going over
there to those places? It just seems hopeless!"*

*I pondered his question for a moment, and then told him
it was just the opposite. "I see people struggling to survive,
to prevail, with courage and determination that would
shame us for any thought we might have of hopelessness.
During every one of my visits, one person after another tells
me: 'This is unacceptable. We are human beings! Go back
and tell your people to help us end this horror.'"*

*So you, readers, are the "people." And we have lots of
work to do.*

We need to write letters, help the divestment movement, go to
candidates' debates and raise questions, call in to television and

radio shows and ask why they aren't covering the issues, write letters to the editor, and many other things. We need to employ again and again the Six Strategies for Effective Change: *Raise Awareness, Raise Funds, Write a Letter, Call for Divestment, Join an Organization,* and *Lobby the Government.*

Since returning from our trips to Africa together, we have spoken at meetings around the United States in which people of all colors and from all walks of life get together and pledge some of their time and energy to fighting genocide and other mass atrocities. It is in rooms like these that social movements are born and incubated. Everyone in those rooms—and potentially everyone reading this book—is part of a larger whole, a long line and history of citizen activism that has the capacity to protect human life, and in the process to change the world.

Our elected leaders and media need to know that we voters and consumers care about crimes against humanity and the people affected by these atrocities, and that it is our national interest to confront the crises.

Our politicians need to know that if they ignore Darfur, northern Uganda, Somalia, Congo, and places like them, there will someday be a political price.

Let's say a normal temperature for any foreign policy issue would be ninety-eight degrees. On Darfur, activists managed to turn the heat up to one hundred degrees, and lots happened, but not enough to immediately stop the genocide. Our goal has to be to develop a committed constituency of American citizens in each congressional district who are willing to dedicate a small portion of their free time to turning the temperature up to 102 degrees, to where the politicians will be unable to ignore their responsibility to protect human life, and the president will be unable to shirk his responsibility to lead the efforts to prevent or confront mass atrocities wherever they are being committed.

We need to tell them, "We're mad as hell and we aren't going to vote for you anymore!"

Remember: There is no organized K Street lobby firm in Washington, D.C., that is working on behalf of genocide. No lobbyists are swarming Congress and the White House looking for support for war criminals or child soldiers or mass rapists.

Our obstacles are the Four Horsemen Enabling the Apoca-lypse: apathy, indifference, ignorance, and inertia. We can and shall overcome these.

The battle is joined. We—the anti-genocide constituency—on the one side versus indifference and other priorities on the other side. Who wins this battle will determine the fate of millions of Africans in the coming year, and millions more in future conflicts.

That is an awesome responsibility we all have, now that we know what is happening and now that we know what needs to be done.

There is a particularly poignant moment in the film *Hotel Rwanda* that summarizes our philosophy about our involvement in confronting genocide. Paul Rusesabagina is addressing the residents who have taken sanctuary in the hotel, and he is ex-horting them to call everyone they know outside of Rwanda to help save their lives. Nothing else has worked. Pictures, pleas, facts, international conventions, and UN resolutions all have produced a cowardly retreat by a world unwilling to stand up to evil. At one point Paul proclaims, *"We must shame them into helping!"*

In 2005, when we were in Darfur with Paul, we agreed that the time had come again to start shaming people into responding.

We need to shame our elected officials by writing letters, by holding demonstrations, and by joining in coalitions and telling these policy makers that they have failed to uphold the responsi-bilities of their office. We also need to shame our friends and fam-ilies into helping us make a difference.

Galvanizing to help protect the lives of millions of Sudanese, Congolese, Ugandans, and Somalis should provide all of us enough empowering shame to at least change the direction of U.S. policy, to become an upstander and not a bystander.

This movement can grow into something more timeless and

relevant to the prevention of future mass atrocities. Ultimately, individual Americans—you!—can make that difference and ensure that "Never Again" means something.

As human beings, we simply cannot allow another 6 million freshly dug graves in Africa because of preventable actions. Mass atrocities can be successfully confronted and ended.

It is—in the end—our choice.

DON:

Bzzt, Bzzt. The vibrating BlackBerry irritatingly drummed the oak, its e-mail alert waking me from my dreams. I hate when I forget to put my electronic leash on Quiet. I'm a light sleeper and already have my wife's tri-weekly snoring bouts to contend with (love you, honey). Now my desire for slumber was in direct conflict with my cat-killing curiosity about what information the new message held. I fooled myself for a couple of minutes that I could delay my satisfaction and wait until I awoke in the morning to read the thing, but who was this feline kidding? I extended my tired paw toward the nightstand and prepared for death. Forcing my eyes to focus, I read the message, deserving exactly what I got:

"Hey, buddy. Got one for you. Last minute because we couldn't get clearance. I'm going to China to meet President Hu and the next day to Egypt to meet with President Mubarak about Darfur. I think it would be something if you could be there. I know it's a long shot. But we got word only 10 minutes ago. Let me know if there's even a chance to do it. Talk to you.

"Sexiest."

Dammit. Why did I look? I should have just deleted the thing out of spite for the late hour it was received. Sure, I had enlisted George's help when I believed the California divestment bill was going south but that was only because I figured Batman and Mr. Freeze might be simpatico—

onscreen, comic-book-character rivalry notwithstanding.
But this request was payback-plus, over the top: Clooney
one-upmanship of the highest order. What nerve! What gall!
What an opportunity! I wouldn't miss it for the world. I hit
him back on the spot.

"I'm in."

Now to sell it to the Fam. The kids were easy. I didn't
even have to spin the trip. Daddy was going abroad to meet
with world leaders, working for peace in Africa. "Cool,
bring us back a scarab beetle."

I anticipated more massaging would be necessary for
wifey but was pleasantly surprised. She consented so
quickly that I seriously thought about hiring a detective to
keep tabs on her while I was away but then played back the
tape of our lives together over the past fourteen years.
Bridgid's record with regards to support of both me and of
those in need is without blemish. I made some calls,
postponed some meetings, packed a bag, and a mere twelve
hours later found myself smack dab in the Middle
Kingdom.

An airport is an airport but as soon as we collect our
bags and hit the streets we realize that we are someplace
entirely different than any of us has ever seen. The city of
Beijing is a sprawling metropolis with enormous, wide-
open streets that can easily accommodate four tanks side by
side, the sun only breaking through the hazy atmosphere of
soft coal smoke for the briefest of moments, making it
impossible to tell even approximately what time it is
without a watch. We weave through the busy streets to the
Grand Hyatt Beijing (just a ten-minute walk from
Tiananmen Square. Spooky) where we pick up the rest of
the delegation, principally Joey Cheek, Olympic Gold
medalist speed skater who donated his $40,000 prize money
to Right to Play, an athlete-driven international
humanitarian organization, and Tegla Loroupe, a long-

distance track and road runner, and a global spokesperson for peace, women's rights, and education. We barely have time to make each other's acquaintance before being hustled to the office of Assistant Foreign Minister He Yafei. Our busy schedule also includes meeting with the local film community as well as a photo-op with the Olympic committee and Chinese athletes too, so there's no time to waste.

We motor over to the Ministry of Foreign Affairs and file inside. The setting is that of an official reception, quite formal, and after being seated and offered tea, Mr. Yafei informs us that regrettably President Hu will be unable to meet with us but he (Yafei) will surely remit all of our concerns to his boss. Disappointed yet undaunted, the delegation jumps right into our pre-planned salvo: Given your (China's) economic interests (re: oil trade) in the government of Sudan, can your government do more to help stem the tide of violence and misery? We are aware of your "back-door" diplomacy efforts, but is there any way we (public figures, talking heads) can publicly give voice to what you are doing, pay you some credit, and generate support? What message can we take back from you to our U.S. leaders and the UN regarding this issue? We gingerly bring up China's appalling human rights record, then segue directly to the Olympic games being held there in 2008, making the point that the world will be watching and having a bloody confrontation raging out of control in a country wherein China invests heavily and has great influence will do little to bolster their shining slogan for the games of "One World, One Dream." Minister Yafei is as affable a man as you could care to meet. He listens patiently, counters intelligently, and advises us to caution our leaders against attempting to militarily force a solution down President al-Bashir's throat, stressing that such an attempt, especially from Western powers, would only exacerbate the deteriorating situation of Darfur. The meeting ends inside of an hour to little fanfare with snapshots and fare-thee-wells carrying us to the door. Before we exit, however, David Pressman, George's advisor and organizer of our trip, reiterates our desire to, as promised, have an audience with President Hu. David is politely rebuffed with assurance that we have, de facto, spoken to the president already.

In the car back to the Hyatt we all decide to call off the remainder of our scheduled meetings/photo-ops in consideration of quid pro quo; we knew how we would have been used and we were fine with that, but the door of propaganda has to swing both ways, and they had just locked theirs, surprise, surprise.

We wrap up our China trip the next day, hop on a Turkish Airlines flight to Istanbul, transfer planes, and head to Egypt to meet with President Mubarak, his son Gamal Mubarak (the General Secretary of the Policy Committee), Gamal's mother, Her Excellency First Lady Suzanne Mubarak, and Foreign Minister Ahmed Aboul Gheit.

The plane ride is long and productive, giving us ample time to compare notes on our first visit and readjust our strategy for our next hosts, who have a decidedly intimate relationship with Sudan, sharing their southern border with her. Egypt is regarded by many as being one of the political and cultural centers of the Middle East and, one would believe, has a vested interest in taking whatever steps are possible to prevent yet another Arab-ruled nation from being pulled apart by internal conflict, especially if the result could be a reduction in the flow of the vital Nile River waters from Sudan to Egypt and the prospect of a surge of refugees streaming into their country from further Sudanese civil war.

We land, immediately pour into our cars, and head to

our first meeting with Gamal Mubarak at the Dar Al-Quwwat al-Janniya (Air Force Club) in Heliopolis. Upon arrival we are brought into a large room with a huge table set for breakfast, a very welcome sight for starving travelers. Moments later our host swoops in. President Hosni Mubarak's youngest son has been described as being quite "presidential" himself—a very fair description. With an MBA from the American University in Cairo, "Mr. Gamal" has all the bearings of a man groomed to eventually take the reins: handsome, erudite, and thoroughly informed on the issues. After the preliminary meet and greet we are invited to sit, and then (really should have seen it coming) déjà vu rears its ugly head. Mr. Gamal announces that we will unfortunately be unable to meet with the president due to scheduling conflicts. I start to wonder if these presidential meetings were ever going to happen in the first place. Were we fools to believe that these heads of state, or any head of state for that matter, would really care what a couple of actors and athletes think? However, in the same fashion as our China meeting, in response to our questions and suggestions, Mr. Gamal thanks us for our passion, informs us that he will look for ways to do everything within his power to advocate for protection for the Darfurian civilians, yet cautions us (the West) against seeking military solutions. He flags our president's unfortunate use of the word "crusade" post–9/11, assuring us that it had indeed reverberated extremely negatively throughout the Arab world, even in Egypt, considered a "friend" of the U.S. Apparently our delegation, if nothing else, can serve as a whipping boy of sorts for the current administration and he gives us an earful. We listen diplomatically before interjecting that ours is not a mission to defend or decry U.S. policies but rather a call to find common ground for solutions.

Our subsequent meetings with American University of

Cairo students, Ahmed Aboul Gheit, and the First Lady, yield only Her Excellency pledging to host a summit in Egypt to raise awareness for the women victims of the Darfur conflict as well as her offering to travel to Chad to more strongly engage Arab interest and support to end the bloodshed. The wrap-up is familiar: photos, handshakes, and "welcome back anytime"s. The remainder of our Egypt leg is uneventful, simply marking time until wheels up, continuing on to New York and the UN.

Inside those hallowed halls, our delegation's sit-down with Secretary-General Kofi Annan, Deputy Secretary-General Mark Malloch Brown, and others proves to be another exercise in frustration. The press reports we saw the day before we arrived, stating that on January 1, 2007, the U.S. and UK would consider enforcing a no-fly zone to patrol the skies over Sudan, seemed to be a ham-handed tactic that no one in the room thinks is feasible or actionable even, yet we find ourselves struggling to nail down effective alternative solutions. Mr. Annan and Mr. Brown agree that we've visited the right players in the game of "who's got the stick" with regard to influence over the Sudanese leadership, but we all doubt seriously that the stick will be effectively utilized. Mr. Annan encourages us not to give up the fight and to be sure to interface with his successor, Ban Ki-moon, and the special envoy to Sudan to be named in January, the very month that the African Union's budget runs out. Happy New Year. Will funds be cobbled together to finance more troops, their numbers still too small to patrol the region, their mandate lacking real power to protect the innocent? Will the U.S. and UK seriously begin flying sorties over the deserts of Darfur? Could that possibly help? Does anyone know what to do? Does anybody really care? I want to scream and break things. But I don't. I'm too polite. Maybe everybody is.

We head home loaded down with more questions than

we departed with and I seriously contemplate getting rid of my BlackBerry, but that wouldn't stop the buzzing in my head. What's next?

As if on cue, my BlackBerry chirps. Here we go again. Do I even dare pick up?

"Buddy, buddy. Welcome back, my man."

"Sup, John?"

"Mission accomplished. The highest ranking delegation to China and Egypt on Darfur, huh?"

"I know, it's crazy," I reply. "No cabinet members, no foreign minister. Just actors and athletes."

Then I give John the lowdown on the state of affairs and my state of mind. His tone changes immediately.

"Look, I hear you on the obstacles, but did you already forget? Not on our watch. There are so many more things that can be done to end these atrocities that haven't yet been tried. Rome wasn't built in a day. The Iraq Study Group had seventy-nine recommendations! Do you think Sudan is less complicated? The movement finally has got Bush's attention, and he's demanding action. Now is the time to pick up the beat, to increase the temperature, to make more noise. What did Martin Luther King used to say?"

"Oh, man, quoting Martin now?"

"You got anybody better? King said, 'The moral arc of the universe bends at the elbow of justice.' And if Dr. King doesn't do it for you, there's this book you and I wrote called Not on Our Watch. *You should read it, again."*

"And you should have heard all that diplomatic pseudo-sympathy on that trip."

"Been there, done that, and will again."

Neither of us talks for a beat. What's left to say? All there is is what's left to do. John breaks the silence.

"And listen, as soon as this thing gets turned around in Darfur, I got two tickets for us to go to Congo."

"Round three, huh?"

"Yep. And bring the rock."
"Yeah, I hear those kids over there got game."

Later that night, in the relative quiet of my house, I play back the tapes of all that's happened vis à vis Darfur since I've become "involved." Times like this, it's easy to feel powerless, easy to feel alone. But when I take off those blinders and look around I see that I am actually surrounded by many people "intending the light," as Joseph Campbell says, hoping against hope to make a difference in their time. I grow inside as we grow in size, not an army of one but one of many taking up the gauntlet thrown at our feet. Millions of lives hang in the balance, their futures determined in part by whether or not we act. Ultimately, I pray that we not stand down from our post. Not us. Not now. Not on our watch.

Taking Action: Things You Can Do Immediately

1. Raise awareness.

    a. Stay informed, and inform others, about what's going on in Darfur.

    The ENOUGH campaign seeks to unite and strengthen the efforts of grassroots activists, policy makers, advocates, concerned journalists, and others by giving them up-to-date information from on the ground in countries of concern and offering practical pressure points to end the violence. If you are concerned about these issues and want to know what you can to do push for change, www.enoughproject.org is the place to find answers.

    The International Crisis Group has field analysis and up-to-date policy recommendations for how to resolve conflicts all over the world, including Darfur. www.crisisgroup.org.

    Eric Reeve's website (www.sudanreeves.org) is a great one-stop shop for news, analysis, and advocacy about the conflict.

    Download the Voices on Genocide Prevention podcast from the United States Holocaust Memorial Museum at http://www.ushmm.org/conscience/podcasts/.

    Encourage friends to go to www.darfurisdying.com and play mtvU's Darfur video game.

    b. Subscribe for the latest news from organizations working to stop the atrocities.

- Genocide Intervention (GI-Net) sends out regular "action alerts" with specific Darfur activism opportunities. http://www.genocideintervention.net/advocate/actionalerts/.

- To subscribe to STAND's national newsletter, sign up here: http://inform.standnow.org/lists/?p=subscribe&id=2.
- Save Darfur has a Weekly Action Network with specific actions you can take each week to help make a difference. http://www.democracy inaction.org/dia/organizationsORG/darfur/signUp.jsp?key=1596.
- Africa Action also features innovative action alerts, at http://www.africaaction.org.

c. Write an op-ed or letter to the editor of your local newspaper.

Save Darfur (www.savedarfur.org) has a great feature that allows you to write letters to the editor of local and national newspapers. http://www.savedarfur.org/page/speakout/dailies.

Here are some of their tips to help get your letter published:

- Most newspapers will only print original letters. Use talking points and sample letters as a starting point for your own message.
- Letters with a personal angle are always compelling. Ask yourself how this issue affects you and your family.
- Keep it brief and to the point. Letters under two hundred words are much more likely to be published.

d. Write to the TV networks and encourage them to cover Darfur.

Visit www.BeAWitness.org and learn more about efforts to push the television networks to devote more time to the crisis in Darfur. Here's a sample letter they will help you send to the networks:

Dear Sir/Madam:

I am writing to urge your network to devote more airtime to covering the ongoing genocide in the Darfur region of Sudan, where as many as 400,000 people have died, thousands of women have been raped, and more than two million people have been forced to flee from their burned and bombed villages to live in squalid refugee camps.

Television has the unique ability to put a human face on statistics. A good news story can bring Darfur, one of the most remote places on earth, directly into America's living rooms. Sadly, television news coverage of Darfur has been woefully deficient. Only one in every 950 minutes of news coverage during 2004 covered Darfur. During June 2005, major news media aired 50 times as many stories about Michael Jackson and 12 times as many stories about Tom Cruise as they did about the genocide in Darfur.

Genocide is newsworthy. By increasing your coverage of events in Darfur, you can help to generate the public attention needed to pressure our government to bring the atrocities to a halt. I urge you to give this crisis the attention it deserves.

Sincerely,

2. Raise funds.

Here are tips for a successful fund-raising event (courtesy of GI-Net):

GENERAL TIPS FOR HOLDING EVENTS

- Decide what type of event will be most effective for the goals you are aiming to accomplish. For example, would a film screening or speaker better suit your purpose for holding the event?
- Test your idea out—ask a few friends what they think. Consider what kind of resources you will need to make it a success.
- Get a team together, rather than working on your own. Make a list of tasks; find out what skills people have, and try to give them tasks they'll enjoy. Make sure everyone knows what his or her responsibilities are.
- Come up with a backup plan. For example, what will you do if it rains?
- Do research and estimate how many people might turn up. What is the minimum number of people you'll need to make money? What's the maximum number of people you can accommodate?
- Think about the best date. Avoid competing with another local function or a major TV event, for example. Agree on a realistic timetable and give each task a deadline.
- Think of ways to keep costs down and your proceeds up. Try to get as much as you can for free—whether it's people's time, a venue, food, publicity, printing, commercial sponsorship, or prizes.
- Bring materials about the current situation in Darfur and the Genocide Intervention Network (GI-Net). You can request flyers, brochures, or other materials by e-mailing fundraising@genocideintervention.net.
- Remember to thank everyone involved and let them all know how much they've raised.
- Above all, make it fun!

QUICK EVENT IDEAS

- Host a Dinner for Darfur. These dinner parties are meant to act as fund-raisers, and are a way to educate your community and give them the tools for action. For an easy guide to hosting an educational fund-raising dinner, go to http://www.genocideintervention.net/fundraise/dinners.php.
- Virtual house parties will get your friends and family involved in the cause with minimal effort.
- Screen *Hotel Rwanda* or a similar film demonstrating the need to stop genocide.
- Selling stylish GI-Net T-shirts is an ideal way to spread the anti-genocide message. If you are willing to commit to selling at least thirty shirts, GI-Net can give them to you for just $7 a shirt. GI-Net recommends that you sell them for $12 a shirt, but you can set whatever

price above $7 you think makes sense for your event. Then you can make a donation with the money you raise.

- The Save Darfur Coalition also has green wristbands that have become one of the emblems of the Darfur movement. Purchase a few, then ask for a donation of $2 or $3 for each one and help make Darfur activists more visible!
- Set up a donation box around your school, workplace, dining hall, or place of worship. Distribute information about mass atrocities.
- Ask local musical groups to perform at a "battle of the bands." Charge admission or set up a donation box at the event.
- Have a bake sale or car wash. Explain prominently that the event is to help protect victims of genocide in Darfur.
- Organize a tournament involving poker, video games, a dance marathon, etc. Charge admission from the participants of the event. You can either give a small portion of the proceeds to the winner or have it be a "benefit tournament" with all winnings sent to the anti-genocide cause.
- Local businesses often look to promote philanthropic causes. Educate them and see if they would be willing to make a donation.
- If there is a Darfur-related event outside your area, encourage your religious organization or other group to sponsor your travel expenses.

3. Write a letter.

There are many different ways to write to elected officials and urge them to take action to stop atrocities in Darfur. Personal letters stand the best chance of being noticed, and we gave you an example of what a letter could look like in Chapter 8 (page 177).

The GI-Net website also has a great tool for quickly generating effective letters. http://www.democracyinaction.org/dia/organizationsORG/ginetwork/campaign.jsp?campaign_KEY=4591.

4. Call for divestment.

The website of the Sudan Divestment Task Force (www.sudandivestment.org) has a wealth of information about the status of ongoing divestment campaigns, and everything you need to know to start a new campaign if none exists where you live.

You can learn the basics of targeted divestment at http://www.sudandivestment.org/divestment.asp.

After you learn the basics, contact the Task Force at info@sudandivestment.org. A Task Force/STAND (Students Taking Action Now: Darfur) representative will work with you to create a customized plan of action for your institution. You will be able to . . .

- Research your institution to find how it may be invested in Sudan
- Submit a targeted divestment proposal to your institution's investment

manager (e.g., treasurer, board of trustees, controller/comptroller, president, state legislator)
• Mobilize a grassroots coalition to support your proposal

5. Join an organization.

Joining an existing organization is the best way to stay up to speed on news, events, and opportunities to get involved in stopping genocide.

a. Students

Students should visit the STAND website to find out how they can get involved. http://www.standnow.org/.

b. Congregations

Congregations can learn more by joining the Save Darfur Congregational Network and taking advantage of their Faith Action Packs, with specific resources to help Christian, Jewish, and Muslim communities mobilize to help the people of Darfur. http://www.savedarfur.org/pages/organize_your_congregation.

For instance, here are samples of scripture, texts, and traditions that they suggest:

PROVERBS 3:27
Withhold not good from them to whom it is due, when it is in the power of thine hand to do it.

ADAPTED FROM AL-QUR'AN, SURAH 5:32
He who has killed an innocent soul, it is as if he had killed all humanity. And he who has saved an innocent soul, it is as if he has saved all humanity.

JAMES 3:17–18
Peacemakers who sow in peace raise a harvest of righteousness.

c. Communities

Community organizations have played a critical role in pushing for action on Darfur. At the Save Darfur website, you can search for groups in your area, or learn how to organize your own group. http://www.savedarfur.org/page/group.

6. Lobby the government.

a. Find out your representative's record on Darfur.

The first step to lobbying congressional officials is to find out what they have or haven't done to make a difference on Darfur. Visit www.darfurscores.org and look at your representative's record on Darfur.

b. Ask focused questions.

Attend public events featuring members of congress and ask them about their position on Darfur. Here are some tips from GI-Net:

- *Investigate local media, blogs, and word of mouth to find out when a political event involving members of Congress or challengers will be held.* If it is an invitation-only function, inquire about how to get invited. Usually organizers will be happy to invite people who sound cooperative and reasonable.
- *Use the Darfur scorecard (www.darfurscores.org) to see where a member of Congress stands on Darfur-related activities.* With this knowledge, you will ask a more pointed and effective question.
- *Your question should be short and pointed.* If you think you might get flustered, write the question down on a note card ahead of time.
- *Look for other chances to get your point across if you can't ask a question directly.* If you were not called on or there was no question-and-answer session, you still have options. If there is a handshake line, join it and ask an abbreviated question while getting your ten seconds with the candidate. Try to approach campaign staff after the speech and ask if you could meet with them about their candidate's Darfur agenda. Ask local media representatives if they would be interested in writing a story mentioning the candidate's Darfur policy.
- *Be sure to follow up with the campaign, either by e-mail or phone, after the event.* This will remind the candidate that yours is an important issue on which he or she needs to take a position.

c. Meet with elected officials.

Making an appointment to meet with a member of Congress isn't as tough as it sounds. You voted for them, and you have a right to tell them exactly how you feel about the issues that matter to you.

Five Helpful Hints for Advocacy Initiatives

There are five elements we would recommend that you keep in mind when you are talking with elected officials or making presentations to interested citizens. For this purpose, we propose the "KIS" organizing framework:

1. *Keep It Simple:* Focus on the basics of your message. Try your best to limit your pitch to three points. If you count more than three, you are officially out of control.
2. *Keep It Short:* Policy makers and most of the public hate history lessons. They will stop listening and start daydreaming. Maintain your focus and keep it concise.

3. *Keep It Sound:* Give a short overview and a clear list of what your audience or interlocutor can do.

4. *Keep It Smart:* Keep the focus on what U.S. policy can do. Don't talk about oranges to the director of apples. Know your audience.

5. *Keep It Special:* Tell an amazing and/or personal short story that everyone will remember to illustrate your point.

◆

Seven Deadly Sins of Human Rights Advocates

Beware of the Seven Deadly Sins of would-be human rights advocates like us. We can get pretty sanctimonious, long-winded, and overzealous. So here are some things to avoid when you are trying to make your case, whether to a politician or to a group of people you are trying to educate.

1. *Don't be too boring!* Advocacy is not like an academic conference. We need to think through how to make our presentations stand out. Tell a story, tell a joke, make what you have to say interesting. Don't paint in black-and-white; paint in color!

2. *Don't be too long-winded!* Most of us who get involved in advocacy could hardly be accused of being shy. We often tend to drone on just a little too long about the issues that fire us up. Zero in on the main points and be concise!

3. *Don't be too unilateral!* We often just make long presentations or speeches at our meetings and events. We need to focus on interaction with our interlocutors or audiences. After initial presentations, engage people by asking questions. Be interactive!

4. *Don't be too complex!* We often overload our message by telling everything about our subject of interest in all its glorious complexity. Pick the highlights. Make a few simple points!

5. *Don't be too unstructured!* There's often so much to be said about our topics that we have the temptation to just blurt it

all out in a stream of consciousness, sort of like hurling mud (or any other similar substance) against a wall and hoping it sticks. Instead, it is important to make a tight situation report and then present a focused set of recommendations. Make it flow!

6. *Don't be too random!* To a U.S. government policy maker or an American audience, we need to remain focused somewhat on what the United States can do. So make sure you focus your audience or interlocutor on the two or three most important things the American government can do, and how that person or group can help make it happen. Be focused!

7. *Don't be too touchy-feely!* We have to match our advocacy agenda to the big picture. We can't just rely on the "because it's the right thing to do" argument, or simply hope that for humanitarian reasons people will respond. We also have to connect our issues to larger national interests and what politicians and Americans care about. For example, if our longer-term counter-terrorism agenda is being undermined by the way in which the United States pursues this agenda in the short term, we need to shout that from the rooftops. If our promotion of freedom is going to be a central objective, then we need to demonstrate how these freedoms are being undermined and not promoted by our counterterrorism policies. Be relevant!